A MOST PECULIAR PEOPLE

A Most Peculiar People

QUOTATIONS ABOUT
WALES AND THE WELSH

compiled and edited by

MEIC STEPHENS

CARDIFF
UNIVERSITY OF WALES PRESS
1992

British Library Cataloguing in Publication Data

A catalogue record for this book is available from the British Library.

ISBN 0-7083-1168-7

Typeset in Wales by Megaron, Cardiff
Printed in England by Biddles Ltd., Guildford

Cyflwynir
y gwaith hwn i'm gwraig
RUTH
Cymraes i'r carn

CONTENTS

PREFACE

The title of this book, which is taken from the well-known squib about the Mumbles (quotation 786), is nicely ambiguous. The Welsh, as observed throughout our history, have been 'a peculiar people' – perhaps not in the biblical sense, as some might claim, but at least in this: certainly different from others, we may also be thought unpredictable, not to say perverse, in our view of ourselves as a distinct national community.

Beginning in Roman times, I have selected extracts from what has been written and said about Wales and the Welsh over a period of some two thousand years, ending in 1990. Many of the quotations, taken from sources both native and foreign, literary and demotic, famous and obscure, refer to the characteristics of the Welsh – our language, religion, social customs, and so on – and, in particular, to our status as a people who have lived for most of our history in a state of crisis, our identity often under threat and our aspirations usually frustrated.

Perhaps a word of caution is needed here. The Welsh, in many ways a controversial people, have been the object of antipathy as well as sympathy, of prejudice as well as panegyric, of scorn as well as admiration, not only on the part of the English but also among ourselves. It is therefore important for a full appreciation of some piquant or delicious remark that the reader should bear in mind who wrote or uttered it, and in what context. Most of the people quoted will be found in the *Dictionary of Welsh Biography*, the *Oxford Companion to the Literature of Wales*, and the *Dictionary of National Biography*; the memory of some others, it must be said, survives only in the obscurity of the publications from which their words have been extracted.

Although Welsh nationality and nationhood are the matters which come into sharpest focus in this book, I have also included, if only by way of relief, a few hundred quotations from the work of Welsh poets and prose-writers which touch on other, more universal themes such as Love, Life, and Death, especially if they seem to have been written in a specifically Welsh context. Nevertheless, the book should not be regarded as an anthology, any more than as a history of Wales, since what makes for a quotation (especially in another language) is often a distorting process that has little to do with literary merit or historical significance. For example, the great poet Dafydd ap Gwilym, who seems to have had almost nothing to say about the Welsh condition, is not represented here; other poets, too, have not found a place for the reason that what seems memorable when expressed in *cynghanedd* often loses its pith and resonance when translated into English. The reader looking for Welsh literary quotations in the original language should turn to *Y Flodeugerdd o Ddyfyniadau Cymraeg*, the collection compiled by Alan Llwyd. Neither that book nor this, however, does away with the need for a comprehensive dictionary which draws on literature in both languages as well as on the social history of the Welsh people in all its variety.

The quotations in *A Most Peculiar People* (2,324 in all) are numbered and arranged, first of all, in chronological order, and then alphabetically under the names of the persons to whom they are attributed. I have not always managed to achieve consistency in the chronology: sometimes, for example, a quotation from a poem is placed according to the date of its first appearance in a periodical, while another may be found under the year of its publication in a book. Quotations referring to historical events are given under the year in which they were published rather than the year to which they relate. Many of the anonymous quotations are drawn from traditional material for which it is impossible to give even a rough date. For each quotation a source is given, sometimes with a brief explanation, but where none is provided the reader should understand that the quotation is taken from the same source as the one preceding it. An asterisk denotes that the quotation has been translated from another language, whether Latin, Welsh, French or some other. The authors quoted (nearly 700) are listed in an index on page 171 and there is a subject index on page 179.

During the compilation of this book I had the assistance of several people whose expertise I am glad to acknowledge now. My friend Dr John Davies was at one stage a collaborator in the work, contributing a few hundred quotations, but gave up in order to undertake another project. Dr John Gwynfor Jones, another historian, found sources for a score of quotations which would otherwise have eluded me. Mr Gwilym Lloyd Edwards was kind enough to let me see the collection of quotations about the Welsh language with which he won a prize at the National Eisteddfod in 1989. My kinsman Mr Ioan Bowen Rees read the typescript and made some valuable suggestions. Among others who took an interest in the work's progress were Mr Sam Adams, Mr Robin Buss, Mr Don Dale-Jones, Dr W. R. P. George, Dr John Harris, Mr Alan Llwyd, Mr Dafydd Orwig, Mr M. Wynn Thomas, the Reverend Patrick Thomas, Dr Merryn Williams, and Mr Rhydwen Williams. I remember, too, with great affection, the help of three friends who did not live to see the book's publication: John Ormond, Michael Parnell, and D. Parry M. Michael.

Lastly, I should like to thank Ms Susan Jenkins and Ms Liz Powell, my editors at the University of Wales Press, for their guidance and practical assistance.

Meic Stephens   June 1992
Whitchurch
Cardiff

THE QUOTATIONS

— **51**BC —

Julius Caesar

1 All the Britons paint themselves with
woad, which gives their skin a bluish
colour and makes them look very dreadful
in battle.*

Commentarii de Bello Gallico (51BC)

— *c.* AD **52** —

Caratacus, Caradoc

2 I had horses, men, arms, wealth. Are you
surprised that I am sorry to lose them? If
you want to rule the world, does it follow
that everybody else welcomes enslavement? Had I surrendered without a blow
before being brought before you, neither
my downfall nor your victory would have
become famous.*

to the Emperor Claudius
recorded by Tacitus, *Annales* (*c.* 115)

— *c.* **98** —

Tacitus

3 And so the Britons were gradually led on
to the amenities that make vice agreeable –
arcades, baths and sumptuous banquets.
They spoke of such novelties as
civilization, when really they were only a
feature of enslavement.*

Agricola (*c.* 98)

— *c.* **115** —

Tacitus

4 The Silures were not . . . easily quelled.

Neither lenity nor rigorous measures could
induce them to submit.*

Annales (*c.* 115)

5 The druids were ranged in order, with
hands uplifted, invoking the gods and
pouring forth horrible imprecations. The
strangeness of the sight struck the Romans
with awe and terror.*

— **440** —

Anonymous

6 Britain, abandoned by the Romans, passed
into the power of the Saxons.*

Chronica Gallica

— **446** —

Anonymous

7 The barbarians push us back to the sea,
the sea pushes us back to the barbarians;
between these two kinds of death, either
we are drowned or slaughtered.*

the Britons' appeal to Aëtius, Consul of the
Western Empire
quoted by Gildas, *De Excidio et Conquestu
Britanniae* (*c.* 540)

— **516** —

Anonymous

8 The battle of Badon, in which Arthur
carried the Cross of our Lord Jesus Christ
for three days and three nights on his
shoulders and the Britons were victors.*

Annales Cambriae

— *c.* **540** —

Gildas

9 Ever since it was first inhabited, Britain has been ungratefully rebelling, stiff-necked and haughty, now against God, now against its own countrymen.*

De Excidio et Conquestu Britanniae (*c.* 540)

10 They [the Saxons] first of all fixed their dreadful claws on the east side of the island, ostensibly to fight for our country, in fact to fight against it. The mother lioness learnt that her first contingent had prospered, and she sent a second and larger troop of satellite dogs . . . Hence the spring of iniquity, the root of bitterness, the virulent plant that our merits so well deserved, sprouted in our soil with savage shoots and tendrils.*

11 The island was still Roman in name, but not by law and custom. Rather it cast forth a sprig of its own bitter planting, and sent Maximus [Macsen Wledig] to Gaul with a great retinue of hangers-on and even the imperial insignia, which he was never fit to bear; he had no legal claim to the title, but was raised to it like a tyrant by rebellious soldiery.*

12 Britain has kings, but they are tyrants; she has judges, but they are wicked.*

13 Britain has priests, but they are fools; very many ministers, but they are shameless; clerics, but they are treacherous grabbers.*

14 Your head is already whitening as you sit upon a throne that is full of guiles and stained from top to bottom with diverse murders and adulteries . . . Vortipor, tyrant of the Demetae.*

15 What of you, dragon of the island. . . You are last on my list, but first in evil, mightier than many in both power and malice. . . strong in arms but stronger still in what destroys a soul, Maglocunus [Maelgwn Gwynedd] . . . The King of all kings has made you higher than almost all the generals of Britain, in your kingdom as in your physique: why do you not show yourself to him better than others in character instead of worse?*

— **589** —

St David

16 Noble brothers and sisters, be glad, and guard your faith and religion, and do the little things which you have heard from me, and which I have shown you. And I shall go the way which our fathers go. And fare you well, and may your conduct be steadfast on earth. For we shall never meet here again.*

reported in *Llyfr Ancr Llanddewibrefi* (1346)

— **late 6th cent.** —

Taliesin

17 There was a great battle Saturday
 morning
From when the sun rose until it grew
 dark.*

'Gwaith Argoed Llwyfain' (trans. Anthony Conran)

18 There was many a corpse beside Argoed
 Llwyfain;
 From warriors ravens grew red,
And with their leader a host attacked.
For a whole year I shall sing their
 triumph.*

19 The wide host of England sleep
 With light in their eyes,
And those that had not fled
 Were braver than were wise.*

'Marwnad Owain ab Urien' (trans. Anthony Conran)

— *c.* **600** —

Aneirin

20 Man in might, youth in years,
Courage in battle.*

of Owain
'Y Gododdin' (trans. Anthony Conran)

21 Diademed in the forefront, wherever he
 went;
Breathless before a girl, he paid for his
 mead.*

of Madog

22 Men went to Catraeth, keen was their
 company.

They were fed on fresh mead, and it
    proved poison –
Three hundred warriors ordered for
    warfare,
And after the revelling there was silence.*

23 Men went to Catraeth with the dawn.
    Their fine spirit shortened their lives,
    Mead they drank, yellow, sweet and
        ensnaring:
    For that year many a minstrel was glad.*

24 Short their lives. Long their kin miss them.
    Seven times their own number of English
        they slew.
    In that contention they made women
        widows.*

25 Although they were being slain, they slew;
    Till the world ends they will be
        honoured.*

26 His sword rang in the heads of mothers.*

of Isac

27 They bore no disgrace, men who stood
    firm.*

28 The poets of the people will judge who are
    the men of courage.*

— post 600 —

Anonymous
29 King Cadfan, the wisest and most
    renowned of all kings.*

inscription on tomb at Llangadwaladr,
Anglesey

30 Aethelfrith led his army to Chester and
    there slew numberless Welshmen, and so
    was fulfilled the prophecy of Augustine,
    wherein he said, If the Welsh will not be at
    peace with us, they shall perish at the hand
    of the Saxons.

The Anglo-Saxon Chronicle

31 If they cry to their god against us, they
    fight against us as surely as do those who
    bear weapons.

of the massacre of the monks of Bangor Is-coed,
c. 615

32 In that year Cadwaladr ap Cadwallon, the
    last king that ruled over the Britons, went
    to Rome and there he died. . . and
    thenceforth the Britons lost the Crown of
    the Kingship, and the Saxons obtained it,
    as Merlin [Myrddin] had prophesied to
    Gwrtheyrn Wrthenau.*

entry for the year 682
Brut y Tywysogyon

33 The body of Cingen dwells underneath.*

the earliest surviving text wholly in Welsh

Beuno
34 For the kinsman of yonder strange-
    tongued man whose voice I heard across
    the river setting on his dogs will obtain
    possession of this place, and it will be
    theirs, and they will hold it in ownership.*

on hearing an Englishman on the bank of the
Severn
recorded in *Llyfr Ancr Llanddewibrefi*(1346)

— 731 —

Bede
35 There are in Britain, in harmony with the
    five books of the divine law, five languages
    and four nations – English, British, Scots
    and Picts. Each of these has its own
    language, but all are united in the study of
    God's truth by the fifth, Latin.*

Historia Ecclesiastica Gentis Anglorum (731)

36 The Britons for the most part have a
    natural hatred for the English and uphold
    their own bad customs against the true
    Easter of the Catholic Church; however,
    they are opposed by the power of God and
    man alike.*

37 Neither the prayers, advice or censures of
    Augustine and his companions could
    obtain the compliance of the Britons, who
    stubbornly preferred their own customs to
    those in universal use among Christian
    churches.*

38 It is to this day the fashion among the
    Britons to reckon the faith and religion of
    Englishmen as naught and to hold no
    more converse with them than with the
    heathen.*

— *c.* **800** —

Nennius

39 The scholars of the island of Britain had no skill and set down no record in books. I have therefore made a heap of all that I have found.*

Historia Brittonum (*c.* 800)

40 Lucius, the British king, received baptism, with all the underkings of the British nation, one hundred and sixty-seven years after the coming of Christ, after a legation had been sent by the Roman emperor and by Eucharistus, the Roman Pope.*

41 The Armorican British, who are overseas, went forth there with the tyrant Maximus on his campaign, and since they were unwilling to return, they razed the western parts of Gaul to the ground and did not leave alive those who piss against the wall.*

42 The eighth battle was in Guinnon fort and in it Arthur carried the image of the holy Mary, the everlasting Virgin, on his shield.*

43 King Maelgwn the Great was reigning among the British in Gwynedd, for his ancestor, Cunedda, with his sons to the number of eight, had come from the North, from the country called Manaw Gododdin, one hundred and forty-six years before Maelgwn reigned.*

— *c.*840 —

44 **Anonymous**
Fee, fie, fo, fum,
I smell the blood of a British man!

traditional rhyme associated with the story of
Jack the Giantkiller

— **9th cent.** —

45 **Anonymous**
Over my heart the shield's worn thin.*

'Canu Llywarch Hen' (trans. Anthony Conran)

46 Ere my back was bent, I was ready with words.*

47 This leaf, chased here and there by the wind,
  Its destiny's drear.
  It is old; it was born this year.*

48 The four chief things I hated
Have come now all at once:
Coughing and old age, sickness and sorrow.*

49 I am old, bent in three, I am fickle and reckless,
  I'm a fool, and uncouth.
  They that once loved me do not now.*

50 Dark is Cynddylan's hall tonight
  With no fire, no bed.
  I weep awhile, then am silent.*

'Stafell Cynddylan' (trans. Anthony Conran)

— *c.* **929** —

Anonymous
51 The Welsh will rise: they will give battle.*

'Armes Prydein' (trans. Joseph P. Clancy)

52 The Welsh must become, through warfare, Trained troops, united, one band, sworn brothers.*

53 Welshmen and Saxons will meet in combat.*

54 Who withers not, fails not, bends not, endures.*

— **1043** —

Anonymous
55 Hywel ab Owain, King of Glamorgan, died in his old age.*

entry for the year 1043
Brut y Tywysogyon

— *c.* **1050** —

Gruffudd ap Llywelyn
56 Speak not of killing. I do but blunt the

horns of the offspring of Wales, lest they should wound their dam.*

of his policy towards other Welsh princely houses

recorded by Walter Map, *De Nugis Curialium* (*c.* 1180)

— *c.* **1060** —

Anonymous

57 Pwyll, prince of Dyfed, was lord over the seven cantrefs of Dyfed.*

Pedair Cainc y Mabinogi (*c.* 1060)

58 And she [Branwen] heaved a great sigh, and with that broke her heart.*

59 Bendigeidfran son of Llŷr was crowned king over this Island and exalted with the crown of London.*

60 Let him who would be a leader be a bridge.*

61 And then Bendigeidfran commanded his head to be struck off. 'And take the head,' he said, 'and carry it to the White Mount in London, and bury it with its face towards France'.*

62 And then they took the flowers of the oak, and the flowers of the broom, and the flowers of the meadowsweet, and from those they called forth the very fairest and best endowed maiden that mortal ever saw, and baptized her with the baptism they used at that time, and named her Blodeuwedd.*

'Culhwch ac Olwen'

63 Four white trefoils sprang up behind her wherever she went, and for that reason she was called Olwen.*

— **1063** —

Anonymous

64 Gruffudd ap Llywelyn, golden-torqued king of the Welsh and their defender, died after many plunderings and victorious battles against his foes, after many feasts

and delights, and great gifts of gold and silver and costly raiment, he who was sword and shield over the fate of all Wales.*

entry for the year 1063
Brenhinedd y Saeson

Florence of Worcester

65 Rhys ap Tewdwr, King of the Welsh, was slain during Easter week in battle near the castle of Brecknock. From that day kings ceased to reign in Wales.*

Chronicon ex Chronicis (*sub* 1093)

— **1110** —

Anonymous

66 And the King said [to Gilbert FitzRichard], 'You were always asking of me a portion of Wales. Now I will give you the land of Cadwgan ap Bleddyn. Go and take possession of it.'*

entry for the year 1110
Brut y Tywysogyon

— **1136** —

Geoffrey of Monmouth

67 Walter, Archdeacon of Oxford, a man of great eloquence and learned in foreign histories, offered me a very ancient history in the British tongue which, in a continuous regular story and elegant style, related the actions of all of them, from Brutus, the first king of the Britons, down to Cadwaladr son of Cadwallon.*

Historia Regum Britanniae

68 Britain, the best of islands, is situated in the Western Ocean, between France and Ireland.*

69 Brutus then called the island Britain from his own name, and his companions he called Britons. A little later the language of the people, which had up to then been known as Trojan or Crooked Greek, was called British, for the same reason.*

70 As the foreign element around them became more and more powerful, they

were given the name Welsh instead of Britons. This word derives either from their leader Gualo, or from their Queen Galaes, or else from their being so barbarous.*

— c. 1137 —

Bernard

71 The Welsh are entirely different in nation, language, laws and habits, judgements and customs.*

Bishop of St David's, letter to Pope Innocent II, c.1137

— c. 1150 —

Anonymous

72 He [Gruffydd ap Cynan] made Gwynedd glitter with lime-washed churches like the firmament with stars.*

Buchedd Gruffudd ap Cynan (c. 1150)

Hywel ab Owain Gwynedd

73 I love, today, England's hatred – open ground
Of the North.*

'Gorhoffedd' (trans. Anthony Conran)

74 I love its sea-coast and its mountains,
Its castle by the wood, and the fine lands,
The meads of its waters, and the valleys,
Its white gulls and lovely women.*

— 1151 —

Geffrei Gaimar

75 There was no more heed paid to the Welsh.*

on the death of Gruffudd ap Llywelyn in 1053
Estoire des Engleis (1151)

— 1157 —

John of Salisbury

76 The English King has set out to conquer the Welsh amidst their Alps and sub-Alps.*

letter

— 1163 —

Anonymous

77 This nation, O King, may now, as in former times, be harassed, and in a great measure weakened and destroyed by your and other powers, and it will also prevail by its laudable exertions, but it can never be totally subdued through the wrath of man, unless the wrath of God shall concur. Nor do I think that any other nation than this of Wales, or any other language, whatever may hereafter come to pass, shall on the day of severe examination before the Supreme Judge, answer for this corner of the earth.*

old man of Pencader to Henry II
recorded by Giraldus Cambrensis, *Descriptio Kambriae* (1193)

— c. 1165 —

Henry II

78 A people called Welsh, so bold and ferocious that, when unarmed, they do not fear to encounter an armed force, being ready to shed their blood in defence of their country, and to sacrifice their lives for renown.*

letter to the Emperor of Byzantium, c. 1165

— 1176 —

Anonymous

79 At Christmas in that year the Lord Rhys ap Gruffudd held court in splendour at Cardigan, in the castle. And he set two kinds of contests there: one between bards and poets, another between harpists and crowders and pipers and various classes of music-craft. And he had two chairs set for the victors.*

entry for the year 1176
Brut y Tywysogyon

— 1180 —

Anonymous

80 In the year one thousand one hundred and eighty there was nothing that might be placed on record.*

entry for the year 1180
Brut y Tywysogion

Walter Map

81 The Welsh will only keep the peace when they can do no mischief.*

De Nugis Curialium (c. 1180)

82 My fellow countrymen, the Welsh, although wholly treacherous to everyone – to each other as well as to foreigners – covet freedom, neglect peace, are warlike and skilful in arms, and are eager for revenge.*

— 1181 —

Chrétien de Troyes

83 The Welsh are all, by nature,
Wilder than the beasts of the field.*

Le Roman de Perceval (1181–90)

— 1191 —

Giraldus Cambrensis, Gerald of Wales

84 As Dyfed with its seven cantrefi is the fairest of all the lands of Wales, as Pembrokeshire is the fairest part of Dyfed, and this spot the fairest of Pembroke, it follows that Manorbier is the sweetest spot in Wales.*

Itinerarium Kambriae (1191)

85 Just as Anglesey can supply all the inhabitants of Wales with corn, so if all the herds were gathered together, Snowdon could afford sufficient pasture for them.*

— 1193 —

Giraldus Cambrensis, Gerald of Wales

86 Cambria, which by a corrupt and common term, though less proper, is in modern times called Wales, is about two hundred miles long and one hundred broad.*

Descriptio Kambriae (1193)

87 The perpetual remembrance of their former greatness, the recollection of their Trojan descent, and the high and continued majesty of the kingdom of Britain, may draw forth many a latent spark of animosity and encourage the daring spirit of rebellion.*

88 The Welsh esteem noble birth and generous descent above all things.*

89 Not only the nobles, but all the people are trained for war, and when the trumpet sounds the alarm, the husbandman rushes as eagerly from the plough as the courtier from his court.*

90 They are as easy to overcome in a single battle, as difficult to subdue in a protracted war.*

91 If they would be inseparable, they would be insuperable.*

92 The English fight for power, the Welsh for liberty; the one to procure gain, the other to avoid loss; the English hirelings for money, the Welsh patriots for their country.*

93 Nature has given not only to the highest, but also to the inferior classes of this nation a boldness and a confidence in speaking and answering even in the presence of their princes and chieftains.*

94 [The Welsh] do not live in towns, villages or castles, but lead a solitary existence deep in the woods.*

95 Even the common people know their family trees by heart and can readily recite from memory the list of their ancestors. . . back to the sixth or seventh generation.*

96 It is to be observed that the British language is more delicate and richer in north Wales, that country being less intermixed with foreigners. Many, however, assert that the language of Ceredigion in south Wales is the most refined.*

97 In their rhymed songs and set speeches they are so subtle and ingenious that they produce, in their native tongue, ornaments of wonderful and exquisite invention both

7

in the words and the sentences. . . They make use of alliteration in preference to all other ornaments of rhetoric, and that particular kind which joins by consonancy the first letters or syllables of words.*

98 In their musical concerts they do not sing in unison like the inhabitants of other countries, but in many different parts. . . You will hear as many different parts and voices as there are performers who all at length unite with organic melody.*

99 They do not engage in marriage until they have tried, by previous cohabitation, the disposition, and particularly the fecundity, of the person with whom they are engaged.*

100 No one of this nation ever begs, for the houses of all are common to all, and they consider liberality and hospitality among the first virtues.*

101 [The Welsh] pay no attention to commerce, shipping or manufacture.*

102 Happy and fortunate indeed would be this nation, nay completely blessed, if it had good prelates and pastors, and but one prince, and that prince a good one.*

— **1198** —

Anonymous

103 With the help and support of all the princes of Wales, [Gwenwynwyn of Powys] gathered a mighty host to seek to restore to the Welsh their ancient status and their proprietary rights and boundaries.*

entry for the year 1198
Brut y Tywysogyon

— **1200** —

Anonymous

104 The world's enigma, Arthur's grave.*

'Englynion y Beddau'

105 Maelgwn ap Rhys . . . sold to the Saxons the lock and stay of all Wales, the castle of Cardigan, for a small worthless price.*

entry for the year 1200
Brut y Tywysogyon

Cynddelw Brydydd Mawr

106 I saw, after battle, bowels on thorns.*

in an *awdl* to Owain Gwynedd

Layamon

107 That wild land which Welshmen love.*

Brut, *c*. 1200

— *c*. **1203** —

Giraldus Cambrensis, Gerald of Wales

108 Because I am a Welshman am I to be debarred from all preferment in Wales?*

letter to the Pope, *c*. 1203

— **1215** —

Anonymous

109 If we have disseised or removed Welshmen from lands or liberties or other things without the legal judgement of their peers in England or in Wales, they shall be immediately restored to them.*

Magna Carta (1215)

— **1216** —

Giraldus Cambrensis, Gerald of Wales

110 I am sprung from the princes of Wales and from the barons of the Marches, and when I see injustice in either race, I hate it.*

De Invectibus (1216)

— **1220** —

Anonymous

111 I am Taliesin. I sing perfect metre, Which will last to the end of the world.*

poem in manuscript
first printed in Ifor Williams, *Lectures on Early Welsh Poetry* (1944)

112 My original country is the region of the summer stars.*

— 1230 —

Anonymous

113 In that year William de Braose the Younger, lord of Brycheiniog, was hanged by the Lord Llywelyn in Gwynedd after he had been caught in Llywelyn's chamber with the King of England's daughter, Llywelyn's wife.*

entry for the year 1230
Brut y Tywysogyon

— 1240 —

Anonymous

114 He [Llywelyn ab Iorwerth] ruled his enemies with sword and spear, gave peace to the monks . . . enlarged his boundaries by his wars, gave good justice to all according to their deserts, and by the bonds of fear or love bound all men duly to him.*

entry for the year 1240
Brut y Tywysogyon

— 1244 —

Anonymous

115 It is not easy in our part of Wales to control Welshmen except by one of their own race.*

his vassals to the Earl of Pembroke, 1244

— 1248 —

Lodewyk van Veltheam

116 [At Ghent] you saw the peculiar habits of the Welsh. In the very depth of winter they were running about with bare legs. . . They were great drinkers. They endangered the Flemings very much. Their pay was too small and so it came about that they took what did not belong to them.*

Voortzetting van den Spiegel Historiael (1248–1316)

— 1256 —

Anonymous

117 The gentlefolk of Wales, despoiled of their liberty and their rights, came to Llywelyn ap Gruffudd and revealed to him with tears their grievous bondage to the English; and they made known to him that they preferred to be slain in war for their liberty than to suffer themselves to be unrighteously trampled upon by foreigners.*

entry for the year 1256
Brut y Tywysogyon

Matthew Paris

118 The Welsh who have been oppressed in manifold ways . . . were at last so outrageously and tyrannically oppressed by the king's agent, Geoffrey Langley, knight, that they aroused themselves for the defence of their country and the observance of its laws.*

Chronica Majora (1256)

119 Wales at this time was in a most straitened condition, and owing to the cessation of agriculture, commerce and the tending of flocks, the inhabitants began to waste away through want; unwillingly too did they bend to the yoke of the English laws; their ancient pride of nobility faded and even the harp of the ecclesiastics was turned to grief and lamentation.*

120 Edward was . . . determined to check the impetuous rashness of the Welsh, to punish their presumption and to wage war against them to their extermination.*

121 The Welsh had sworn on the gospels boldly and faithfully to the death for the liberty of their country and the laws of their ancestors, declaring they would rather die with honour than drag on an unhappy life in disgrace. This manly and brave determination might justly shame the English, who lazily bent their necks to foreigners and to every one that trampled on them, like vile and timid rabble, the scum of the human race.*

122 Far from showing obedience to the king's son, Edward, [the Welsh] only ridiculed and heaped insults and derision upon him, and he in consequence conceived the idea of giving up Wales and the Welsh as untameable.*

— 1265 —

Thomas Wykes

123 The English soldiers, being accustomed to
bread, could not do without it when they
were in the land of the Welsh with nothing
but meat or milk food on which that
savage people is used to feed.

Chronicle

— 1273 —

Llywelyn ap Gruffudd

124 The King well knows that the rights of
Llywelyn's principality are entirely
separate from the rights of the King's
realm, although Llywelyn holds his
principality under the King's royal
power.*

letter to Edward I, 11 July 1273

— 1275 —

Anonymous

125 In the Marches of Wales, or in any other
place where the King's writ does not run,
the King who is sovereign lord will do
right to all such as will complain.*

the Statute of Westminster, 1275

— 1282 —

Anonymous

126 And then was effected the betrayal of
Llywelyn in the belfry at Bangor by his
own men.*

entry for 1282
Brut y Tywysogyon

127 The King's host came without warning
upon Llywelyn ap Gruffudd and slew him
and many of his host on the feast day of
Pope Damasus, the eleventh day of the
month of December, a Friday, and then all
Wales was cast to the ground.*

Brehinedd y Saesson, 1282

128 Glory to God in the highest, peace to men
of goodwill, mastery to the English, victory
to Edward, honour to the Church, joy for

the Christian faith and eternal extinction
for the Welsh. The good news has reached
our ears that the old serpent Llywelyn,
who was once the prince of Wales, the
father of all deceit, the child of revolt, the
author of treason and the chief of all evil,
has been defeated on the field of battle.*

clerk in letter to Edward I, Dec. 1282

Gruffudd ab yr Ynad Coch

129 The heart's gone cold under a breast of
       fear;
Lust shrivels like dried brushwood.
See you not the way of the wind and the
       rain?
See you not oaktrees buffet together?
See you not the sea stinging the land?
    See you not truth in travail?
See you not the sun hurtling through the
       sky
    And that the stars are fallen?
Do you not believe in God, demented
       mortals?
    Do you not see the whole world's
       danger?
Why, O my God, does the sea not cover
       the land?
    Why are we left to linger?*

elegy to Llywelyn ap Gruffudd (trans. Anthony
Conran)

Roger Lestrange

130 Know, sir, that Llywelyn ap Gruffudd is
dead, his army broken and all the flower of
his men killed.*

letter to Edward I, Dec. 1282

— 1284 —

Anonymous

131 The Divine Providence. . . has now. . .
wholly and entirely transferred under our
proper dominion the land of Wales with its
inhabitants . . . and has annexed and
united the same into the Crown . . . as a
member of the said body.*

the Statute of Rhuddlan, 1284

132 [For] thefts, larcenies, burnings, murders,
manslaughter and manifest and laborious
robberies . . . we will that they shall use the
laws of England . . . Concerning

moveables, as of contracts, debts, sureties, covenants, trespasses, chattels and all other moveables of the same sort, they may use the Welsh law whereto they have been accustomed.*

— 1296 —

Anonymous

133 Welshmen are Welshmen.*

clerk of the court at Beaumaris, Feb. 1296

— 1300 —

Anonymous

134 In this year King Edward of England made Lord Edward, his son and heir, Prince of Wales and Count of Chester. When the Welsh heard this, they were overjoyed, thinking him their lawful master, for he was born in their lands.*

entry for the year 1300
Historia Anglicana

— 1311 —

Pierre de Langtoft

135 When elsewhere it is summer, it is winter in Wales.*

a rhyming summary of the history of England, 1311

— 1317 —

Llywelyn Bren

136 I will give myself up for the people, for it is better that one man should die than the whole people go into exile or perish by the sword.*

quoted in *Fiesta Edwardi de Carnarvan* (1317)

— *c.* 1320 —

Casnodyn

137 A slender, exquisite lady of beautiful Welsh speech.*

poem to Gwenllian, wife of Sir Gruffudd Llwyd, *c.* 1320

— *c.* 1330 —

Anonymous

138 The Welsh habit of revolt against the English is a long-standing madness . . . and this is the reason. The Welsh, formerly called the Britons, were once noble, crowned with the whole realm of England; but they were expelled by the Saxons and lost both name and kingdom . . . But from the sayings of the prophet Merlin they still hope to recover England. Hence it is they frequently rebel.*

Vita Edwardi Secundi (*c.* 1330)

— *c.* 1339 —

Anonymous

139 Englishmen were encouraged to intermingle with the Welsh so that the peace will be better assured and security improved by Englishmen so placed.

Calendar of Close Rolls, 1339–41

— 1344 —

Anonymous

140 The people of Wales inhabiting, as they do, wild places, are themselves untamed and fierce, so that they will hardly receive discipline from those expert in their own tongue . . . If they had a prelate ignorant of it they would be more disobedient and rebellious.

the Canons of St Asaph
quoted in Calendar of Papal Petitions, 1344

— 1345 —

John de Weston

141 Since his coming into Wales he has found the country most marvellous and strange.

to the officers of the Prince of Wales, 21 Aug. 1345

— 1346 —

Anonymous

142 I have made no mention of my own name lest these words should be marred by envy.

But rather let the reader pray that the name of him who wrote them should be written in Heaven and never blotted out from the book of life.*

Llyfr Ancr Llanddewibrefi (1346)

— *c.* **1350** —

Ranulf Higden

143 That which now is Wales by name
Was erst called Cambria, and Fame
Says 'twas from Camber, Brutus's son,
A king who reigned here long agone.*

'Of Wales' (trans. Peter Roberts)

144 Its bishops too are now but two;
In better times it had three more,
And princes of its own could boast;
But now the Saxons rule the roast.*

— **1372** —

Owain Lawgoch

145 [Wales] is and should be mine by right of succession, by kindred and by inheritance.*

declaration to his supporters, from Paris, 10 May 1372

— **1386** —

Anonymous

146 A burgess cannot be convicted or adjudged by any Welshman, but only by English burgesses and true Englishmen.

the charter of Laugharne, 1386

Sypyn Cyfeiliog

147 Come whenever you wish, take what you see,
    And once come, stay as long as you like.*

poem to Dafydd ap Cadwaladr of Bachelltre, Mont.

— **1401** —

Anonymous

148 It is ordained . . . that no Englishman shall be convicted by any Welshman . . . within the land of Wales.*

Rotuli Parliamentorum (1401)

149 It is ordained . . . that from henceforth no Welshman shall be armed nor bear defensible armour.*

150 It is ordained that no Englishman married to a Welshwoman . . . shall be put into any office in Wales or in the Marches.*

— **1402** —

Anonymous

151 [Glyndŵr] almost destroyed the King and his armies, by magic as it was thought, for from the time they entered Wales to the time they left, never did a gentle air breathe on them, but throughout whole days and nights, rain mixed with snow and hail afflicted them with cold beyond endurance.*

Annales Henrici Quarti (1402)

— **1404** —

Adam of Usk

152 At Machynlleth, Owain [Glyndŵr] and his mountain men, even in their miserable plight, usurping the methods of conquerors and the rights of kings, although to his own confusion, held, or simulated or pretended to hold parliaments.*

Chronicon (1404)

— **1406** —

Owain Glyndŵr

153 My nation has been trodden underfoot by the fury of the barbarous Saxons.*

letter to King Charles VI of France, March 1406

— **1411** —

Anonymous

154 The liberties of Brecon shall be restricted to those whom we deem to be Englishmen and to such of their heirs as are English on both their mother's and their father's side.

the charter of Brecon, 1411

— 1415 —

Anonymous

155 Very many say that he [Owain Glyndŵr]
died: the seers say that he did not.*

Annals of Owain Glyndŵr (1415)

— 1420 —

Siôn Cent

156 My hope is on what is to come.*

'Gobeithiaw a ddaw ydd wyf'

157 All men end by lying down.*

'I'r Byd'

— *c.* 1436 —

Anonymous

158 Beware of Wales, Christ Jesus must us
keep,
That it make not our child's child to weep.

The Libel of English Policy (*c.* 1436)

— *c.* 1450 —

Deio ab Ieuan Du

159 The red dragon will show the way.*

poem thanking Siôn ap Rhys of Glyn Nedd for
the gift of a bull

Guto'r Glyn

160 Where are the old men? Dead, at last?
I tonight am left the oldest.*

poem to the abbot of Glyn Egwystl (trans.
Anthony Conran)

161 Keep Horsa's offspring from Flint,
Rowena's race from Gwynedd,
No posts for Saxons, my lord,
No pardon for a burgher.*

poem to William Herbert, Earl of Pembroke

162 Take Glamorgan and Gwynedd,
Make one land from Conwy to Neath,
If England's dukes resent it,
Wales will rally to your side.*

163 Woe that we are born in servitude.*

poem to Edward IV

— 1485 —

Anonymous

164 Sir Rice ap Thomas draws Wales with
him:
A worthy sight it was to see
How the Welshmen rose wholly with him
And shogged him to Shrewsbury.

'The Red Rose of England'

165 The Welsh may now be said to have
recovered their independence, for the most
wise and fortunate Henry VII is a
Welshman.*

report of Venetian envoy, 1485

Henry VII

166 To free this our Principality of Wales of
such miserable servitude as they have long
piteously stood in.

letter to Welsh gentry seeking their support,
1485

Richard ap Hywel

167 I dwell with my people.*

— *c.* 1520 —

Anonymous

168 Aberdare, Llanwynno through,
all Merthyr to Llanfabon,
there was never a more disastrous thing
than cutting the woods of Glyn Cynon.*

'Coed Glyn Cynon'

— *c.* 1527 —

Lewys Morgannwg

169 What is the world without a poet's hope?*

elegy to Iorwerth Fynglwyd

— 1534 —

Eustace Chapuys

170 The distress of the people is incredible,
especially the Welsh, from whom by Act of
Parliament the king has just taken away
their native laws, customs and privileges,
which is the very thing they can endure
least patiently.*

to Emperor Charles V, 1534

— **1536** —

Anonymous

171 An act for Laws and Justices to be ministered in Wales in like form as it is in this realm.

title of the Act of Union, 1536

172 His Highness . . . of the singular love and favour that he bears towards his subjects of this said dominion of Wales, and intending to reduce them to the perfect order, notice and knowledge of the laws of this his Realm, and utterly to extirpate all and singular the sinister usages and customs differing from the same . . . hath . . . ordained, enacted and established that his said country or dominion of Wales shall stand and continue for ever from henceforth incorporated, united and annexed to and with his Realm of England.

Act of Union, 1536

173 Persons born or to be born in the said Principality . . . of Wales shall have and enjoy and inherit all and singular Freedoms, Liberties, Rights, Privileges and Laws . . . as other the King's subjects have, enjoy or inherit.

174 The people of the dominion [of Wales] have and do daily use a speech nothing like nor consonant to the natural mother tongue used within this realm.

175 No person or persons that use the Welsh speech or language shall have or enjoy any manor, office or fees within the realm of England, Wales or other the king's dominions upon pain of forfeiting the same offices or fees unless he or they use and exercise the speech or language of English.

— *c.* **1540** —

John Price

176 North Wales has been a great while the chiefest seat of the last Kings of Britain because it was and is the strongest country within this isle.

Description of Cambria (*c.* 1540)

— **1547** —

John Price

177 And now, since God has given the printing press in our midst to multiply knowledge of His blessed words, it is proper for us, as all Christendom has done already, to participate in that virtue with them, so that as good a gift as this should not be without fruit for us more than for others.*

Yny Lhyvyr Hwnn (1547)

William Salesbury

178 Go barefoot on pilgrimage to his Grace the King and his council to beseech that the Holy Scriptures should be available in your language.*

Oll Synnwyr Pen Kembero Ygyd (1547)

179 And take this advice from me: unless you save and correct and perfect the language before the extinction of the present generation, it will be too late afterwards.*

180 If you do not wish to be worse than animals . . . obtain learning in your own language; if you do not wish to be more unnatural than any other nation under the sun, love your language and those who love it. If you do not wish utterly to depart from the faith of Christ . . . obtain the holy scripture in your own tongue as your happy ancestors, the ancient British, had it.*

— **1551** —

William Salesbury

181 Woe unto the priests of the world who do not rebuke vice and do not preach. Woe unto him who does not guard his flock and he a shepherd. Woe unto him who keeps not his sheep from Roman wolves with his crooked staff.*

Kynniver llith a ban (1551)

— **1567** —

Richard Davies

182 There flourished and reigned all manner of falsehood, idolatry, excess, superstition, charms and incantations; faith was extinguished and all kinds of evil and godlessness were fostered.*

of religion in pre-Reformation Wales
Epistol at y Cembru (1567)

183 Holy Scripture and the Word of God were common in former times among the Welsh.*

184 So depreciated was the Welshman's language and so much neglected that the printing press could bring forth no fruit to be accounted to the Welshman in his own tongue until this very day or just a short while ago.*

Gruffydd Robert

185 My distinguished lord, the heart of every Welshman leaps with true joy when he hears a man of your eminence speaking his language.*

to the Earl of Pembroke
Dosparth byrr ar y rhan gyntaf o ramadeg gymraeg (1567)

186 It is very strange that the Welsh are so uncaring towards me [the Welsh language] and I so useless to them, especially . . . as I am so abundant in letters, so rich in words, so ancient in my origins.*

187 You will have some people, as soon as they see the Severn or the belfries of Shrewsbury, and hear an Englishman say goodmorrow, who begin to abandon their Welsh.*

188 He who denies his father or his mother or his country or his language will never be a man of civilization and virtue.*

— *c.* **1570** —

Anonymous

189 Take ten, he said, and call them Rice,
Take another ten and call them Price,
Take fifty others and call them Hughes,
A hundred more and dub them Pughes,
Now Roberts name a hundred score
And Williams name a legion more, .
And call, he moaned in languid tones,
Call all the others Jones.

attributed to a Tudor judge, *c.* 1570
quoted by H. Morris Jones, *Doctor in the Whip's Room* (1955)

— **1572** —

Humphrey Llwyd

190 Even in direst poverty they never forget their gentle origins.*

Commentarioli Descriptionis Britannicae Fragmentum (1572)

191 Of late, the [Welsh people] are applying themselves to settle in towns, learn mechanics, engage in commerce, cultivate the soil, and undertake all other public duties equally with Englishmen.*

— **1573** —

Humphrey Llwyd

192 Their tongue [Ceredigion's] is esteemed the finest, of all the other people in Wales. And Gwynedd, the purer, without permixion, coming nearest unto the ancient British. But the Southern most rudest, and coarsest, because it has greatest affinity with strange tongues.

The Breviary of Britayne (1573)

— **1583** —

Sir Henry Sidney

193 A better people to govern than the Welsh [Europe] holdeth not.

letter to Sir Francis Walsingham, 1 March 1583

— **1586** —

Anonymous

194 There is not a land in all Christendom of comparable area having so many saints within it as were found among the Welsh in times gone by.*

Y Drych Cristionogawl (1586)

— **1587** —

Thomas Churchyard

195 Wales is this day (behold throughout the shires)
In better state than 'twas these hundred years.

The Worthiness of Wales (1587)

Morris Kyffin

196 Ye British poets, repeat in royal song
(With weighty words used in King
    Arthur's days)
Th'imperial stock from whence your
    Queen hath sprung;
Install in verse your Princess' lasting
    praise:
  Pencerddiaid, play on ancient harp
    and crowde;
  Atceiniaid, sing her praises piercing
    loud.

Let hills and rocks rebounding echoes yield
Of Queen Elizabeth's long lasting fame;
Let woody groves and watery streams be
    filled,
And creeks and caves, with sounding of the
    same:
  O Cambria, stretch and strain thy
    utmost breath
  To praise and pray for Queen
    Elizabeth.

The Blessedness of Britain (1587)

— **1588** —

Anonymous

197 The translation of the Bible into the Welsh
or British tongue which by Act of
Parliament should long since have been
done, is now performed by one Dr Morgan
and set forth in print.

Acts of the Privy Council, 22 Sept. 1588

William Morgan

198 If there are those who in order to
safeguard unity insist that it would be
better to urge our fellow-countrymen to
learn English rather to translate the
Scriptures into our langage, I would wish
them to be more careful lest, in their zeal
for unity, they become an impediment on
the path to truth.*

Y Bibl Cyssegr-lan (1588)

199 There is no doubt that likeness in religion
is a far stronger bond of union than
uniformity of language.

to Elizabeth I, 1588

— *c.* **1590** —

John Davies (of Hereford)

200 We have been long afflicted and oppressed

By those that sought our whole race to
    destroy.

'Cambria'

201 Caerleon where King Arthur lived of yore
Shall be rebuilt, and double gilt once
    more.

202 I speak for those whose tongues are strange
    to thee
In thine own tongue: if my words be unfit,
That blame be mine: but if Wales better be
By my disgrace, I hold that grace to me.

— **1591** —

Gervase Babington

203 I am the Bishop of Aff, because all the land
has gone.

of the bishopric of Llandaff
quoted in Glanmor Williams (ed.), *Early Modern
Glamorgan* (1974)

— **1592** —

Siôn Dafydd Rhys

204 For our part, we Welsh are sometimes so
disgusting and so frippish, and (different
from every other people in the world) so
light-headed, that we affect a slight shame
about uttering our own language; yes, and
how fortunate some of us can be that we
can snobbishly pretend that we have
utterly lost our ability to speak Welsh, and
must now put up with speaking English, or
French, or Italian or absolutely any other
tongue as long as it is not Welsh.*

Cambrobrytannicae Linguae Institutione (1592)

— **1593** —

John Penry

205 I am a poor young man born and bred in
the mountains of Wales.

letter to Lord Burghley just before his execution,
22 May 1593

— **1594** —

Morris Kyffin

206 A Churchman from Wales declared at the

Eisteddfod that the printing of Welsh books should not be allowed, for the Welsh should be made to learn English and to forget their Welsh . . . Could the Devil himself have expressed it better?*

Deffynniad Ffydd Eglwys Loegr (1594)

207 A necessary, masterly, godly, learned work for which the Welsh will never be able to repay and thank him in accordance with his deserts.*

of William Morgan's translation of the Bible into Welsh

208 A wretched people [the Welsh], they know little, have seen less, and they cannot be taught.*

George Owen

209 There is a certain ardent affection in the hearts of Welshmen towards Her Majesty which makes them inwardly to rejoice that God has blessed our nation . . . with a prince of our own natural country and name.

A Dialogue of the Present Government of Wales (1594)

— 1595 —

Sir Phillip Sidney

210 In Wales, the true remnant of the ancient Britons, there are good authorities to show the long time they had poets, which they called bards: so through all the conquests of Romans, Saxons, Danes, and Normans, some of whom did seek to ruin all memory of learning among them, yet do their poets to this day, last; so as it is not more notable in soon beginning than in long continuing.

An Apology for Poetry (1595)

— 1597 —

William Shakespeare

211 But I will never be a truant, love,
Till I have learned thy language, for thy tongue
Makes Welsh as sweet as ditties highly penn'd
Sung by a fair queen in a summer's bower,
With ravishing division, to her lute.

Mortimer to Lady Mortimer
Henry IV, part I (*c.* 1597)

212 Now I perceive the devil understands Welsh.

Hotspur

213 Lie still, ye thief, and hear the lady sing in Welsh.

Lady Percy to Hotspur

I had rather hear Lady my brach howl in Irish.

Hotspur to Lady Percy

214 At my nativity
The front of heaven was full of fiery shapes
Of burning cressets; and at my birth
The frame and huge foundation of the earth
Shaked like a coward.

Owen Glendower

215 Three times hath Henry Bolingbroke made heat
Against my power; thrice from the banks of Wye
And sandy-bottomed Severn have I sent him
Bootless home and weather-beaten back.

216 Heavens defend me from that Welsh fairy! lest he transform me to a piece of cheese.

Falstaff of Sir Hugh Evans
The Merry Wives of Windsor (1597)

217 I am not able to answer the Welsh flannel.

Falstaff

— 1598 —

Anonymous

218 It is very certain that if [Ireland] should be cut off from . . . England, it would make the old brutes of Wales to look about them more than they do now.

Calendar of State Papers Domestic, 1598–9

219 These mountains may not unfitly be termed the British Alps, as being the most vast of all Britain.

of Snowdonia
Description of Wales (1599)

William Shakespeare

220 Though it appear a little out of fashion,
There is much care and valour in this
Welshman.

King Henry of Fluellyn
Henry V (1599)

221 There is a river in Macedon, and there is
also moreover a river at Monmouth . . .
and there is salmons in both.

Fluellyn to King Henry

222 If your majesty is remembered of it, the
Welshmen did good service in a garden
where leeks did grow, wearing leeks in
their Monmouth caps, which, your
majesty knows, to this hour is an
honourable badge of the service; and, I do
believe, your majesty takes no scorn to
wear the leek upon St Tavy's day.

223 I wear it for a memorable honour, for I am
Welsh, good countryman.

King Henry to Fluellyn

224 You thought, because he could not speak
English in the native garb he could not
therefore handle an English cudgel: you
find it otherwise; and henceforth let a
Welsh correction teach you a good English
condition.

Gower to Pistol, of Fluellyn

— **1600** —

Anonymous

225 There is no history written by the bards
since the death of Llewelyn ap Gruffudd,
the last prince of Cambria, for they had no
princes of their own to set forth their acts.*

Y Tri Chof (17th cent.)

226 As ragged as a Welsh curate.

traditional saying, 17th cent.

227 Alas, alas, poor Radnorshire,
Never a park, not even a deer,
Never a squire of five hundred a year
Save Richard Fowler of Abbey Cwm-hir.

228 Upon the Sundays and holidays, the
multitude of all sorts of men and women

and children of every parish do use to meet
in sundry places . . . where their harpers
and crowthers sing them songs of the
doings of their ancestors, namely of their
wars against the kings of this realm and the
English nation.

manuscript, 'The State of North Wales touching
Religion', *c.* 1600

Edward ap Raff

229 The world has all gone English.*

poem, *c.* 1600

— **1603** —

George Owen

230 No country in England so flourished in one
hundred years as Wales hath done since
the government of Henry VII to this time,
insomuch that if our fathers were now
living they would think it some strange
country inhabited with a foreign nation, so
altered is the countrymen, the people
changed in heart within and the land
altered in hue without, from evil to good,
and from bad to better.

The Description of Pembrokeshire (1603)

231 The whole country was brought into small
pieces of ground and intermingled up and
down with another, so as in every five or
six acres you shall have ten or twelve
owners.

232 Some [Welsh students at Oxford and
Cambridge] prove to be learned men and
good members in the commonwealth of
England and Wales; some worthy
labourers in the Lord's vineyard, many of
them have proved excellent in the Civil
Laws, some in Physic, and other laudable
studies, wherein they are found nothing
behind other nations.

233 [Henry Tudor] drew the hearts of
Welshmen to him as the lodestone doth the
iron . . . there hath not been found in
England any country or province more
obedient in heart than this country of
Wales.

234 For now the poor tenant that lived well in
that golden world is taught to sing unto his
lord a new song.

— 1612 —

Sir John Davies

235 [Henry VIII] united the dominion of Wales to the Crown of England . . . by means whereof that entire country in a short time was securely settled in peace and obedience, and hath attained to that civility of manners and plenty of all things, as now we find it not inferior to the best parts of England.

Why Ireland was never entirely subdued (1612)

— 1619 —

Ben Jonson

236 Remember the country has always been fruitful of loyal hearts to your majesty, a very garden and seed-plot of honest minds and men . . . Though the nation be said to be unconquered and most loving liberty, yet it was never mutinous, and please your majesty, but stout, valiant, courteous, hospitable, temperate, ingenious, capable of all good arts, most lovingly constant, charitable, great antiquaries, religious preservers of their gentry and genealogy, as they are zealous and knowing in religion.

For the Honour of Wales (1619)

— c. 1620 —

Sir John Wynn

237 A great temporal blessing it is and a great heart's ease to a man to find that he is well descended.

History of the Gwydir Family (c. 1620)

238 Civility and learning flourished in that town, so as they were called the lawyers of Caernarfon, the merchants of Beaumaris, and the gentlemen of Conwy.

239 It was Owen Glyndŵr's policy to bring all things to waste, that the English should find not the strength nor resting place in the country.

— 1621 —

Anonymous

240 Their Lord they shall praise,
Their language they shall keep,
Their land they shall lose,
Except wild Wales.*

of the Britons
quoted by John Davies, *Antiquae Linguae Britannicae* (1621)

John Davies (of Mallwyd)

241 It is impossible to believe that God would have seen fit to keep this language until these days, after so many crises in the history of the nation . . . had He not intended His Name to be called and His great works to be proclaimed in it.*

Antiquae Linguae Britannicae (1621)

242 I have known Englishmen who know not a word of Welsh, who have been able to read Welsh (without knowing anything except the force of the letters) with such perfection and such clarity that any Welshman could understand . . . so definite and perfect are our rules of writing that we yield not to any language on this point.*

243 Lately, it is true, because of daily intercourse with the English and because our young men receive their education in England . . . some English words and a number of English idioms have pushed their way in and are increasingly pushing their way in day by day.*

244 There is not so great a difference between the language of the works of Aneirin and Taliesin and the acceptable way of speaking today that those who are fairly learned in the Welsh language cannot understand them.*

245 It is a matter of astonishment that a handful of the remaining Britons, in so confined a corner, despite the oppression of the English and the Normans, have for so many centuries kept not only the name of their ancestors but also their own original language to this very day, without any change of importance, and without corruption.*

246 Although [the Welsh language] claimed unto herself a number of Latin words when she was under the yoke of Rome, and

although she borrowed words from other languages as a result of the intercourse of peoples, she has equivalent words of her own for which she is not indebted to any foreign language.*

247 The Britons called themselves . . . *Cymry*, that is, the original inhabitants, and they called their language *Cymraeg*, the original or innate speech, not because they believed that the nation and the language sprang from the earth like a toadstool, but because the beginnings of the nation and the language were older than anyone could remember.*

James Howell

248 'Twas a tough task, believe it, thus to tame
   A wild and wealthy language, and to
      frame
   Grammatic toils to curb her, so that she
   Now speaks by rules, and sings by prosody;
   Such is the strength of art rough things to
      shape
   And of rude commons rich enclosures
      make.

'Upon Dr Davies's British Grammar', *c*. 1621

— **1627** —

Anonymous

249 Wales is fading, the bards are in their
      graves.*

poem, 1627

— **1630** —

Rowland Vaughan

250 O blood-red Brythons, take the labour and trouble to set out your rich speech, unless you are of the same opinion as the anglicized Welsh, who believe it is better that our language should be annihilated and exterminated so that this whole island should speak the language of the English.*

Yr Ymarfer o Dduwioldeb (1630)

— **1632** —

Anonymous

251 There were three jovial Welshmen,

As I have heard men say,
And they would go a-hunting, boys,
   Upon St David's Day;
And all the day they hunted,
   But nothing could they find
Except a ship a-sailing,
   A-sailing with the wind.

ballad, *c*. 1632

John Davies (of Mallwyd)

252 If the guardian of your tender youth see fit, Your Highness should be imbued from the cradle, at the same as with other languages, with the ancient language of this island, which is now restricted to your own Welsh people . . . for knowing languages is no indignity for princes.*

dedication to Charles, Prince of Wales
Dictionarium Duplex (1632)

253 The Welsh books which could have shown us the meaning of the ancient words. . . have nearly all disappeared through the fury of war, the hatred of enemies, the ravages of fire and the neglect of our fellow countrymen.*

254 I openly condemn the efforts of those who labour to trace almost every Welsh word to a Latin source . . . It is obvious that most Welsh words are innate to the Welsh nation and that they do not spring from Latin or any other European language.*

255 Poets, in every language, through some peculiar privilege of theirs, claim to themselves the right to judge words . . . But the writings of poets in general, and particularly those of Welsh poets, are such that they are incomparable in the complexity of their sentences and the obscurity of their words.*

— **1634** —

John Milton

256 A noble peer of mickle trust and power
   Has in his charge, with tempered awe to
      guide
   An old and haughty nation proud in arms.

of the Earl of Bridgewater and his lands in Wales

Comus (1634)

— **1645** —

James Howell

257 This life at best is but an inn,
And we the passengers.

Epistolae Ho-Elianae (1645)

John Williams

258 [The drovers are] the Spanish fleet of
North Wales which bring hither that little
gold and silver we have.

letter to Prince Rupert, Jan. 1645

— **1646** —

Shôn ap Owen

259 Three Welshmen, two soldiers; three
Englishmen, two thieves; three
Frenchmen, two traitors.

A True Copy of the Welsh Sermon (1646)

— **1649** —

Anonymous

260 We, on the part of your Highness's
subjects, inhabiting that part of the island
which our invaders first called Wales . . .
do crave to be received and adopted into
the same laws and privileges which your
other subjects enjoy.

gentlemen of Wales to Henry VIII
recorded by Lord Herbert of Cherbury, *Life and
Reign of Henry the Eighth* (1649)

— **1650** —

Henry Vaughan

261 They are all gone into the world of light!

'They are all gone into the world of light!'

262 I saw Eternity the other night
Like a great Ring of pure and endless
light,
All calm, as it was bright,
And round beneath it, Time in hours,
days, years,
Driv'n by the spheres
Like a vast shadow mov'd, in which the
world
And all her train were hurl'd.

'The World'

263 My Soul, there is a Countrie
Far beyond the stars,
Where stands a wingèd Centrie
All skilful in the wars;
There above noise, and danger,
Sweet peace sits crown'd with smiles,
And one born in a manger
Commands the beauteous files.

'Peace'

264 Lord! What a busy, restless thing
Has thou made man;
Each day and hour he is on wing,
Rests not a span.

'The Pursuite'

— **1652** —

John Edwards

265 Among all the countries of the world, there
is no nation more lacking in love and more
hostile to its own language than the Welsh,
although our language, because of its
antiquity and richness, deserves as much
respect as any other language.*

Madruddyn y Difinyddeaeth Diweddaraf (1652)

— **1653** —

Morgan Llwyd

266 O people of Wales! unto you is my cry. O
inhabitants of Gwynedd and
Deheubarth! my voice cries out to you.
The dawn has broken and the sun is rising
upon you.*

Gwaedd yng Nghymru (1653)

267 Enter your secret chamber, which is the
light of God within you.*

268 The fire has been kindled in Wales. The
door of your forest (O land of the present-
day Britons) is open to the fierce flames.
And the axe is already at your root. If you
do not bear good fruit this very hour, you
shall be stopped from being a people.*

Llyfr y Tri Aderyn (1653)

269 A man's time is his inheritance, and woe to
him who spends it in vain.*

270 Lord, I desire to be dissolved,
And from my self be free;

For in the womb of this dark world
  I have been long from Thee.

'Sweet Master Christ'

271 Let Wales and England rousèd be!
    O churches, sleep no more,
and be not drunk with wealth or wrath –
  hark how the nations roar.

'Awake, O Lord, Awake thy Saints'

272 O Wales, poor Rachel, thou shalt bear;
    sad Hannah, now rejoice.
The last is first, the summer comes
  to hear the turtle's voice.

Christ is in arms. The day is hot:
  now Beelzebub, retreat.
When that great summer is once past
  next comes that harvest great.

'The Summer'

— *c.* **1660** —

John Jones

273 Mr Sheriff, I must return you many thanks
for your civility.

the regicide's last words before execution,
17 Oct. 1660

Huw Morys

274 While life lasts, spend your summer;
You will have heaven for wintering.*

'Cyngor'

— **1662** —

Anonymous

275 Men who are made heralds in other
countries are born heralds in Wales; so
naturally are all there inclined to know
and keep their descents, which they derive
from great antiquity; so that any Welsh
gentlemen (if this be not a tautology) can
presently climb up, by the stairs of his
pedigree, into princely extraction.

The History of the Worthies of England (1662)

Rowland Watkyns

276 The many-headed Hydra, or the People,
  Now build the church, then pull down
      bells and steeple.

'The Common People'

277   I do prefer by far
An unjust peace before the justest war.

'Peace and War'

278 For every marriage then is best in tune
When that the wife is May, the husband
    June.

'To the most Courteous and Fair Gentlewoman,
Mrs Elinor Williams'

— **1663** —

George Herbert

279 Who sweeps a room as for Thy laws
Makes that and th'action fine.

'The Elixir'

280 Teach me, my God and King,
In all things Thee to see,
And what I do in any thing
To do it as for Thee.

281 Throw away thy rod,
Throw away thy wrath,
  O my God,
Take the gentle path.

'The Temple'

282 Who would have thought my shrivelled
    heart
Could have recovered greenness?

'The Flower'

283 I struck the board, and cried, 'No more,
    I will abroad.'

'The Collar'

284 Love bade me welcome; yet my soul drew
    back,
  Guilty of dust and sin.

'Love'

285 Softness, and peace, and joy, and love, and
    bliss,
  Exalted manna, gladness of the best,
  Heaven in ordinary, man well dressed,
The Milky Way, the bird of paradise . . .
  Church-bells beyond the stars heard, the
    soul's blood,
  The land of spices; something
    understood.

'Prayer'

— 1667 —

Charles Edwards

286 The English, who formerly were ravenous wolves, have for us become cherishing shepherds.*

Y Ffydd Ddi-ffuant (1667)

Samuel Pepys

287 I do observe, it being St David's Day, the picture of a man, dressed like a Welchman, hanging by the neck upon one of the poles . . . which is one of the oddest sights I have seen a good while.

entry in diary, 1 March 1667

Katherine Phillips

288 This spoke King Arthur who, if fame be true,
Could have compelled Mankind to speak it too.

'On the Welch Language'

— 1681 —

Rhys Prichard

289 'Tis to the Welsh a foul disgrace
They're in religion still so young
That not a tenth of all the race
The Scriptures read in their own tongue.*

Cannwyll y Cymru (1681)

— 1682 —

Ifan Llwyd ap Dafydd

290 Welsh in its own land is the most alien language under the heavens.*

Ystorie Kymru (latter half of the 17th cent.)

William Richards

291 The land is mountainous and yields pretty handsome clambering for goats, and hath variety of precipices to break one's neck, which a man must do sooner than fill his belly, the soil being barren and an excellent place to breed famine in.

Wallography (1682)

292 Their native gibberish is usually prattled throughout the whole of Taphydom except in their market towns, whose inhabitants, being a little raised . . . do begin to despise it. 'Tis usually cashiered out of gentlemen's houses . . . so that, if the stars prove lucky, there may be some glimmering hopes that the British language may be quite extinct and may be English'd out of Wales.

— 1688 —

Thomas Jones

293 And thus it pleased the Almighty to deal with us the Britons; for these many ages have eclipsed our power and corrupted our language and almost blotted us out of the Books of Records.

The British Language in its Lustre (1688)

— 1690 —

Anonymous

294 The guile and softness of the Saxon race
In gallant Briton's soul had never place;
Strong as his rocks and in his language pure,
In his own innocence and truth secure:
Such is the bold, the noble mountaineer,
As void of treason as he is of fear.

the Brogyntin Poet
'On the Welsh', *c.* 1690

— 1697 —

John Vanbrugh

295 A Welch woman? Prithee, of what country's that?

Aesop to Quaint

That, Sir, is a country in the world's backside where every man is born a gentleman, and a genealogist.

Quaint to Aesop
Aesop (1697)

— 1700 —

Anonymous

296 Here lies buried under these stones
Shon ap Wiliam ap Shinkin ap Shones;
Her was born in Wales and killed in France,
Her went to Cot by a very mis-shance.

'Epitaph on a Welch Man', early 18th cent.

297 When Merlin's oak shall tumble down,
Then shall fall Carmarthen town.

traditional rhyme, early 18th cent.

E.B.

298 The fag end of Creation; the very rubbish
of Noah's flood; the highest English hills
are as cherrystones to the Welsh Alps, so
that there is not in the whole world a
people that live so near to and yet so far
from Heaven, as the Welsh do.

A Trip to North Wales (1700)

299 The language is inarticulate and guttural
and sounds more like the gobbling
of geese or turkeys than the speech of
rational creatures.

300 Nothing can be imagined so troublesome
as a Welshman possessed with the spirit of
genealogy.

— 1701 —

Ellis Wynne

301 The duties of Kings and Judges and the
Rulers of State and Church, apart from
being heavy and complex, are alas,
irrelevant to the Welsh language.*

Rheol Buchedd Sanctaidd (1701)

— 1703 —

Ellis Wynne

302 On a fine evening in a warm and mellow
summer I betook me up one of the
mountains of Wales, with spy-glass in
hand, to enable my feeble sight to see the
distant near, and to make the little to loom
large.*

Gweledigaethau'r Bardd Cwsg (1703)

— 1721 —

Erasmus Saunders

303 There is, I believe, no part of the Nation
more inclined to be religious, and to be
delighted with it, than the poor
inhabitants of these Mountains.

View of Religion in the Diocese of St David's (1721)

—1724 —

Daniel Defoe

304 The devil lives in the middle of Wales.

Tour through the Whole Island of Great Britain
(1724)

John Dyer

305 Ever charming, ever new,
When will the landscape tire the view!

'Grongar Hill'

306 A little rule, a little sway,
A sunbeam in a winter's day,
Is all the proud and mighty have
Between the cradle and the grave.

307 Content me with an humble shade,
My passions tam'd, my wishes laid;
For while our wishes wildly roll,
We banish quiet from the soul.

308 O may I with myself agree
And never covet what I see.

— 1727 —

Daniel Defoe

309 They [the Welsh] value themselves much
on their antiquity, the ancient race of their
houses, families and the like, and above all,
their ancient heroes . . . and, as they
believe their country to be the pleasantest
and most agreeable in the world, so you
cannot oblige them more than to make
them think that you believe so too.

A Tour through the Whole Island of Great Britain
(1727)

310 The only support we had in this heavy
journey was, (1) that we generally found
their provisions very good and cheap and
very good accommodations in the inns.
And (2) that the Welsh gentlemen are very
civil, hospitable, and kind; the people are
very obliging and conversible, and
especially to strangers.

William Gambold

311 Its misfortune is that it is not at all known
in foreign countries, unless in a small
province of France; and very little known
in this our own island, the Principality of

Wales excepted. Yet herein the language
as well as its proprietors did but share in
the common fate of all conquered nations;
for it is very obvious that the language of
such must as well give way to the language
of the conquerors, as the necks of the
inhabitants must truckle under the yokes
of their subduers.

preface to his *Welsh Grammar* (1727)

David Meredith
312 Long in barb'rous Welsh I went astray
And talked by rote, as country fiddlers
play . . .
'Till your ingenious pen improved my
sense
And shew'd me number, gender, mood,
and tense.

epigraph to William Gambold's *Welsh Grammar*
(1727)

— 1728 —

James Thomson
313 Where the broken landscape, by degrees
Ascending, roughens into rigid hills;
O'er which the Cambrian Mountains, like
far clouds
That skirt the blue horizon, dusky rise.

The Seasons (1728)

— 1730 —

Richard Savage
314 Cambria, my darling scene!

'To John Powell'

— 1732 —

Thomas Fuller
315 Blessed is the eye
That is between Severn and Wye.

Gnomologia (1732)

— 1736 —

Lewis Morris
316 It has been the continual blind complaint
of some uneasy men . . . that the preserving

of Welsh . . . is keeping up a discord
between the subjects of the Monarchs of
Great Britain; if so, God forbid we should
ever talk Welsh . . . But amity and concord
amongst men does not consist in the
Language they speak . . . but in the
congruity of their opinions in Religion and
Politics.

letter to William Morris, April 1736

317 Good Lord, to what a poor degree our
Language is dwindled in that county . . . I
could not understand ye Hodge Podge
which they speak.

of the Welsh of Glamorgan
letter to Edward Samuel, 1 Oct. 1736

— 1739 —

John Wesley
318 I have seen no part of England so pleasant
for sixty or seventy miles together as those
parts of Wales I have been in. And most of
the inhabitants are indeed ripe for the
Gospel. I mean (if the expression appears
strange) they are earnestly desirous of
being instructed in it, and as utterly
ignorant of it they are as any Creek or
Cherokee Indians.

entry in journal, 20 Oct. 1739

— 1740 —

Griffith Jones
319 What length of time . . . how many
hundreds of years must be allowed for the
general attainment of English, and the
dying away of the Welsh language? . . .
And in the meantime, while this is adoing
. . . what myriads of poor ignorant souls
must launch forth into the dreadful abyss
of eternity, and perish for want of
knowledge.

in *Welch Piety* (1740)

320 She [the Welsh language] has not lost her
charms, her chasteness, remains
unalterably the same . . . still retains the
beauties of her youth, grown old in years,
but not decayed. I pray that due regard
may be had to her great age, her intrinsic

25

usefulness, and that her long standing repute may not be stained by wrong imputations . . . Let her stay the appointed time to expire a peaceful and natural death, which we trust will not be till the consummation of all things, when all the languages of the world will be reduced into one again.

Lewis Morris

321 Ye sailors bold both great and small
That navigate the ocean,
Who love a lass that's fair and tall,
Come hearken to my motion;
You must have heard of Milford Haven,
All harbours it surpasses,
I know no port this side of heaven
So famed for handsome lasses.

'The Fishing Lass of Hakin'

— 1742 —

Lewis Morris

322 Kington, Herefordshire: all English here.
New Radnor is not four miles from hence,
where there is nothing but Welsh.

letter to William Morris, 11 Feb. 1742

— 1745 —

Lewis Morris

323 I am ashamed of my self and country of Wales, that we have neither the skill nor courage to write the history of our own ancestors, nay far from that, that few of us in these days . . . take any pleasure in reading the histories those brave people have left us.

letter to Thomas Carte, 30 March 1745

— 1746 —

Anonymous

324 Let England boast Bath's crowded springs,
Llandrindod happier Cambria sings.

'A Journey to Llandrindod Wells, in Radnorshire'

325 In all cases where the kingdom of England, or that part of Great Britain called England, hath been or shall be mentioned in any Act of Parliament, the same has been and shall from henceforth be deemed and taken to comprehend and include the Dominion of Wales.

Act of Parliament, 1746

William Shenstone

326 Yet for those mountains, clad with lasting snow,
The freeborn Briton left his greenest mead,
Receding sullen from his mightier foe,
For here he saw fair Liberty recede.

'Elegy XXI'

— 1749 —

John Torbuck

327 'Tis a tongue (it seems) not made for any mouth; as appears by an instance of one in our company, who having got a Welsh poly-syllable into his throat, was almost choked with consonants, had we not, by clapping him on the back, made him disgorge a guttural or two, and so saved him.

A Collection of Welsh Travels and Memoirs of Wales (1749)

328 They are all so well versed in the history of their descents, that you shall hear a poor beggar woman derive her extraction from the first maid of honour to Nimrod's wife, or else she thinks she is a nobody.

— 1750 —

Lewis Morris

329 I am a jovial miner,
I wander up and down,
I have no settled station
In country or in town,
    Then a-mining we will go . . .

'The Miner's Ballad', c. 1750

330 They talk of peace in palaces,
I'm sure there's no such thing;
Then who hath most contentment
A miner or a king?
    Then a mining we will go . . .

William Williams, Pantycelyn

331 Guide me, O Thou great Jehovah,

Pilgrim through this barren land;
I am weak, but Thou art mighty,
   Hold me with thy powerful hand.
Bread of Heaven, bread of Heaven
Feed me till I want no more.

Open now the crystal fountain,
   Whence the healing stream doth flow;
Let the fire and cloudy pillar
   Lead me all my journey through.
Strong Deliverer, strong Deliverer,
   Be Thou still my strength and shield.

When I tread the verge of Jordan,
   Bid my anxious fears subside;
Death of Deaths, and Hell's destruction,
   Land me safe on Canaan's side.
Songs of praises, songs of praises,
   I will ever give to thee.*

'Guide me, O Thou great Jehovah' (trans. the
author and Peter Williams), *c.* 1750

332 Pilgrim I am in a desert land,
      Wandering far and late,
   In expectation, every hour,
      I near my Father's gate.*

'Pererin' (trans. Anthony Conran)

333 I gaze across the distant hills
      Thy coming to espy;
   Beloved, haste, the day grows late,
      The sun sinks down the sky.

'I Gaze across the Distant Hills'

— 1752 —

Richard Morris

334 [That] the mad Methodists . . . have in a
   manner bewitched the major part of the
   inhabitants . . . is generally attributed to
   the indolence and . . . ignorance of too
   many of the parochial ministers.

letter to the Bishop of Bangor, 5 Jan. 1752

Goronwy Owen

335 Our language excels most others in
   Europe, and why does not our poetry? It is
   to me very unaccountable. Are we the only
   people in the world that know not how to
   value so excellent a language?

letter to William Morris, 7 May 1752

— 1753 —

Goronwy Owen

336 Perhaps it were to be wished that the

Rules of Poetry in our language were less
nice and accurate; we should then
undoubtedly have more writers, but
perhaps fewer good ones . . . As English
poetry is too loose, so ours is certainly too
much confined and limited.

letter to Richard Morris, 21 Feb. 1753

Thomas Richards

337 Yet our name hath not been quite blotted
   out from under Heaven. We hitherto not
   only enjoy the true name of our Ancestors
   but have preserved entire and uncorrupted
   . . . that primitive language, spoken as well
   by the ancient Gauls and Britons some
   thousands of years ago.

Thesaurus (1753)

— 1755 —

Evan Evans, Ieuan Brydydd Hir, Ieuan Fardd

338 The most ancient pieces of poetry in the
   British language are both better
   understood and relished than those in any
   living languages whatsoever of equal
   antiquity.

letter to William Morris, *c.* 1755

339 A good book, remember,
   Is a man's best friend and a lantern.*

'Llyfr'

Lord Lyttleton

340 Nature is in all her majesty there; but it is
   the majesty of a tyrant, frowning over the
   ruins and desolation of a country . . .
   There is not upon those mountains a tree
   or shrub, or a blade of grass; nor did we see
   any habitation or culture in the whole
   wide space. Between them is a solitude fit
   for Despair to inhabit, whereas all we had
   seen before in Wales seemed formed to
   inspire the meditations of Love.

of the mountains of Merioneth
letter to Mrs Bower
Account of a Journey into Wales (1755)

Richard Morris

341 You are, alas, almost the only chieftain in
   Wales who has a true love for his country
   and his language.*

letter to William Vaughan of Corsygedol,
14 June 1755

— 1756 —

Lord Lyttleton

342 The Vale of Festiniog is the perfectly beautiful of all we have seen. With the woman one loves, with the friend of one's heart and a study of books, one might pass an age in this vale and think it a day.

letter, quoted by Samuel Palmer, *The Vale of Festiniog* (1756)

John Shebbeare

343 I found more remains of ancient vassalage amongst the common people, and a greater simplicity of manner, than is to be met with in England.

of the Welsh
Letters to the English Nation (1756)

— 1758 —

Lewis Morris

344 Ieuan Fardd [Evan Evans] . . . has discovered some old MSS lately, that nobody of this age or the last ever as much dreamed of. And his discovery is to him and me as great as that of America by Columbus. We have found an epic poem in the British called Gododdin, equal at least to the Iliad, Aeneid or Paradise Lost.

letter to Edward Richard, 5 Aug. 1758

— 1760 —

Christopher Smart

345 For I am of the seed of the Welch woman and speak the truth from my heart.

epigraph to 'Jubilate Agno', *c.* 1760

346 For I will consider my Cat Jeoffry,
    For he is the servant of the Living God,
      duly and daily serving Him.

— 1761 —

Lewis Morris

347 The English tongue is as much a foreign language to me as the French is; we have whole parishes in the mountainous parts of Wales where there is not one word of English spoken.

letter to Samuel Pegge, 11 Feb. 1761

Edward Thomas

348 Cambria perceives
    The task unequal, and unstrings her lyre.

epithalamium on the marriage of George III, 1761

— 1763 —

John Wesley

349 It is common in the congregations attended by Mr W[illiam] W[illiams], and one or two other clergymen, after the preaching is over, for anyone that has a mind to give out a verse of a hymn. This they sing over and over with all their might, perhaps above thirty, yea, forty times. Meanwhile the bodies of two or three, sometimes ten or twelve, are violently agitated and they leap up and down, in all manner of postures, frequently for hours together.

entry in journal, 27 Aug. 1763

— 1764 —

Evan Evans, Ieuan Brydydd Hir, Ieuan Fardd

350 But you have one advantage over us, which is, that a great part of your ancient poets are either in print, or in such public libraries where a free access may be had of them, whereas ours remain still in private hands, and are with great difficulty to come at by those that can make proper use of them. This is a great pity.

letter to Bishop Percy, 13 Jan. 1764

351 Our bishops look upon me . . . with an evil eye because I dare have any affection for my country, language and antiquities, which in their opinion had better been lost and forgotten.*

letter to Lewis Morris, 12 May 1764

— 1766 —

Evan Evans, Ieuan Brydydd Hir, Ieuan Fardd

352 As Bishops we have only worthless grasping self-seekers, who endeavour to deprive us of the light of God's word in our own language.*

letter to Richard Morris, 23 June 1766

— 1767 —

Bishop Percy

353 Evan Evans [Ieuan Fardd], the Welsh author, called on me in the evening and borrowed five guineas.

entry in journal, 23 May 1767

— 1768 —

Dr Bowles

354 Wales is a conquered country, it is proper to introduce the English language, and it is the duty of the bishops to endeavour to promote English.

on being charged that as a monoglot Englishman he could not communicate with his monoglot Welsh-speaking parishioners in a parish in Anglesey, 1768

— 1769 —

Thomas Llewelyn

355 The uniqueness of the old language is more ancient and more undubitable, and even more truly and peculiarly Welsh, than even their ancient mountains.

Historical and Critical Remarks on the British Tongue (1769)

— 1770 —

Joseph Craddock

356 I doubt whether so extensive a circular prospect is to be seen in any part of the terraqueous globe.

Letters from Snowdon (1770)

— 1771 —

John Walters

357 I do not hesitate to profess to the world that I prefer *this* to any of the languages ancient or modern, that I have any acquaintance with . . . for which my affection increases every hour.

A Dissertation on the Welsh Language (1771)

358 To be a passive and unconcerned spectator of . . . the extirpation of the language of one's ancestors, betrays a tameness of spirit and a servility of disposition by no means becoming a gentleman, or one that hath any ancestry to boast of.

— 1772 —

Evan Evans, Ieuan Brydydd Hir, Ieuan Fardd

359 The false historians of a polished age
Show that the Saxon has not lost his rage.
Though tamed by arts, his rancour still
    remains:
Beware of Saxons still, ye Cambrian
    swains.

'The Love of our Country'

360 Let England in her Alfred's high renown
Boast of a monarch worthy of her crown;
But let not Cambrian science be forgot –
How Asser taught, how Alfred learning
    got.
Monsters ingrate, how can you
    barbarous call
The men that taught the brightest of
    you all?

— 1773 —

Rhys Jones

361 As for our own countrymen who are too apt to neglect and forget their mother-tongue, it is to be hoped it is more out of ignorance and affectation than hatred and ill-will.

'To the reader'
Gorchestion Beirdd Cymru (1773)

362 God has shown more love and favour to the Welsh than to almost any other nation under the sun . . . Although we were conquered by the Romans, and driven by the Saxons from the lowlands of England to the Welsh highlands, and later conquered by the Normans, and although laws were passed specifically to delete our language totally from the face of the earth; yet the Most High has given us strength and resilience to withstand all the incursions of our enemies, however frequent they have been; and to retain our language and some of our possessions also,

despite them all; and let us hope that we shall remain so for ever more.

Edward Williams, Iolo Morganwg

363 Why, Cambria, did I quit thy shore,
The scenes I loved so dear?
With wounded feelings rankling sore
I languish, and thy loss deplore
In Folly's hateful sphere.

'Stanzas written in London in 1773'

— 1774 —

Samuel Johnson

364 Wales is so little different from England that it offers nothing to the speculation of the traveller.

letter to James Boswell, 1774

365 After dinner, the talk was of preserving the Welsh language. I offered them a scheme . . . I recommended the republication of David ap Rhees's Grammar.

A Diary of a Journey through North Wales (1774)

— 1775 —

Edmund Burke

366 From that moment, as by a charm, the tumults subsided; obedience was restored; peace, order and civilization followed in the train of liberty. When the day star of the English constitution had risen in their hearts, all was harmony within and without.

on the Act of Union, 1536
speech in the House of Commons, 22 March 1775

Evan Evans, Ieuan Brydydd Hir, Ieuan Fardd

367 To the gluttonous great ones of our land
Corruption came from England.*

elegy to William Vaughan of Corsygedol, 1775

— 1776 —

Edward Williams, Iolo Morganwg

368 [As] the North Wales poets [have] always taken a liberty, bordering on

unwarrantable licentiousness, of using their local words and phrases in their works, certainly a Silurian writer must be allowed the same privilege.

letter to Owain Myfyr (Owen Jones), 25 Jan. 1776

— 1777 —

John Wesley

369 At Pembroke in the evening we had the most elegant congregation I have seen since we came into Wales. Some of them came in dancing and laughing as into a theatre, but their mood was quickly changed and in a few minutes they were as serious as my subject – Death.

entry in journal, 19 July 1777

— 1778 —

Thomas Pennant

370 The season of the Welsh poetry has long since been over and so I trust that the attempt will never be revived.

letter to Revd John Lloyd, Jan. 1778

— 1779 —

Evan Evans, Ieuan Brydydd Hir, Ieuan Fardd

371 A poor sight the hall of Ifor Hael –
mounds
In a swamp are lying;
Thorn and blasted thistle own it,
Bramble where was greatness.*

'Llys Ifor Hael' (trans. Anthony Conran)

— *c.* 1780 —

Anonymous

372 Taffy was a Welshman,
Taffy was a thief,
Taffy came to my house
And stole a leg of beef.

I went to Taffy's house,
Taffy was in bed,
I picked up a poker
And hit him on the head.

traditional rhyme, *c.* 1780

Edmund Burke

373 That nation [the Welsh] is brave and full of spirit.

speech in the House of Commons, 11 Feb. 1780

— **1781** —

Anonymous

374 This Society will present gold medals, or bounties, for the improvement of agriculture and the planting of trees in the Principality and to those assiduous in promoting trade, manufacture and commerce.

the Honourable Society of Cymmrodorion in letter to Members of Parliament, 1781

Thomas Pennant

375 There were very few castles in North Wales before its conquest by the English.

Tours in Wales (1781)

376 This town [Caernarfon] is justly the boast of North Wales, for the beauty of its situation, the goodness of its buildings, the regularity of the plan and, above all, the grandeur of the castle, the most magnificent badge of our subjection.

377 The elements seem to have warred against this mountain: rains have washed, lightnings torn, the very earth deserted it, and the winds made it the constant object of their fury.

of Glyder Fawr

378 At length she [Marged Uch Ifan] gave her hand to the most effeminate of her admirers, as if predetermined to maintain the superiority which nature had bestowed on her.

— **1782** —

Anonymous

379 We have no coal exported from this port, nor ever shall, as it would be too expensive to bring it down here from the internal part of the country.

Customs officer, Cardiff, 1782

William Gilpin

380 [Cardiff] has more of the furniture of

antiquity about it than any town we had seen in Wales.

Observations on the River Wye (1782)

— **1784** —

Edward Davies

381 No better cider does the world supply
Than grows along thy borders, gentle
 Wye;
Delicious, strong, and exquisitely fine,
With all the friendly properties of wine.

'Chepstow: a Poem' (1784)

— **1788** —

Gilbert White

382 At this very time, woollens instead of linen prevail among the poorer Welsh, who are subject to foul eruptions.

The Natural History of Selborne (1788)

— **1790** —

Evan Lloyd

383 If Milton was right when he called Liberty a mountain nymph, I am now writing to you from her residence; and the peaks of our Welsh Alps heighten the idea, by wearing the clouds of heaven like a cap of Liberty.

letter to John Wilkes, 1790

— **1792** —

Anonymous

384 This being the day on which the autumnal equinox occurred, some Welsh bards, resident in London, assembled in congress on Primrose Hill, according to ancient usage.

The Gentleman's Magazine (Oct. 1792)

Nicholas Owen

385 A man who had always lived in any of the level counties of England, were he transported in his sleep, and set down here, would suffer more astonishment from the change than I believe it is in the power of the human mind to conceive.

Caernarvonshire, a Sketch of its History, Antiquities, Mountains and Productions (1792)

J. M. W. Turner

386 This combination of mountainous scenery is truly sublime and surpasses any thing I have seen.

Diary of a Tour in Part of Wales (1792)

Edward Williams, Iolo Morganwg

387 Is there Peace?*

the cry of the Archdruid during ceremonies of the Gorsedd of Bards, 1792

388 The truth against the world.*

motto of the Gorsedd of Bards of the Isle of Britain, 1792

— **1794** —

Samuel Taylor Coleridge

389 At Bala is nothing remarkable except a lake of eleven miles in circumference.

letter to Robert Southey, 15 July 1794

— **1796** —

Anonymous

390 Pistyll Rhaeadr and Wrexham steeple, Snowdon's mountain without its people, Overton's yew-trees, St Winifred's wells, Llangollen's bridge and Gresford's bells.

'The Seven Wonders of North Wales', late 18th cent.

391 A vast treasure is contained in the Welsh language, in manuscripts and the oral traditions of the people, of which barely a notice has hitherto been given to the world.

in *The Cambrian Register* (1796)

David Williams

392 The manners of Wales still border on intemperance; though it be not an indispensable duty of hospitality, as it has been, to drench the guest into insensibility, indisposition or death.

History of Monmouthshire (1796)

— **1797** —

Henry Penruddocke Wyndham

393 The ancient history of Wales is a calendar of usurpations, depredations, and murders.

A Gentleman's Tour through Monmouthshire and Wales (1797)

394 A Welsh guide blunders through his route, and lest his knowledge should be suspected, will make no enquiry about it, till he himself is really alarmed; and then he becomes more terrified than those he pretends to conduct.

395 I have since seen, in the most retired spots of this country, a wretched cottage nearly bursting with the fullness of its congregation; and multitudes, in a heavy rain, swarming about the outside, imbibing, with gasping mouths, the poisonous tenets of a mechanical preacher.

396 While the English roads are crowded with travelling parties of pleasure, the Welsh are so rarely visited that the author did not meet with a single party during his six weeks journey in Wales.

397 Cardiff is a populous but ill-built town, nor is there any thing very pleasing in its environs.

398 The romantic beauties of nature are so singular and extravagant in the Principality, particularly in the counties of Meirioneth and Caernarvon, that they are scarcely to be conceived by those who have confined their curiosity to other parts of Great Britain.

399 I don't recollect to have seen one beggar before in the whole tour; the common people were indeed poor enough, but they seemed contented with their lot, and were always willing to answer our enquiries, without the least expectation of reward; they never asked for it; and when we sometimes gave the half-clothed wretch a shilling, they received it with an awkward surprise, and were so astonished that they could only express their thanks in tears of gratitude.

— **1798** —

Pratt

400 I have seen groups of poor people in the sequestered spots of both North and South Wales . . . at the sight of an unexpected man of the world, they will run into a rocky cavity, like a rabbit into its hole, or

plunge into the thickest shade as if they
were escaping from a beast of prey.

Gleanings through Wales, Holland and Westphalia
(1798)

William Wordsworth
401 How oft, in spirit, have I turned to thee,
O sylvan Wye! thou wanderer through the
   woods,
How often has my spirit turned to thee!

'Lines composed a few miles above Tintern
Abbey', 1798

— **1799** —

Anonymous
402 If, therefore, in the colloquial intercourse
of the scholars, one of them be detected in
speaking a Welsh word, he is immediately
degraded with the 'Welsh lump', a large
piece of lead fastened to a string, and
suspended round the neck of the offender.
The mark of ignominy has had the desired
effect: all the children of Flintshire speak
English very well.

reported by Richard Warner, *A Second Walk
through Wales* (1799)

David Samwell
403 In Walbrook stands a famous inn,
   Near ancient Watling Street,
Well stored with brandy, beer and gin,
   Where Cambrians nightly meet.

If on the left you leave the bar
   Where the Welsh landlord sits,
You'll find the room where wordy war
   Is waged by Cambrian wits.

'The Padouca Hunt'

Edward Williams, Iolo Morganwg
404 North Wales is now as Methodistical as
south Wales, and south Wales as Hell.

letter to Owain Myfyr (Owen Jones), 1799

— **1800** —

Ann Griffiths
405 Lo, between the myrtles standing,
   One who merits well my love,
Though His worth I guess but dimly,

High all earthly things above;
   Happy morning
When at last I see him clear!*

'Wele'n sefyll rhwng y myrtwydd'

— **1801** —

Anonymous
406 We do not designedly separate, nor do we
deem ourselves to be dissenters from the
Established Church. In our doctrinal
tenets we fully agree with the Articles of
the Church of England. What appears in
our religious organization as inclining
towards Dissent has taken place of
necessity rather than choice. It is not our
intention to form a schism, a sect or a
party. God forbid.*

statement of the Calvinistic Methodists at their
Quarterly Association, Bala, June 1801

William Coxe
407 The inhabitants [of western Monmouth-
shire] unwillingly hold intercourse with
the English, retain their ancient prejudices
and still brand them with the name
of Saxons.

An Historical Tour through Monmouthshire (1801)

— **1802** —

Edward Jones
408 The sudden decline of the national
minstrelsy and customs of Wales is in a
great degree to be attributed to the
fanatick imposters, or illiterate plebian
preachers, who have too often been
suffered to over-run the country,
misleading the greater part of the common
people from their lawful church, and
dissuading them from their innocent
amusements, such as singing, dancing, and
other rural sports, with which they had
been accustomed to delight in from the
earliest times. . . The consequence is,
Wales, which was formerly one of the
merriest and happiest countries in the
world, is now become one of the dullest.

preface to *The Bardic Museum* (1802)

409 Seeing with regret the rapid decrease of
performers on the harp in Wales, with the

consequent decline of that elegant and expressive instrument, as well as of our National Music and Poetry, gave me the first idea of reviving the ancient Eisteddfod ... which meeting I caused to be convened at Corwen, in Meirionethshire, about the year 1788.

— 1803 —

William Owen Pughe

410 Every one feels that partiality for his native country so distinctly working in his breast, as to require no kind of argument for its existence; but it probably assumes a more active sway over the mind of a people whom the revolutions of the world have deprived of independency, and whose name appears on the verge of oblivion among the nations, who in their turn are rising into pre-eminence.

introduction to *A National Dictionary of the Welsh Language* (1803)

— 1804 —

John Evans

411 The Welsh language lays claim to high antiquity, as being a branch of the Jaspian, or that dialect of the Hebrew spoken by the posterity of Japhet.

Letters written during a Tour through North Wales in the Year 1798 and at other Times (1804)

Benjamin Heath Malkin

412 Yet, when we consider how highly they valued their independence, and how respectable is that sentiment in a nation, we cannot but regret that the union of interests was necessarily to be obtained at the expense of patriotic feeling, and with some diminution of that consequence, so proudly maintained by their ancestors.

The Scenery, Antiquities, and Biography of South Wales (1804)

413 On the whole, the pleasure of a tour in Wales is in some degree tinged with melancholy, on observing the honest and amiable manners of its inhabitants, to find so many appearances of a fallen country.

414 North Wales is becoming English.

415 Radnorshire is generally considered, in a picturesque point of view, as the least interesting of the Welsh counties.

416 The language of Radnorshire is almost universally English. In learning to converse with their Saxon neighbours, they have forgotten the use of their vernacular tongue.

417 This town [Merthyr Tydfil], as it may properly be termed, is now by far the largest in the whole principality.

418 The workmen of all descriptions at these immense works [at Cyfarthfa, Merthyr Tydfil] are Welsh men. Their language is entirely Welsh. The number of English amongst them is very inconsiderable.

419 It is very remarkable that great immoralities do not prevail in any part of Wales, not even in places contiguous to large manufactories, especially if the English language happens to be but little spoken.

420 Such was, and in many parts continues to be, the proverbial barrenness of Cardiganshire, that the people of the neighbouring counties in ancient times branded it with the appellation of the Devil's Grandmother's Jointure.

421 Almost all the Welsh sects among the lower orders of the people have in truth degenerated into habits of the most pitiable lunacy in their devotion. The various subdivisions of methodists, jumpers and I know not what, who meet in fields and houses, prove how low fanaticism may degrade human reason.

422 The greatest fault imputed to the common people by their superiors is the want of a due regard to their own interests, without which they are never likely to be industrious, though they may be faithful servants to their employers.

423 Wales yields not, in the shadow of a thought, to England, in loyalty to the reigning family. Indeed, the King seems to be the only Saxon to whom they are thoroughly reconciled.

— 1805 —

Theophilus Evans

424 The treachery of the Saxons, whom the original Britons introduced into the island as friends and allies, and their cruelty in exterminating in cold blood the nobility of the ancient inhabitants . . . still rankles in the bosoms of the indigenous sons of freedom.

The History of Brecknockshire (1805)

Sir Walter Scott

425 The Welch antiquaries have considerably injured their very high claims to confidence by attempting to detail very remote events with all the accuracy belonging to the facts of yesterday. You will have one of them describe you the cut of Llywarch Hen's beard or the whittle of Urien Rheged with as much authority as if he had trimmed the one or cut his cheese with the other. These high pretensions weaken greatly our belief in the Welch poems, which probably contain great treasure.

letter to a friend, 1805

426 They swore their banners broad should gleam,
In crimson light, on Rhymney's stream;
They vow'd Caerphili's sod should feel
The Norman charger's spurning heel.

'The Norman Horse Shoe'

— 1810 —

Thomas Jones

427 I have the vanity to say that I was the first man that thought of reviving the Eisteddfod. It had engaged my thoughts from the age of fourteen to my twenty-sixth year.

letter to Edward Charles, 1810

— 1811 —

Julia Ann Hatton

428 In vain by various griefs oppressed,
I vagrant roam devoid of rest,
With aching heart, still lingering stray
Around the shores of Swansea Bay . . .

Then Kilvey Hill, a long adieu,
I drag my sorrows hence from you:
Misfortune with imperious sway
Impels me far from Swansea Bay.

'Swansea Bay'

Thomas Love Peacock

429 On the top of Cadair Idris, I felt how happy a man may be with a little money and a sane intellect, and reflected with astonishment and pity on the madness of the multitude.

letter to E. J. Hookham, 9 April 1811

— 1812 —

Thomas Love Peacock

430 Oh beauteous Meirion! Cambria's mountain-pride!

The Philosophy of Melancholy (1812)

Percy Bysshe Shelley

431 Steal, if possible, my revered friend, one summer from the cold hurry of business, and come to Wales.

letter to William Godwin, 25 April 1812

432 Hail to thee, Cambria, for the unfettered wind
Much from thy wilds even now
methinks I feel
Chasing the clouds that roll in wrath behind
And tightening the soul's laxest nerves to steel!
True! Mountain Liberty alone may heal
The pain which Custom's obduracies bring,
And he who dares in fancy even to steal
One draught from Snowdon's ever-sacred spring
Blots out the unholiest rede of wordly witnessing.

'On Leaving London for Wales'

433 The society in Wales is very stupid. They are all aristocrats and Christians but as to that I tell you I do not mind in the least: the unpleasant part of the business is that they hunt people to Death who are not so likewise.

letter to James Hogg, Dec. 1812

— 1813 —

Walter Davies, Gwallter Mechain

434 The spirit of emigration [has] infatuated a great part of the Principality.

A General View of the Agriculture and Domestic Economy of North Wales (1813)

J. G. Wood

435 The Rhondda is the wildest region of Glamorganshire, where the English language is scarce ever heard.

The Principal Rivers of Wales (1813)

— 1814 —

Anonymous

436 Only a few of the parishioners have actively joined their *Seiats*, and nine out of ten follow the itinerant preachers without caring to what denomination and sect they belong.

the vicar of Llanynghenedl to the Bishop of Bangor, 1814

437 North Wales, the more immediate field of his missionary labours for thirty years, will probably retain traces of his various strenuous exertions to promote the Kingdom of Christ till time shall be no more.

inscription on tomb of Thomas Charles of Bala at Llanycil

438 Sweet meadow grazing, good beer and comfortable lodgings. *

sign in Welsh on the Drover's House, Stockbridge, Hants., *c.* 1814

— 1815 —

John Jones

439 It was his pride to be thought the oracle and patron of all that is curious or valuable in the literary remains of the Ancient Britons.

of Owen Jones, Owain Myfyr
letter to *The Monthly Magazine* (vol. 34, Feb. 1815)

— 1817 —

Samuel Taylor Coleridge

440 Among the peasantry of North Wales, the ancient mountains, with all their terrors and all their glories, are pictures to the blind, and music to the deaf.

Biographia Literaria (1817)

— 1818 —

Anonymous

441 Resolved: that all the pews in the Church be made uniform and of the same height as the Iron Masters' pews, except those of Mr Crawshay, Mr Forman, Mr Hill and Mr Guest.

minute-book of the parish of Merthyr Tydfil, 6 May 1818

Felicia Dorothea Hemans

442 The boy stood on the burning deck
   Whence all but he had fled;
The flame that lit the battle's wreck
   Shone round him o'er the dead.

'Casabianca'

— 1819 —

Michael Faraday

443 The building appeared to be a school and the children were chanting a Welch psalm. I never heard sounds that charmed me as these did. Never did music give me such pleasure before. I regretted the moment when they ceased to vibrate and left us to sink down into common life again.

Journal of a Walking Tour through Wales (1819)

— 1820 —

Anonymous

444 Three tries for a Welshman.*

traditional saying, *c.* 1820

445 Three jolly Welshmen, coming out of Wales,
Riding on a nanny goat, selling sheeps' tails.

traditional children's rhyme, Salop, *c.* 1820

446 What are you waiting for – the Prince of Wales?*

traditional complaint to young women showing no inclination to marry, Russia, *c.* 1820

447 We, who are natives and the real owners, cannot stretch a foot without being trod on.

protest of Tredegar workers against 'the children of Hengist and Horsa' (the English masters), *c.* 1820

Robert Jones

448 There has been riot and commotion in England, Scotland and Ireland, because [those countries] neither feared God nor honoured the King . . . but our nation remained wonderfully faithful to the Government in all troubles.*

Drych yr Amseroedd (1820)

Sir Walter Scott

449 You hear the Welsh spoken much about you, and if you can pick it up without interfering with more important labours, it will be worth while.

letter to his son Charles, 19 Dec. 1820

— **1821** —

Lord Macaulay

450 All trades and professions here are in the most delightful confusion. The druggist sells hats and the shoemaker is the sole bookseller, if that dignity can be allowed him on the strength of the three Welsh Bibles and the Guide to Caernarvon which adorn his window. The grocer sells ropes and the clothes brush is a luxury as yet unknown in Llanrwst.

letter to his mother, 1821

— **1822** —

Thomas de Quincey

451 Wales, as is pretty well known, breeds a population somewhat litigious.

Confessions of an English Opium-Eater (1822)

— **1823** —

Thomas Love Peacock

452 The mountain sheep are sweeter
But the valley sheep are fatter;
We therefore deemed it meeter
To carry off the latter.

'The War-Song of Dinas Vawr'
The Misfortunes of Elphin (1823)

Thomas Jefferey Llewelyn Prichard

453 Heard ye the voice of the muse of the mountain?
The lays of the land of the mineral fountain?
Hear ye the songs of the Welsh mountaineer,
The son of old Cymry – held filially dear;
Oh list to the minstrel who sweeps the Welsh *telyn*,
Hear! hear ye the harpings of Jefferey Llewelyn.

epigraph to *Welsh Minstrelsy* (1823)

— **1824** —

John Humphreys Parry

454 While the national peculiarities, whether in manners or literature, of Scotland and Ireland, have been industriously explored, and in many instances successfully developed, Wales has been regarded with an indifference not easily to be reconciled with that spirit of enterprise by which the literary public of Great Britain is known to be animated.

The Cambrian Plutarch (1824)

— **1827** —

John Jones

455 The general pursuit of the Welsh is agriculture; but without approximation to excellence, for the cattle are subjected to privations and the soil to ingratitude.

A History of Wales (1827)

— **1828** —

Anonymous

456 The mother of the steam coal trade.

epithet of Lucy Thomas, Abercanaid, Merthyr Tydfil

— **1829** —

Anonymous

457 How mad the dull mysticism, how atrocious the gloomy passion, of Wales must seem amid the lucid common sense and unimpassioned judgement of England, may easily be conceived.

in *Blackwood's Magazine* (Nov. 1829)

Felix Mendelssohn

458 Here I am in Wales . . . and a harper sits in the vestibule of every inn and never stops playing so-called folk-melodies, that is, infamous, common, faked stuff.*

letter to Carl Friedrich Zelter, 1829

— 1830 —

Anonymous

459 Only two things can save a cornered hare – God and a Cardiganshire jury.

traditional saying, *c.* 1830

460 An Act for the more effectual administration of Justice in England and Wales.

title of the Act abolishing the Great Session of Wales, 1830

Henry Gastineau

461 [Wales] is situated between fifty-one degrees, twenty-minutes, and fifty-three, twenty-five of north latitude; and between two degrees, forty-one minutes, and four, fifty-six west longitude, from Greenwich.

Wales Illustrated (1830)

462 During centuries this country was the theatre for the display of the most heroic courage and conspicuous martial prowess ever exhibited to the world.

463 Wales, whether considered with reference to the nature of the country, its picturesque scenery, geographical features, or rare productions, independent of its history, as a people whose circumstances, actions, and fate, stand single and unparalleled in the annals of the world, possesses peculiar interest, and is of the highest importance.

— 1831 —

Anonymous

464 My Lord, the union is so important to me

that I would live on sixpence a week rather than give it up.

miner to magistrate at Merthyr Tydfil, 1831

465 I saw the Merthyr riots,
And the great oppression of the workers;
Sixty were killed outright
And some of the soldiers wounded...
But dear heaven! the worst trick
Was the hanging of Dic Penderyn.*

ballad, 1831

Mrs Arbuthnot

466 There has been a great riot in Wales and the soldiers have killed twenty-four people. When two or three were killed at Manchester, it was called the Peterloo Massacre and the newspapers for weeks wrote it up as the most outrageous and wicked proceeding ever heard of. But that was in Tory times; now this Welsh riot is scarcely mentioned.

entry in diary, June 1831

Richard Lewis, Dic Penderyn

467 O Lord, what an iniquity!*

last words on scaffold, Cardiff, 13 Aug. 1831

— 1832 —

Anonymous

468 [The visit of Princess Victoria] will confirm inviolate our tiny Principality from that progression towards democracy . . . which is lamentably stalking in some other parts of the Empire.

The Cambrian Quarterly Magazine (vol. 4, 1832)

John Blackwell, Alun

469 In these days of sedition and threatened anarchy, the principality has always been tranquil and happy as Goschen.

address to the Beaumaris Eisteddfod, 1832

Felicia Dorothea Hemans

470 My thoughts, wild Cambria, dwell with thee!

'The Cambrian in America'

Robert Owen

471 If we cannot yet reconcile all opinions, let us endeavour to unite all hearts.

motto of his newspaper, *The Crisis*, 1832

William Price (of Llantrisant)

472 The chapel preachers never lead the people except at funerals.

speech at Llantrisant, *c.* 1832

— **1833** —

Marquess of Bute

473 J. B. Pryce has hinted that I might show indulgence to the tenant at Pantygorddinan as, it seems, he belongs to the classic race of Bards . . . I must say this is not a ground to be recognised in the management of an estate.

letter to E. P. Richards, 7 Oct. 1833

M. A. Leigh

474 The custom of jumping, during the performance of public worship, originated in the western parts of Wales about the year 1700, amongst the followers of Harris, Rowland, and others . . . The jumping usually commences at the conclusion of the service and is accompanied by loud groans and violent gesticulations, which are frequently continued till the parties sink down completely exhausted.

Guide to Wales and Monmouthshire (1833)

475 Caerwys . . . in Flintshire was formerly a place of considerable importance, as the country assizes were held there, and was also noted as the seat of the Eisteddfod, a species of British bards poured forth their extemporaneous effusions, or awakened their harps to melody in trials of skills, instituted by law, and held here with great form and ceremony.

476 Merthyr Tydfil is remarkable for the number and extent of its iron-works, the whole of the surrounding district, eight miles in length and four in breadth, abounding in iron ore and coals. Scarcely anything can be conceived more awfully grand than the descent, on a dark night, into the Vale of Merthyr Tydvil, from any of the surrounding hills, where on a sudden the traveller beholds, as it were, numberless volcanoes breathing out their undulating pillars of flame and smoke.

477 The custom of bundling, or courting in bed, for which the Welsh have frequently

been bantered, is only known in the most retired parts of North Wales; and even there, is not practised in the manner which the terms suggest to the minds of those who have had the happiness of living surrounded by all the comforts and conveniences of a more civilized state.

Henri Martin

478 The Celt is ever ready to revolt against the despotism of fact.*

Histoire de France (1833)

E. P. Richards

479 The continuance of the [Welsh] language is of no benefit to the country; it is kept up . . . to keep the dissenters together.

letter to the Marquess of Bute, 11 Dec. 1833

— **1834** —

Lady Charlotte Guest

480 The bishop's address. . . turned chiefly on reproof of Dissenters, who, to our shame, have done more for religion in Wales than our Church has ever attempted.

entry in journal, 6 Oct. 1834

— **1835** —

David Rowland

481 Samaria? What was Samaria? Samaria was their ash-tip. An ash-tip where they threw all their sticks and rubbish. A hot-bed of Paganism and Heresy and everything. Yes, my friends, Samaria was the Merthyr Tydfil of the Land of Canaan.*

sermon, *c.* 1835

— **1837** —

Anonymous

482 The refusal of the county magistrates [of Merioneth] to act with a man who had been a grocer, and is a Methodist, is the dictate of a genuine patriotism.

Report on Certain Boroughs (1837)

Lady Charlotte Guest

483 The Tory landlords brought their Tenants

up themselves like flocks of sheep and made them break their pledge-words. They absolutely dragged them to the Poll, threatening to turn them out of their farms unless they voted plumpers for Lord Adare.

entry in journal, 4 Aug. 1837

484 We all went to the Cymreigyddion Meeting which was brilliantly attended . . . But it seemed to me that there was not the same display of genuine and native enthusiasm among the lower order of Welsh Literati themselves, which had been so animating and gratifying in 1835. I am afraid the Society is beginning to be tamed down to the conventional rules of English taste.

entry in journal, 18 Oct. 1837

— **1838** —

Lady Charlotte Guest

485 This evening, I went to the Cambrian Ball in my regular Welsh peasant's dress. . . such a thing I believe had never been seen before in London and it caused quite a sensation.

entry in journal, 19 May 1838

486 My dear children, Infants as you yet are, I feel that I cannot dedicate more fitly than to you these venerable relics of ancient lore, and I do so in the hope of inciting you to cultivate the Literature of 'Gwyllt Gwalia', in whose beauiful language you are being initated, and amongst whose free mountains you were born. May you become early imbued with the chivalric and exhalted sense of honour and the fervent patriotism for which its sons have ever been celebrated.

dedication 'to Ivor and Merthyr'
of her translation of the Mabinogion, 1838

Thomas Roscoe

487 A wild and mountainous region where nature seemed to reign in stern and unbroken silence.

of the Rhondda valleys
Wanderings through South Wales (1838)

Robert Southey

488 Within the stones of Federation there,

On the green turf, and under the blue sky,
A noble band, the Bards of Britain stood,
Their heads in reverence bare, and bare of foot,
A deathless brotherhood!

'The Gorsedd' (1838)

— **1839** —

Thomas Jenkins

489 See – around a thousand hills,
  How my sons unite;
Like your purest mountain rills,
  Forming for the fight.

'Liberty's Address to the Welsh'

Lord Melbourne

490 [South Wales] is the worst and most formidable district in the kingdom. The affair we had there in 1831 was the most like a fight of anything that took place.

letter to the Marquess of Normanby, Nov. 1839

Thomas Jefferey Llewelyn Prichard

491 It is true that others have made Wales the scene of action for the heroes of their tales; but however talented such works might be, to the Welshman's feeling they lacked nationality, and betrayed the hand of the foreigner in the working of the web.

preface to *The Adventures and Vagaries of Twm Shon Catti* (2nd edn., 1839)

Lord Tennyson

492 It is remarkable how fluently little boys and girls can speak Welsh.

letter to Emily Sellwood, 1839

493 I cannot say I have seen much worth the trouble of the journey, excepting the Welsh women's hats, which look very comical to the English eye, being in truth men's beaver-hats, with the brim a little broad and tied under the chin with a black ribbon. Some faces look very pretty in them.

Henry Vincent

494 I could not help thinking of the defensible nature of the country in the case of foreign invasion! A few thousand of armed men on the hills could successfully defend them. Wales would make an excellent Republic.

in *The Western Vindicator* (6 April 1839)

Hugh Williams

495 Come, hail, brothers, hail the shrill sound
of the horn;
For ages deep wrongs have been hopelessly
borne;
Despair shall no longer our spirits dismay,
Nor wither the arm, when upraised for the
fray;
The conflict of freedom is gathering nigh,
We live to secure it, or gloriously die.

'The Horn of Liberty'

— 1840 —

W. H. Smyth

496 Providence ordained the universal deluge
to create the south Wales coalfield.

*Nautical Observations on the Port and Maritime
Vicinity of Cardiff* (1840)

— 1841 —

William Jones

497 Wales is divided into 844 parishes, in
which there are about 1,000 churches and
chapels.

*The Character of the Welsh as a Nation in the Present
Age* (1841)

498 Never has the Welsh language been more
encouraged than during the last twenty-
five years, and never, in the same compass
of time, has the English spread itself so
much over the principality.

499 On the whole I am inclined to the opinion
that the extinction of the language is
impracticable; consequently, the
discouragement of it must be both
impolitic and wicked.

500 I fear the opinion held by many is true,
that not twenty females in Wales are
acquainted with the grammar of their
native tongue.

501 A strong feeling of prejudice is entertained
by each religious party against all the
others which co-exist.

502 Whilst adultery is a crime seldom heard of,
instances in which parties preparing for

marriage forestall the privileges of that
sacred state are shamefully numerous.

503 To exist after so many and persevering
attempts at their extinction, and to retain
the vernacular use of their primitive,
nervous, and enchanting language, after so
many revolutions in their civil and
religious circumstances, are facts in which
they will ever glory; and no good reason
appears why our English neighbours
should deny us the consolation of these
facts, or laugh at us, with so much sarcastic
malevolence, when the matter is discussed
in their society.

504 Merthyr, the Gehenna of Wales, where
black beings dwell, amidst fire and smoke,
who dive into deep caverns, where
opportunities are afforded them to concoct
their treasonable designs against the
inhabitants of the upper world.

505 But for their dissensions and questionable
views of politics, the Independents would
have much that would be deserving of
commendation.

506 There is a large number of good people
among them [the Baptists], and were it not
for the tendency of their system to general
anarchy, they would not be an
uninteresting portion of society.

507 Of all the communities of Wales they [the
Calvinistic Methodists] are the most
zealous advocates of total abstinence from
intoxicating drinks.

508 The Methodists of the Wesleyan
Persuasion are not a very numerous body
of people in Wales.

509 It is devoutly to be wished that the
[Anglican] clergy of Wales were more
vernacularly acquainted with the language
in which they officiate.

510 The people of the South are fond of
conversation, and are even garrulous; one
of them will talk as much in five minutes as
a Northwalian will in fifteen, especially
when he is a little excited.

511 In Meirionethshire there is much
innocence and simplicity, and the

inhabitants stand pre-eminent among their countrymen for their chastity.

512 The Denbighshire people appear more demure in their habits than the inhabitants of any other part of Wales.

513 The Marquis of Anglesey is a splendid exception to many of the higher classes in North Wales.

514 The poor of Wales are not to be considered an abandoned race of people. Some of them undoubtedly are very immoral; but many may be found who are quiet, resigned, and devoted to religion; and Christianity appears to be producing its benign and transforming influence on their minds.

515 It should be borne in mind that the animated and popular style of preaching used by Dissenters has been one of the chief means by which the people have been withdrawn from the Church; and if ever they are expected to return, it can only be achieved by that most important ordinance of the Almighty, the preaching of his truths in such a way as to tell on the heart of the audience.

516 The labouring classes of Wales are not to be considered as sunk in ignorance and barbarism. In scientific knowledge it is allowed they are lamentably deficient, but in religious information and moral conduct they equal, if they do not surpass, those of any other country in the world.

— 1842 —

Philip Davies

517 I have been driving horses below ground three years and was twelve months before that at a trap door. When at the traps I used frequently to fall asleep.

collier boy, aged 10, of Dinas, Rhondda
evidence to the Commission of Inquiry into the
Employment of Children in Mines, 1842

Thomas Price, Carnhuanawc

518 I know not on the face of the earth a region more beautiful, more blissful, and all in all more desirable than the land of Wales.*

Hanes Cymru (1842)

— 1843 —

Anonymous

519 The people, the masses, to a man throughout the three counties of Carmarthen, Cardigan and Pembroke are with me. O yes, they are all my children . . . Surely, say I, these are members of my family, these are the oppressed sons and daughters of Rebecca.

statement by the Daughters of Rebecca
in *The Welshman* (1 Sept. 1843)

520 It is a shameful thing for us Welshmen to have the sons of Hengist [the English] holding dominion over us.

the Daughters of Rebecca
reported in *The Times* (6 Sept. 1843)

William Day

521 The landlords are most of them of the old Church and King school. The tenantry are almost all Dissenters, with a spice of the fanaticism of the Covenanters about them.

letter to George Cornewall Lewis (9 July 1843)

— 1844 —

Anonymous

522 The people's ignorance of the English language practically prevents the working of the laws and institutions and impedes the administration of justice.

report of the Commissioners of Inquiry for
South Wales (1844)

Lord Tennyson

523 I have walked thrice up Snowdon, which I found very much easier to accomplish than walking on level ground.

letter to Edmund Lushington, 29 July 1844

— 1846 —

William Rees, Gwilym Hiraethog

524 The Welsh Members of Parliament should resolve themselves into an united Welsh party.*

in *Yr Amserau* (26 March 1846)

William Williams MP

525 The people of that country laboured under

a peculiar difficulty from the existence of an ancient language.

speech in the House of Commons, 10 March 1846

526 If the Welsh had the same advantages for education as the Scotch, they would, instead of appearing as a distinct people, in no respect differ from the English. Would it not, then, be wisdom and sound policy to send the English schoolmaster among them. . . A band of efficient schoolmasters is kept up at much less expense than a body of police or soldiery.

— **1847** —

Anonymous

527 The Welsh language is a vast drawback to Wales, and a manifold barrier to the moral progress and commercial prosperity of the people. It is not easy to over-estimate its evil effects.

Report on the State of Education in Wales, 'the Blue Books' (1847)

528 The Welsh language is peculiarly evasive, which originates from its having been the language of slavery.

Edward Lloyd Hall, in evidence

529 Perjury is common in courts of justice, and the Welsh language facilitates it.

Clerk to the Magistrates at Lampeter, in evidence

530 From my experience of Ireland, I think there is a very great similarity between the lower orders of Welsh and Irish – both are dirty, indolent, bigoted and contented.

Curate of St Mary's, Brecon, in evidence

531 In the works the Welsh workman never finds his way into the office. He never becomes either clerk or agent . . . His language keeps him under the hatches, being one in which he can neither acquire or communicate the necessary information.

532 So long as children are familiar with no other, they must be educated to a considerable extent through the medium of [Welsh] . . . Out of school, can the language of lessons make head against the language of life?

533 The young people often meet at evening schools for the preparation of the *pwnc*, and this leads to immoralities between the young persons of both sexes, who frequently spend the night afterwards in hay-lofts together.

vicar of Troedyraur, in evidence

534 I assert with confidence, as an undeniable fact, that fornication is not regarded as a vice, scarcely as a frailty, by the common people in Wales. It is considered as a matter of course – as the regular conventional progress towards marriage.

chaplain of the Bishop of Bangor, in evidence

535 The want of chastity is the besetting evil of this country . . . The parents do not see the evil in it. They say their daughters have been 'unfortunate' and maintain their illegitimate grand-children as if they were legitimate.

vicar of Denio, in evidence

536 The Welsh are peculiarly exempt from the guilt of great crimes. There are few districts in Europe where murders, burglaries, personal violence, rapes, forgeries or any felonies on a large scale are so rare. On the other hand, there are perhaps fewer countries where the standard of minor morals is lower.

537 Brynmawr contains 5,000 people, nearly all of whom are of the lowest class . . . Not the slightest step has been taken to improve the mental or moral condition of this violent and vicious community.

538 I regard the degraded condition [of the people of Monmouthshire] as entirely the fault of their employers, who give them far less tendance and care than they bestow on their cattle, and who with few exceptions, use and regard them as so much brute force instrumental to wealth, but as nowise involving claims on human sympathy.

539 The masters are looked upon generally as the natural enemies of the men; the intimate relation between capital and labour, and the identical interest which links their fate, are neither understood nor believed; both classes imagine that they are necessarily antagonistic.

540 [The Cymreigyddion] holds meetings at Abergavenny where a band of literati promote Welsh literature by making English speeches once a year in its defence.

Charles Frederick Cliffe

541 These hills are of the carboniferous group and will no doubt ultimately be invaded, and perforated with coal levels. We trust that it may not happen in our day.

The Book of South Wales (1847)

542 The people of this solitudinous and happy valley [the Rhondda] are a pastoral race, almost wholly dependent on their flocks and herds for support . . . The air is aromatic with wild flowers and mountain plants, a sabbath stillness reigns.

— **1848** —

T. E. Clarke

543 Weep, sons of Cambria, weep at the loss of such a benefactor [the second Marquess of Bute], and may the lasting monuments of his genius and beneficence, his boundless generosity, high character and philanthropic mind, excite a nation's feeling of admiration and regret.

Guide to Merthyr Tydfil (1848)

Evan Jones, Ieuan Gwynedd

544 We have raised a periodical Welsh literature for ourselves, in the course of forty years, which circulates about 60, 000 copies monthly.

A Vindication (1848)

— **1849** —

Anonymous

545 That until the middle of the nineteenth century the Celtic tongue in its varieties of Gaelic, Welsh, Irish and Manx, should be employed as a vernacular, is matter not less of surprise than of national discredit . . . No thought appears to have been bestowed on the fact that large masses of the population were isolated from general progress on account of their inability to speak English.

in Chambers' Edinburgh Journal (vol. 2, 1849)

546 One thing, however, must be said for the Welsh, that under all the disadvantages of a local tongue, they have not languished as a people, nor become burdensome to their Anglo-Saxon neighbours.

Michael D. Jones

547 By settling together [in the USA], we will be far happier than being scattered as we are now; we would have a better ministry and our nation would be saved from extinction.*

in *Y Cenhadwr Americanaidd* (Jan. 1849)

Queen Victoria

548 Welsh should be taught in Wales as well as English.

letter to Lord Landsdowne, 1849

— **1850** —

Thomas Carlyle

549 Ah me! 'Tis like a vision of Hell, and will never leave me, that of these poor creatures broiling, or in sweat and dirt, amid their furnaces, pits, and rolling mills. For here is absolutely no aristocracy or guiding class; nothing but one or two huge iron masters, and the rest are operatives, petty shopkeepers, Scottish hawkers. The town [Merthyr Tydfil] might be, and will be, one of the prettiest places in the world. It *is* one of the sootiest, squalidest, and ugliest; all cinders and dust-mounds and soot. Their very greens they bring from Bristol, though the ground is excellent all round. Nobody thinks of gardening in such a locality – all devoted to metallic gambling.

letter to his wife, Aug. 1850

Richard Hall

550 Pontypool! thou dirtiest of dirty places.

'Pontypool'

Charles Kingsley

551 We've the stones of Snowdon And the lamps of heaven.

'Letter to Thomas Hughes'

Lady Llanover

552 Mothers of Wales, speak Welsh to your

children . . . It is from you, and not from their fathers, that they will learn to love God in their own language.*

in *Y Gymraes* (vol. 1, 1850)

T. W. Rammell

553 For all intents and purposes of civic government, Merthyr Tydfil is as destitute as the smallest rural village in the empire.

report to the Board of Health, 1850

— 1851 —

Anonymous

554 Who list to read the deeds
    by valiant Welshmen done,
Shall find them worthy men of arms
    as breathes beneath the sun;
They are of valiant hearts,
    of nature kind and meek,
An honour on St David's Day
    it is to wear the Leek.

'The Praise of St David's Day'
(reprinted 1851 from an earlier black-letter broadside)

Henry Austin Bruce, Lord Aberdare

555 I consider the Welsh language a serious evil, a great obstruction to the moral and intellectual progress of my countrymen.

speech, 1851

— 1852 —

Matthew Arnold

556 The calm sea shines, loose hang the vessel's sails;
Before us are the sweet green fields of Wales,
And overhead the cloudless sky of May.

Tristram and Iseult (1852)

Thomas Frankland Lewis

557 The people saw that their only remedy was to take the law into their own hands. The Rebecca conspiracy was organised with much skill and carried through with much fidelity . . . It was never diverted from its original purpose, and the instant that purpose seemed likely to be attained. . .the association was dissolved. The Rebecca

Riots are a very creditable portion of Welsh History.

in conversation with Nassau Senior, 1852
quoted by David Williams, *The Rebecca Riots* (1955)

— 1853 —

Anonymous

558 The name of John Jones is in Wales a perpetual incognito.

report of the Registrar General, 1853

559 Cardiff is gaining a world-wide reputation as one of the most immoral of seaports.

in *Merthyr Guardian*, (8 Jan. 1853)

Lady Charlotte Guest

560 I was under the painful necessity of discharging an otherwise very good school mistress today for having gone to a convivial party at a Unitarian preacher's house where there was dancing, on a Good Friday.

entry in journal, 3 June 1853

561 If the men threaten, or make any demonstration of a strike, I will resist them to the end. Every wheel in these works shall stop simultaneously if I see any indication of a compulsive course being followed . . . I will be their master.

entry in journal, 11 July 1853

John Williams, Ab Ithel

562 Wales is strictly and emphatically independent. . . Victoria is peculiarly our own Queen – Boadicea rediviva – our Buddug the second . . . We can address our English friends, We have more right in Victoria than thee, a larger quantity of Celtic than of Saxon blood flowing through her royal veins.

speech at the Abergavenny Eisteddfod, 1853

— 1854 —

Nathaniel Hawthorne

563 At Bangor we went to a handsome hotel and hired a carriage and two horses for

some Welsh place, the name of which I forget; neither can I remember a single name of any of the places through which we posted on that day, nor could I spell them if I heard them pronounced, nor pronounce if I saw them spelt.

Note Book (1854)

Thomas Jefferey Llewelyn Prichard

564 And be it further observed, there is decidedly more Welsh nationality in an English production, when vigorously embracing a subject, historic or traditional, that is purely Cambrian, than in a composition in the Welsh language on affairs that are in no respect connected with Wales or Welshmen.

Heroines of Welsh History (1854)

William Thomas, Islwyn

565 Everything is sacred, all these mountains Have in them heavenly poetry.*

'*Y Storm*'

566 Poetry, O Poetry! Who shall put
    Limits on you? Wide as the heavens
Is the spread of your empire.*

— 1855 —

János Arany

567 Edward the king, the English king,
    Rode on a milk-white charger;
'I wish to know the worth,' said he,
    'Of my Welsh lands over the border.

Is the grass rich for sheep and ox,
    Are the soil and rivers good,
And are my provinces watered well
    By rebel patriots' blood?

And what of the people, the wretched
    people,
    Do they seem a contented folk,
Or, as I ordered, did they subdue them
    Like oxen to the yoke?'

'Your Majesty, Wales is the fairest jewel
    You have in all your crown;
River and field and valley and hill
    Are the best you may come upon.

And as for the people, the wretched
    people,
    They are so contented, Sir,

Like so many graves their hamlets stand,
    And none there ever stir.'*

'A Welski Bardók' (trans. Neville Masterman)

— 1856 —

William Barnes

568 It seems to me that for a man to study the early British History of our land without Welsh is, as it were, to dig the earth with a sharp stick instead of a spade.

'Ancient Britons'
lecture delivered to the Dorchester Working Men's Mutual Improvement Society, 28 Oct. 1856

Evan James

569 The old land of my fathers is dear to me,
    Land of poets and singers, men of
        renown;
Her brave warriors, patriots most
        excellent,
    Spilt their blood for freedom.

Chorus:
My country, my country!
I stand up for my country:
While the sea is a wall to the well-loved
    place
O! long may the old language survive.*

the national anthem of Wales (literal trans.)
'Hen Wlad fy Nhadau', 1856

Michael D. Jones

570 Our national weakness is our servility, but in a Welsh Colony we can be imbued with a new spirit.*

speech at Bala, 15 Aug. 1856

— 1857 —

Michael D. Jones

571 Welsh among Spaniards will not meet with the same fate as among North Americans, who are energetic and who draw every nation into their own mould.

public letter in response to offer by the Argentinian Government of land in Patagonia for use as a Welsh Colony, 19 Dec. 1857

Charles Kingsley

572 And they went up Snowdon, too, and saw

little beside fifty fog-blinded tourists, five-and-twenty dripping ponies, and five hundred empty porter bottles; wherefrom they returned, as do many, disgusted, and with great colds in their heads.

Two Years Ago (1857)

Edward Williams, Iolo Morganwg

573 Strike a Welshman if you dare,
Ancient Britons as we are,
We were men of great renown
Ere a Saxon wore a crown.

attributed by T. D. Thomas in his biography of the writer, 1857

— **1858** —

Enoch G. Salisbury MP

574 Gentlemen, I am a Welshman, and I love my country . . . How is the renovation of the Welsh race to be brought about? By the promotion of railways. I, for one, am not ashamed to say – and I say it here boldly – that I shall be delighted to see the Welsh people anglicized. I am quite sure that the way to anglicize the Welsh people is by the promotion of railways and commerce among them, and making the English and the Welsh thoroughly one people.

speech at opening of the Vale of Clwyd Railway, 14 Oct. 1858

— **1860** —

Anonymous

575 The Biarritz of the Cambrian Coast.

advertisement for Aberystwyth, 1860s

Walter White

576 Welshpool is a town of English aspect, excepting the names over the doors, and market day, when hats such as the Long Parliament wore may be seen on the heads of the women who come in from the country.

All Round the Wrekin (1860)

— **1861** —

John Ceiriog Hughes

577 Still do the great mountains stay,
And the winds above them roar.*

'Alun Mabon' (trans. Anthony Conran)

578 To the customs of old Wales
Changes come from year to year;
Every generation fails,
One has gone, the next is here.
After a lifetime tempest-tossed
Alun Mabon is no more,
But the language is not lost
And the old songs yet endure.

579 Every star in heaven is singing,
All through the night;
Hear the glorious music ringing
All through the night
Songs of sweet ethereal lightness
Wrought in realms of peace and whiteness,
See, the dark gives way to brightness,
All throught the night.*

'Ar Hyd y Nos' (trans. A. G. Prys-Jones)

— **1862** —

Anonymous

580 What should we do with English here?

girl in Cardiganshire
recorded by George Borrow, *Wild Wales* (1862)

George Borrow

581 I proposed Wales from the first, but my wife and daughter who have always had rather a hankering after what is fashionable, said they thought it would be more advisable to go to Harrowgate or Leamington.

Wild Wales (1862)

582 I sat silent and melancholy, till looking from the window I caught sight of a long line of hills, which I guessed to be the Welsh hills, as indeed they proved, which sight causing me to remember that I was bound for Wales, the land of the bard, made me cast all gloomy thoughts aside and glow with all the Welsh enthusiasm with which I glowed when I first started in the direction of Wales.

583 All conquered people are suspicious of their conquerors. The English have forgot that they ever conquered the Welsh, but some ages will elapse before the Welsh forget that the English have conquered them.

584 The Welsh are afraid lest an Englishman should understand their language, and, by

hearing their conversation, become acquainted with their private affairs, or by listening to it, pick up their language which they have no mind that they should know – and their very children sympathize with them.

585 No language has a better supply of simple words for the narration of events than the Welsh, and simple words are the proper garb of narration, and no language abounds more with terms calculated to express the abstrusest ideas of the metaphysician.

586 As to its sounds – I have to observe that at the will of a master it can be sublimely sonorous, terribly sharp, diabolically guttural and sibilant, and sweet and harmonious to a remarkable degree.

of the Welsh language

587 Gentility will be the ruin of the Welsh, as it has been of many things.

588 Wherever I have been in Wales, I have experienced nothing but kindness and hospitality, and when I return to my own country I will say so.

589 The man then asked me from what part of Wales I came, and when I told him I was an Englishman, was evidently offended, either because he did not believe me, or, as I more incline to think, did not approve of an Englishman's understanding of Welsh.

590 Wales is a bit crazed on the subject of religion.

591 I found nothing to blame and much to admire in John Jones the Calvinistic Methodist of Llangollen.

592 Oats and Methodism! What better symbols of poverty and meanness?

— 1863 —

Hussey Vivian

593 At this time we are one whole compact people. Remember that you are all Englishmen though you are Welshmen. Depend upon it – we must consider ourselves Englishmen.

speech at the Swansea Eisteddfod, 1863

— 1864 —

Anonymous

594 The farmer in Wales as well as the labourer must be taken to mean a person generally badly lodged and insufficiently fed and clothed.

report of medical officer to the Privy Council, 1864

Matthew Arnold

595 The people travelling about in Wales, and their quality, beggar description. It is a social revolution which is taking place, and to observe it may well fill one with reflection.

letter to his mother, 1864

R. J. Derfel

596 No man can love Mankind unless he love his own nation.*

'Gwladgarwch y Cymry'
Traethodau ac Areithiau (1864)

597 The greatest oppression for a conquered nation is to set foreigners who do not understand its language as spiritual pastors to it.*

'Pethau Wnawn pe Gallwn'

598 In every country the providence of God blesses patriots.*

'Enllibwyr ein Gwlad'

599 It is our language that keeps us a distinct nation, and because of that it is reasonable that we should keep our language.*

'Cadwriaeth yr Iaith Gymraeg'

600 I love my country to a fault, if that were possible.*

'Yr Eisteddfod'

Anthony Trollope

601 It's a superb carpet, my lady, and about the newest thing we have. We put down four hundred and fifty yards of it for the Duchess of South Wales at Cwddglwch castle, only last month.

The Small House at Allington (1864)

— 1865 —

David Davies (of Llandinam)

602 I am a great admirer of the old Welsh

language, and I have no sympathy with those who revile it. Still, I have seen enough of the world to know that the best medium to make money by is the English language. I want to advise every one of my countrymen to master it perfectly; if you are content with brown bread, you can of course, remain where you are. If you wish to enjoy the luxuries of life, with white bread to boot, the only way to do so is by learning English well. I know what it is to eat both.

speech at the National Eisteddfod, Aberystwyth, Sept. 1865

Abraham Lincoln

603 Sir, we omitted the Welsh because they have proved themselves real friends of our cause.

explaining why the Welsh were not ejected with other foreigners during the American Civil War quoted in *Western Mail* (Jan. 1954)

Thomas Price

604 Englishmen, English capital and enterprise, English customs and unhappily English vices, are rushing in upon us like mighty irresistible torrents carrying away before them our ancient language, social habits, and even our religious customs and influence over the masses.*

speech to the Congregational Union, 1865

Griffith Richards

605 It would be an enormous advantage to the Welsh and to the English if the Welsh language became extinct before tomorrow morning and the Welsh became absorbed into the English nation.*

in *Y Cronicl* (vol. 23, 1865)

— 1866 —

Anonymous

606 The Welsh language is the curse of Wales. Its prevailence and the ignorance of English have excluded, and even now exclude, the Welsh people from the civilization, the improvement, and the material prosperity of their English neighbours . . . Their antiquated and semi-barbarous language, in short, shrouds them in darkness.

editorial
in *The Times* (8 Sept. 1866)

607 The Eisteddfod is one of the most mischievous and selfish pieces of sentimentalism which could possibly be perpetrated. It is simply a foolish interference with the natural progress of civilization and prosperity. If it is desirable that the Welsh should talk English, it is monstrous folly to encourage them in a loving fondness for their old language.

608 Wales, it should be remembered, is a small country, unfavourably situated for commercial purposes, with an indifferent soil, and inhabited by an unenterprising people. It is true it possesses valuable minerals, but these have been chiefly developed by English energy and for the supply of English wants. A bare existence on the most primitive food of a mountainous race is all that the Welsh could enjoy if left to themselves.

editorial
in *The Times* (14 Sept. 1866)

609 We, the Welsh, have been loyalists for centuries . . . more so than the English themselves.*

editorial
in *Y Gwladgarwr* (18 Aug. 1866)

610 It is the crown of Welshmen that no other nation harbours ill feeling against them in any sense.*

Matthew Arnold

611 When I see the enthusiasm these Eisteddfods can awaken in your whole people, and then think of the tastes, the literature, the amusements of our own lower and middle class, I am filled with admiration.

reply to invitation to visit the Eisteddfod at Chester, 1866

612 On this side Wales – Wales, where the past still lives. Where every place has its tradition, every name its poetry, and where the people, the genuine people, still knows this past, this tradition, this poetry, and lives with it, and clings to it; while, alas, the prosperous Saxon on the other side, the invader from Liverpool and Birkenhead, has long forgotten his.

On the Study of Celtic Literature (1866)

613 The fusion of all the inhabitants of these islands into one homogeneous, English-speaking whole, the breaking down of barriers between us, the swallowing up of separate provincial nationalities, is a consummation to which the natural course of things irresistibly tends; it is a necessity of what is called modern civilization, and modern civilization is a real, legitimate force; the change must come, and its accomplishment is a mere affair of time.

614 It must always be the desire of a government to render its dominions, as far as possible, homogeneous . . . Sooner or later the difference of language between Wales and England will probably be effaced . . . an event which is socially and politically so desirable.

615 The practical contribution of Welsh culture to that of England and the world at large must be made in English.

616 For all modern purposes, I repeat, let us all as soon as possible be one people; let the Welshman speak English, and if he is an author, let him write in English.

617 An Eisteddfod is, no doubt, a kind of Olympic meeting; and that the common people of Wales should care for such a thing, shows something Greek in them, something spiritual, something humane, something (I am afraid one must add) which in the English common people is not to be found.

618 The sooner the Welsh language disappears as an instrument of the practical, political, social life of Wales, the better; the better for England, the better for Wales itself.

619 If I were asked where English poetry got these three things, its turn for style, its turn for melancholy, and its turn for natural magic . . . I should answer, with some doubt, that it got much of its turn for style from a Celtic source; with less doubt, that it got much of its turn for melancholy from a Celtic source; with no doubt at all, that from a Celtic source it got nearly all its natural magic.

Friedrich Engels
620 There is no country in Europe where there

are not different nationalities under the same government. The Highland Gaels and the Welsh are undoubtedly of different nationalities from the English, although nobody will give to these remnants of peoples long gone by the titles of nations any more than to the Celtic inhabitants of Brittany in France.*

What have the Working Classes to do with Poland? (1866)

Thomas Gee
621 Let English be the language of commerce and Welsh the language of religion.*

in *Baner ac Amserau Cymru* (1 Aug. 1866)

John Griffiths
622 The literature of Wales is remarkable for the purity of its sentiments and the high tone of its morality. Infidelity or scepticism have found no room for their utterance. We have hardly a single publication among the hundreds of thousands that find circulation in the Principality that can give offence to the high moral sentiments produced by our common Christianity.

speech at the Music Hall, Chester, 6 Feb. 1866

Henry Richard
623 Clansmen battling for their respective chieftains.

of Welsh politicians
Letters on the Social and Political Condition of Wales (1866)

— **1867** —

Anonymous
624 The Welsh are cordially liked and heartily respected by all their fellow-subjects, as a gallant and most gifted race. Year by year the English know them better, and year by year the English like them more. There is really not even a lingering trace of national jealousy. Long ago, we fought our last fight with the Welsh, and luckily for them we won it.

editorial
in *The Daily Telegraph* (13 Sept. 1867)

625 The Eisteddfod, with its mottoes and hieroglyphics, must be in a desperately

shaky condition if it cannot stand a little of that gentle raillery to which usage has now given the appropriate name of 'chaff'.

Thomas Rees

626 Ever since the incorporation of Wales with England, the loyalty of the Welsh nation to their Saxon rulers has been perfectly unswerving, notwithstanding the occasional effusions of frenzied poets and hot-headed orators against the Saxon invaders.

Miscellaneous Papers on Subjects relating to Wales (1867)

627 Novels, the disgrace of English literature and the curse of multitudes of English readers, do not take with Welsh readers.

in *The Carmarthen Journal* (6 Sept. 1867)

H. L. Spring

628 The Welsh are a conquered race, and have very little regard for their conquerors, and even some of the most ignorant of them are so stupid as to entertain the notion of reclaiming their country from the English.

Lady Cambria (1867)

629 Had the mineral wealth of the principality been discovered by the natives, and could it have been properly put to use before they were subdued to English rule, they might have preserved their language and have been the foremost amongst British subjects in wealth, manufactures and arts; but as the English have, through Providence, been the means of opening out her resources, it is plain that the English element must universally prevail.

John Thomas, Ieuan Ddu

630 If Welshmen have a fault, 'tis that their slices
    Of their right's last loaf to a mere crumb is brought;
And but infers at last the English tongue
    Alone can save our skins from English wrong.

'Harry Vaughan'

— 1868 —

John Ceiriog Hughes

631 To rouse the old land to its former glory.*

'Cadlef Morgannwg'

James Kenward

632 The most important and valuable of all things connected with Wales is her language.

For Cambria (1868)

633 The continued introduction of railways will operate largely in the degradation of the language and be a potent agent of denationalization.

634 I call upon the young men of Wales to rise energetically to meet the present emergency. Do not believe that the existence of two languages in our country is an unmixed evil, any more than that the existence of two climates or two kinds of scenery is one. You who were born and also live on Cambrian soil, be the earnest and consistent advocates of your nation's rights, the vindicators of its fame, the representatives of its genius and worth.

635 How can you believe in Homer if you doubt Taliesin?

636 An Englishman wishing to cast in his lot with Welsh interest is distracted by the dissension everywhere prevalent.

Thomas Nicholas

637 I see no valid reason . . . why the Welsh should rest content with the obscurity which blind adherence to a speech which can never become the vehicle of science and commerce must entail upon them.

The Pedigree of the English People (1868)

Queen Victoria

638 [If a royal residence is established in Ireland] every other place in the Queen's dominions – Wales and the colonies even – might get up pretensions for residence, which are out of the question.

remark to Disraeli, 1868

— 1869 —

Anonymous

639 At the last election there was not more interference by the Conservative than by the Radical Landlords, with the freedom of voting by their tenants, and certainly

nothing to be compared with the systematic intimidation by the Dissident Preachers.

agent of the Cawdor estate, letter, 21 May 1869

Henry Richard MP
640 No question relating to Wales has occupied the attention of Parliament in the memory of man.

speech in House of Commons, 1869

— 1870 —

Anonymous
641 Wales, England – and Llanrwst.*

traditional saying, *c.* 1870

Richard Davies, Mynyddog
642 Talk in Welsh
And sing in Welsh;
Whatever you do,
Do everything in Welsh.*

'Gwnewch Bobpeth yn Gymraeg'

John Evans, Y Bardd Cocos
643 Four fat lions without any hair,
Two on this side and two over there.*

of the monumental lions on the Britannia Bridge, Anglesey, *c.* 1870

William Ewart Gladstone MP
644 There is a complete, constitutional, legal and . . . historical identity between the Church in Wales and the Church of England.

speech in House of Commons, 1870

William Herbert, Earl of Pembroke
645 The name Herbert is becoming vulgar. I am thinking of changing my name to Jones.

on hearing that a Mr Jones of Llanarth had changed his name to Herbert, *c.* 1870

Francis Kilvert
646 A lovely evening and the Black Mountains lighted up grandly, all the furrows and water courses clear and brilliant, people coming home from market, birds singing, buds bursting, and the spring air full of beauty, life and hope.

entry in diary, 24 Feb. 1870

647 I have an ambition to write some songs which shall be sung by the girls of Hay and Glasbury, and at village concerts and about the hills.

13 May 1870

648 Hay Fair today and tomorrow and I am right glad to escape the noise, bustle, dust, drunkenness and the general upturn of the country.

17 May 1870

649 To me there seems to be a halo of glory round this place [Clyro] . . . Many sweet and sacred memories hover about these hill homes and make the place whereon one stands holy ground.

7 June 1870

650 At Maesllwch Castle last week four guns killed seven hundred rabbits in one afternoon.

25 Oct. 1870

651 Oh these kindly hospitable houses about these hospitable hills. I believe I might wander about these hills all my life and never want a kindly welcome, a meal, or a seat by the fire.

26 Oct. 1870

Andrew Lang
652 Westward I watch the low green hills of Wales,
   The low sky silver gray,
The turbid Channel with the wandering sails
   Moans through the winter day.

'Clivedon Church'

Karl Marx
653 Very gallant young fellows these Celts, also born dialecticians, everything is conceived in Triads.*

letter to Friedrich Engels, 11 May 1870

— 1871 —

Anonymous
654 In the best interest of the Welsh it is desirable to do everything lawful to wean

them from their provincial tongue. There can be no doubt its use is gradually dying out and it is permissible to hasten a process which has simultaneously arisen among the people themselves from the course of events.

editorial
in *The Times* (14 Nov. 1871)

655 Every resident of the *Wladfa* who has lived there for six months and who is eighteen years of age or over, shall be considered an elector.*

constitution of the Welsh colony in Patagonia
in *Baner ac Amserau Cymru* (12 July 1871)

Francis Kilvert

656 I like wandering about these lonely, waste and ruined places. There dwells among them a spirit of quiet and gentle melancholy more congenial and akin to my own spirit than full life and gaiety and noise.

entry in diary, 6 March 1871

657 Mr Marsden [the vicar of Glascwm, Rads.] told me that only four years ago died the last old woman who could speak her native Radnorshire Welsh, her northern tongue which she had learnt as a child from her mother and grandmother, never having lived out of her own parish. No one else in the parish could talk Welsh to her except Mr Marsden and her great delight was when he would read to her from a Welsh book.

22 May 1871

658 It is a fine thing to be out on the hills alone. A man can hardly be a beast or a fool alone on a great mountain.

29 May 1871

659 Oh, Aberedw, Aberedw. Would God I might dwell and die by thee.

660 I have always had a vision of coming into a Welsh town about sunset and seeing the children playing on the bridge, and this evening the dream came true.

12 June 1871

661 Cader Idris is the stoniest, dreariest, most desolate mountain I was ever on.

13 June 1871

662 An angel satyr walks these hills.

20 June 1871

663 The land was rejoicing in the sunshine, the jewelled green of the meadows, the brilliant blue of the Beacon.

26 Sept. 1871

664 At Llangadock for the first time on the journey we saw a Welshwoman in a tall peaked hat.

16 Oct. 1871

665 Clyro Petty Sessions, and the Magistrates abolished the New Inn, a happy time for the village.

30 Oct. 1871

— **1872** —

R. D. Blackmore

666 Certainly you may ask, Llewellyn; it is a woman's and a Welshman's privilege.

The Maid of Sker (1872)

667 How [he] knew me to be a Welshman, I could not tell then, and am not sure now. It must have been because I looked so superior to the rest of them.

668 However, it was the old, old thing. The Welsh must do all the real work, and the English be paid for sitting upon them after they are dead.

Francis Kilvert

669 An election of a Guardian for the parish is coming on and the place is all in an uproar of excitement. Church versus Chapel and party feelings running very high. The dissenters are behaving badly.

entry in diary, 29 March 1872

670 Talk of being priest-ridden, 'tis nothing to being ridden by political dissenting preachers.

20 April 1872

Henry Morton Stanley

671 Doctor Livingstone, I presume?

on finding the explorer at Ujiji, 10 Nov. 1871
How I found Livingstone (1872)

R. D. Thomas

672 Unless the Government of Britain and the rich landowners do not make some better arrangement quickly to pay more wages to the honest workers of Wales . . . and give them more justice and civil and religious liberty . . . the Principality will be emptied . . . O our dear compatriots in holy Wales! We should love to see you *all* here.*

Hanes Cymru America (1872)

673 I do not like to deny historic fact, but I would like to be able to have sure proof that descendants of Madawg are still living somewhere in America. And if there are, in their low and subjected condition, any Welsh Indians, it would be more of a benefit and advantage to us as a nation to make truly worthy efforts in our compassion and in our religious efforts to enlighten them and benefit them.

— **1873** —

Anonymous

674 The Metropolis of Wales.

epithet for Cardiff, first used 1873

William Ewart Gladstone MP

675 The continued prevalence of the Welsh language is chiefly due to the misguided and ungenerous policy of the British Government.

speech at the Mold Eisteddfod, 1873

Francis Kilvert

676 I found old Giles without coal, thanks to that strike of the South Wales colliers and the baneful tyrannical influence of that cursed Union.

entry in diary, 20 Jan. 1873

— **1874** —

Herber Evans

677 Civilization is at an end.

on hearing of the defeat of the Liberal candidate in Caernarfonshire, 1874

Gerard Manley Hopkins

678 Looking all around me but most in looking

far up the valley I felt an instress and charm of Wales.

entry in journal, 6 Sept. 1874

— **1875** —

Francis Kilvert

679 Wales, sweet Wales. I believe I must have Welsh blood. I always feel so happy and natural and at home among the kindly Welsh.

entry in diary, 12 April 1875

680 A strange fascination, a beautiful enchantment hangs over Builth and the town is magically transfigured still.

13 April 1875

681 Tintern Abbey at first sight seemed to me to be bare and almost too perfect to be entirely picturesque.

July Eve, 1875

682 I have heard great talk of the Wye at Chepstow but no one who has only seen the river at Chepstow and Tintern can imagine the beauty and character of the Wye as a mountain stream between Rhayader and Hay.

Sir Lewis Morris

683 Dear motherland, forgive me, if too long
I hold the halting tribute of my song;
Letting my wayward fancy idly roam
Far, far from thee, my early home.
There are some things too near,
Too infinitely dear
For speech; the old ancestral hearth,
The hills, the vales that saw our birth,
Are hallowed deep within the reverent
breast:
And who of these keeps silence, he is best.

'To my Motherland'

— **1877** —

Anonymous

684 The whole mental machinery of the Welsh and the Irish seems better oiled than that of the Saxon.

in *The Cornhill Magazine* (vol. 36, 1877)

William Ewart Gladstone MP

685 I speak of the country of Wales . . . There
is no part that can exceed it from one end
of this island to the other in the ardent,
and I may say, passionate love for
instruction.

speech at Nottingham, 1877

Gerard Manley Hopkins

686 Lovely the woods, waters, meadows,
    combes, vales,
All the air things wear that build this
    world of Wales;
Only the inmate does not correspond.

'In the Valley of the Elwy'

Michael D. Jones

687 The greater part of the demand among us
for English chapels arises from the haughty
pride of men made servile by adulation of
the English.*

in *Y Ddraig Goch* (June 1877)

— **1878** —

Anonymous

688 Few of them show intelligence. I find that
when the question is translated to Welsh,
they understand it better.

entry in log-book of National School, Llanrug,
1 Nov. 1878

William Thomas, Islwyn

689 Thank you, Martha, for all you did for me.
You have been very kind. I am going to
Anne now.*

to his wife on his death-bed, referring to Anne
Bowen, his first love, 1878

— **1879** —

Anonymous

690 God forgive me.

inscription on gravestone of Robert Thompson
Crawshay, iron-master, at Faenor, near
Merthyr Tydfil, 1879

— **1880** —

Anonymous

691 The Parnell of Wales.

epithet applied to Thomas Edward Ellis, 1880s

**Robert Ambrose Jones, Emrys ap
Iwan**

692 It is better for a nation to be the object of
English hatred than of their scorn.*

'Dr Edwards a'r Achosion Seisnigol'
in *Baner ac Amserau Cymru* (1880)

693 Oh how we love a bit of stroking. We
should rather, Mr Gladstone, be without
bread than without soap. If you tickle us in
a tender spot we lie still as a litter of piglets
on a dung-heap. We half-worship you
since you called us 'patient and loyal
Welshmen', and especially since you
described our country as 'poor little
Wales'.*

letter in *Baner ac Amserau Cymru* (1880)

William Price (of Llantrisant)

694 You the coalowners are the Welsh
Pharaohs who think you can suck the life-
blood of the colliers for ever. You have
grown fat and prosperous; you own the big
houses; you wear the finest clothes; your
children are healthy and happy; yet you
do not work. How then have you got those
things by idleness? . . . Take heed, you men
whose bodies are bloated by the life-blood
of the poor, take heed before it is too late.
Remember that the oppression of the
Pharaohs did not last for ever, and neither
will the oppression of the blood-sucking
Pharaohs of Wales.

quoted by Rhys Davies, 'A Drop of Dew'
in *Wales* (no. 31, Oct. 1949)

— **1881** —

Anonymous

695 Whereas the provisions in force against the
sale of fermented and distilled liquors
during certain hours of Sunday have been
found to be attended with great public
benefit, and it is expedient and the people
of Wales are desirous that in the
Principality of Wales these provisions be
extended to the other hours of Sunday.

preamble to the Sunday Closing Act (Wales),
1881

696 Such is the attachment of the Welsh to
their own language and literature, so

deeply interwoven are they with their daily life, their religious worship and even their amusements, that . . . the Welsh language will long be cherished by the large majority of the Welsh people.

report of the Committee on Intermediate and Higher Education in Wales, 1881

William Ewart Gladstone MP

697 Where there is a distinctly formed Welsh opinion upon a given subject, which affects Wales alone . . . I know of no reason why a respectful regard should not be paid to that opinion.

speech in House of Commons, 1881

David Lloyd George

698 I eyed the Assembly in a spirit similar to that in which William the Conqueror eyed England on his first visit to Edward the Confessor, as the region of his future domain.

recalling his first visit to House of Commons, 1881

— 1882 —

Robert Ambrose Jones, Emrys ap Iwan

699 I believe it is the suppressed condition of the Welsh that is the reason why their music is so sentimental.*

'Llythyr Alltud'
in *Baner ac Amserau Cymru* (13 Dec. 1882)

— 1883 —

J. Viriamu Jones

700 No nobler task could fall to the lot of any Welshman.

on being appointed first Principal of University College, Cardiff
quoted by K. V. Jones, *Life of John Viriamu Jones* (1915)

Clement Scott

701 Bring, novelists, your notebook, bring,
     dramatists, your pen,
And I'll tell you a simple story of what
     women do for men;
It's only a tale of a lifeboat, the dying and
     the dead,

Of a terrible storm and shipwreck that
     happened off Mumbles Head.

'The Women of Mumbles Head'

Thomas Davies

702 The inaccessibility of Aberystwyth to the outside world must be accepted as a dispensation of Providence. Such a town deserves to be isolated.

letter to Thomas Charles Edwards, 1884
quoted by E. L. Ellis, *The University College of Wales, Aberystwyth 1872–1972* (1972)

— **1885** —

Anonymous

703 The Society for the Utilization of the Welsh Language for the Better Teaching of English.

first title of Cymdeithas yr Iaith Gymraeg, 1885

704 There is an effort made by certain well-meaning but ill-advised friends of Wales to bring the Welsh language to the front and make it a class subject in our elementary schools. The true and disinterested friends of the country admit that its low social and educational condition is due to the prevalence of the Welsh language. No one objects to the study of the old language but it is quite a different matter to make it a part of the curriculum of our day schools. The children of those who earn their living by manual labour attend school for the purpose of fitting themselves the more successfully to compete in the battle of life. A knowledge of Welsh can be of no possible help to them. It is in fact a positive disadvantage.

editorial
in *Western Mail* (12 May 1885)

Daniel Owen

705 These strikes are strange things, May. They are things that have come from the English; they do not belong to us, and I greatly fear that they will bring great evil to the country and to religion.*

Abel Hughes
in *Rhys Lewis* (1885)

706 That's the difference between Church and Chapel . . . You Church people think

yourselves good when you are bad, and the Chapel people think themselves bad when they are good.*

Wil Bryan

— 1886 —

Basil Jones

707 Wales is at present nothing more than the Highlands of England without a Highland Line; it is a geographical expression.

speech, 1886

— 1887 —

Anonymous

708 The common idea of a landlord is a man who has the mouth of a hog, the teeth of a lion, the nails of a bear, the hooves of an ass, the sting of a serpent, and the greed of the grave. The landowners of our country are, in general, cruel, unreasonable, unfeeling and unpitying men . . . Many of them have been about the most presumptuous thieves that have ever breathed.*

editorial
in *Baner ac Amserau Cymru* (2 Nov. 1887)

William Ewart Gladstone MP

709 I affirm that Welsh nationality is as great a reality as English nationality.

speech at Swansea, 4 June 1887

710 Wales has not told her own tale . . . It is time your representatives . . . subject to the claim of imperial patriotism, laid their Welsh heads together and considered what are the fair claims of Wales.

David Lloyd George

711 Do you not think that this tithe business is an excellent lever wherewith to raise the spirit of the people?

letter to T. E. Ellis, 1887

Colonel Mainwaring

712 I should like it to be entered on record that the now popular game of lawn tennis was the old Welsh game of Cerrig y Drudion.

at meeting of the Cambrian Archaeological Association, 26 Aug. 1887

Llewelyn Turner

713 The separate language shuts out the people of Wales from a share in the finest freehold that has ever been the heritage of this or any other age or clime in the world – that owned by the English-speaking races.

in *North Wales Gazette* (27 Dec. 1887)

— 1888 —

William Abraham MP, Mabon

714 No colliery can be opened without the consent of the landlord and the consent must be given on his terms [and] even if the capital of the speculation had all been expended uselessly, the landlord must have his pound of flesh.

in *The Cambrian* (28 March 1888)

John Ceiriog Hughes

715 All Wales is a sea of song.*

title of poem
Yr Oriau Olaf (1888)

Henry Jones

716 I am so little eager for an independent Wales that I would as soon re-establish Druidism in Anglesey as set up an independent Parliament in Caernarvon. Union with England is essential to our existence . . . but union, even the closest, does not mean that Wales is to be Anglicized.

'Some of the Social Wants of Wales'
Transactions of the Welsh National Society, 1888–9

717 We must either cohere for national ends or become a mere part of England.

William Jones

718 What of the character of the Prince [of Wales]? Has he made himself known as a Sunday School teacher or anything of that sort? I don't know of a more poor lot on the face of history than the English Kings and Monarchs. Their histories are stinking in the nostrils of the Welsh nation.

speech at meeting of Bangor Municipal Council, 1888

David Randall MP

719 I solicit your suffrages as a Welsh Nationalist.

election address, Gower, 1888

— 1889 —

Anonymous

720 Of the three Celtic races which have contributed so largely to the development and prosperity of this country [the United States of America] . . . the Welsh, modest, unassuming, with no desire to shine or to challenge the pretensions of their brothers, with quiet industry and unaffected dignity, have worked and laboured in various fields, winning for themselves neither fame nor fortune, but a quiet safe place and secure in the respect and confidence of their fellow men . . . They mingled freely with the others and much of their race individuality has been lost. This has always been characteristic of the Welsh.

in *The New York Times* (1889)

721 As long as men are lunatic enough to maintain oppressive and wasteful monarchies, so long will the poor be downtrodden and the wealthy exalted. *

in *Baner ac Amserau Cymru* (17 Aug. 1889)

722 Buddug [Victoria] and her progeny have always been cold and indifferent towards Wales and that has begotten among the people an equivalent coldness and indifference, to say the least.*

in *Y Genedl Gymreig* (21 Aug. 1889)

Owen M. Edwards

723 To me the best proof of the healthy strength of Wales is the fact that it is only in literature and music has her life been portrayed so far.*

O'r Bala i Geneva (1889)

E. Pan Jones

724 Look for a moment at those districts where the Welsh language has been supplanted by the English language. The inhabitants have degenerated in body and mind . . . and religion is like the shadow of a shadow.

speech at Llanover, 1889

Robert Ambrose Jones, Emrys ap Iwan

725 I should prefer, of the two, to see my countrymen using splendid English than poor Welsh.*

'Picio'r Gwallt yr Hanner Cymry'
Y Geninen (April/July 1889)

David Lloyd George

726 In North Wales we measure a man from his chin up.

in speech at his adoption meeting as Liberal candidate for Caernarfon Boroughs, 3 Jan. 1889

Sir Lewis Morris

727 Dear lady, we are feeble folk and weak
But our old tongue and loyal hearts we
   keep;
We cherish still the love we may not speak,
   The old affection deep.

ode welcoming Queen Victoria to Wales, 1889

Queen Victoria

728 [Tell] the Prince of Wales how this naturally sensitive and warmhearted people feel the neglect shown them by [him] and his family . . . It is very wrong of him not to come here . . [as] he takes his title from this country, which is very beautiful.

letter to Sir Henry Ponsonby, 27 Aug. 1889

Walt Whitman

729 The Welsh people are an animated, gesticulating people.

letter to Ernest Rhys, 24 Sept. 1889

T. Marchant Williams

730 Poets and pothouses always run together in my mind . . . Did you ever come across a bard who was a useful member of society?

The Land of my Fathers (1889)

— 1890 —

Anonymous

731 It came to pass in days of yore,
   The Devil chanced upon Llandore;
Quoth he, By all this fume and stink,
   I can't be far from home, I think.

traditional rhyme, 1890s

Owen M. Edwards

732 Much of the misunderstanding between parties in Wales arises from the fact that no party understands the history of the Wales of the past . . . I would like to depict . . . the olden days just as they were – and not from the angle of a Liberal or Tory, Methodist or Independent.*

in *Cymru Fydd* (vol. 3, 1890)

Thomas Edward Ellis MP

733 Over and above all, we shall work for a Legislature, elected by the manhood and womanhood of Wales, and to them responsible. It will be the symbol and cementer of our unity as a nation, our instrument in working out our social ideals and industrial welfare, the pledge of our heritage in the British Empire, the deliverer of our message and example to humanity, the rallying point of our nationality and fulfiller of our hopes.

speech at Bala, 1890

David Lloyd George

734 The Tories have not yet realized that the day of the cottage-bred man has at last dawned.*

speech during Parliamentary election, 1890

735 I feel so sanguine that were self-government granted to Wales she would be a model to the nationalities of the earth of a people who have driven oppression from their hillsides and initiated the glorious reign of freedom, justice and truth.

speech to South Wales Liberal Federation, Feb. 1890

736 The current of the time is sweeping to nationalism. Wales, in throwing in her lot with Ireland in the self-government struggle, has struck a blow not only for the national rights of another Celtic country, but also for her own.

maiden speech in House of Commons, 13 June 1890

— **1891** —

Joseph Bailey MP

737 Wales has never been a nation.

speech in House of Commons, 20 Feb. 1891

Owen M. Edwards

738 If we are to understand the history of Wales, and to know the Welshman's soul, we have to start with the mountains.*

in *Cymru* (no. 1, 15 Aug. 1891)

739 I believe there is nothing that will strengthen a Welshman's character as much as knowing the history of his own country; I believe there is no better way of educating a Welshman than with his own literature; I believe that by keeping his Welshness a Welshman will be most ready to do good, and most successful and happiest and nearest to God.*

William Ewart Gladstone MP

740 The Nonconformists of Wales are the people of Wales.

speech in House of Commons, 1891

— **1892** —

William Abraham MP, Mabon

741 Wales ought to be considered by England as the nearest of kin . . . the loveliest, nay, I would almost say the best of her children.

speech in House of Commons, 1892

Owen M. Edwards

742 No nation on earth is of pure blood, and where the blood is most mixed is the most genius and progress.*

'Hanes Cymru'
in *Cymru* (vol. 2, no. 7, 15 Feb. 1892)

T. E. Ellis MP

743 In 1880 Wales declared instinctively and passionately for freedom to struggling peoples and subject races. In 1886, that year of apostasies and disasters, Wales declared for Irish national freedom more decisively than did even Ireland herself. Today, Wales herself appeals for freedom, and we are confident that the democracy of England will give to this appeal an early, a generous, and an enthusiastic response.

speech at Newcastle-upon-Tyne, 1892

D. Emrys Jones

744 A great bulk of the bardic effusions seem to be the veriest twaddle. The whole bardic tribe, with their conceits, presumption and arrogance, wanted some process of reincarnation, and a considerable period of quiescence might elapse without any detriment to Welsh poetry.

in *The North Wales Chronicle* (22 Oct. 1892)

Arthur Price

745 All hope of Welsh Nationalism doing

anything for some time ended when Ellis grasped the Saxon gold.

of T. E. Ellis's acceptance of the office of Junior Whip
letter to J. E. Lloyd, 1892

David Thomas MP
746 Nor have we any desire to stimulate the Welsh language by artificial means. The Welsh language is very well able to take care of itself.

speech in House of Commons, Feb. 1892

— 1893 —

Anonymous
747 [The river Rhondda] contains a large proportion of human excrement, stable and pigsty manure, congealed blood, offal and entrails from the slaughterhouses, the rotten carcases of animals, cats and dogs in various stages of decomposition, old cast-off articles of clothing and bedding, old boots, bottles, ashes, street refuse and a host of other articles. The water is perfectly black from small coal in suspension.

report of Ystradyfodwg Urban Sanitary Board, 1893

Robert Ambrose Jones, Emrys ap Iwan
748 It is Welshmen whose minds are poor that find Welsh to be poor.*

'Cymraeg y Pregethwr'
address to students at Bala Theological College, 25 Feb. 1893

William Ewart Gladstone MP
749 The treatment of Monmouthshire in Wales is, I appreciate, quite modern, though it may be very proper.

letter to Asquith, 10 Nov. 1893

Marie Trevelyan
750 The thoughtful mind sees in these people [the Welsh] many good qualities of head and heart. Their characteristics are patient, plodding and indomitable perseverance.

Glimpses of Welsh Life and Character (1893)

Queen Victoria
751 There is no 'Church of Wales'.

letter to W. E. Gladstone (Feb. 1893)

— 1894 —

Owen M. Edwards
752 The literary activity of Wales is to be found chiefly in the Welsh-speaking districts. It is from these districts that most of its teachers come. It is in these districts that the great poets have lived. It will be one of the aims of this magazine to lay before the English-speaking Welshman the treasures of his ancestors' thoughts.

Wales (May 1894)

753 It is not race or language that has made Wales a separate country and the Welsh a peculiar people. Wales owes its separate existence to its mountains; it is to the mountains that the Welsh people owe their national characteristics.

Keir Hardie
754 The life of one Welsh miner is of greater commercial and moral value than the whole Royal crowd put together, from the Royal Great Grandmamma down to the puling Royal Great Grandchild.

in *Labour Leader* (30 June 1894)

Robert Jones, Emrys ap Iwan
755 There is nothing deserves to be called literature unless the nation and the generations bear witness to having a part in it.*

'Y Clasuron Cymraeg'
in *Y Geninen* (Jan. 1894)

David Lloyd George MP
756 Yes, Home Rule for Hell! I like every man to speak up for his own country.

in speech at meeting in Cardiff in response to heckler who had shouted ' 'Ome Rule for 'Ell', 4 Oct. 1894

Herbert Lewis
757 We have nothing to gain by subservience to the Liberal Party and . . . we shall never get the English to do us justice until we show our independence of them.

letter to T. E. Ellis, 1894

W. Llewelyn Williams
758 The educated and the leisured classes have been brought up in ignorance of the Welsh

language, and often with a distinct prejudice against it as a mere patois, unworthy of the respect of an educated and cultured man. Welshmen writing in the vernacular have, therefore, only a very limited circle to appeal to.

address to the Honourable Society of Cymmrodorion, 1894

— 1895 —

Owen M. Edwards

759 There is little criticism in Wales, and much slander and puff.

in *Wales* (vol. 2, no. 19, Nov. 1895)

Robert Ambrose Jones, Emrys ap Iwan

760 Let the Welshman have what is his, and the foreigner what is the foreigner's! In the name of reason, what is fairer?*

'Paham y Gorfu yr Undebwyr' in *Y Geninen* (Oct. 1895)

761 If someone says that we are a nation equal and not subjected to the English, then why have we no Welsh Parliament?*

762 The true Welshman is he who believes and professes that the most important of all political questions is that of keeping Wales Welsh in language and spirit.*

David Lloyd George MP

763 It is quite impossible to have one legislature to serve the needs of Celt and Teuton.

'National Self-Government for Wales' in *Young Wales* (1895)

764 The Celt is Liberal in his politics because he is Conservative in his temperament.

765 I maintain strongly that all our demands for reform, whether in Church, Land, Education, Temperance or otherwise, ought to be concentrated in one great agitation for national self-government.

letter to Thomas Gee, 1895

Sir John Rhŷs

766 Why provide them with bathrooms? The young men are only up for eight weeks.

on hearing the suggestion that baths might be installed in Jesus College, Oxford, *c.* 1895

Lord Rosebery

767 In Wales [the Church of England] is very much what Gibraltar is to Spain, a foreign fortress placed on the territory of a jealous, proud and susceptible nation.

letter to Queen Victoria, Jan. 1895

W. Jenkyn Thomas

768 The best way to promote Welsh interests in Parliament is to leaven the Liberal Party from within and not to form a Welsh party distinct from, and independent of, that organization.

in *Young Wales* (March 1895)

W. Llewelyn Williams

769 What avails it to form a National Party in Parliament if our Nationalism is sapped and undermined in every school in Wales?

in *Young Wales* (1895)

— 1896 —

Anonymous

770 Wales for ever!*

traditional saying, *c.* 1896

771 There is no traitor in this house.*

sign in windows of Union families during the Penrhyn Lock-out, Bethesda, 1896–1903

Robert Bird

772 There are, from Swansea to Newport, thousands upon thousands of Englishmen, as true Liberals as yourselves, who will never submit to the domination of Welsh ideas.

speech at meeting of Cymru Fydd, Newport, 16 Jan. 1896

Owen M. Edwards

773 Whenever Wales awakes, her religious feeling will awaken too; with Arthur comes St David, always.*

'Dewi Sant' *Cartrefi Cymru* (1896)

A. E. Housman

774 The flag of morn in conqueror's state

Enters at the English gate;
The vanquished eve, as night prevails,
Bleeds upon the road to Wales.

'The Welsh Marches'

Idrisyn Jones

775 We plead, then, that the two great
languages might remain the heritage of
Wales; English as the language of the
secular, and Welsh as the language of the
religious life, so that in all temporal affairs
on the one hand and in spiritual on the
other, our country might prosper.

'The Moral Importance of Retaining the Welsh
Language'
in *Young Wales* (Aug. 1896)

J. Viriamu Jones

776 The history of Wales during the last
twenty-five years has been little else than
the history of its educational progress.

Wales (1896)

J. P. Mahaffy

777 We can see in the signal example of Wales
how a country adjoining the most civilized
in Europe, and under its laws, can be kept
barbarous by upholding its own obsolete
language.

'The Modern Babel'
in *The Nineteenth Century* (vol. 40, Nov. 1896)

— 1897 —

Anonymous

778 Cardiff proudly terms itself a Victorian
town.

statement by Cardiff Corporation to Queen
Victoria, 1897

779 Mr [Joseph] Conrad did not neglect to
state that he valued the *Western Mail* very
highly for its liveliness and originality,
adding that in the circles in which he
moves this is a common opinion.

report on the writer's visit to Cardiff
in *Western Mail* (1 Jan. 1897)

David Davies

780 As a people we have been winking and
smiling and frowning in the dark for

centuries, under the mistaken impression
that the race for which the winks and
smiles and frowns were particularly meant
could see them.

'Wales and the Welsh'
in *Young Wales* (vol. 3, 1897)

Owen M. Edwards

781 Notes about flowers and animals are very
acceptable. I have had too many letters
concerning semi-political matters lately.
Let the particular mission of *Wales* be
borne in mind.

editorial
in *Wales* (vol. 4, no. 35, March 1897)

— 1898 —

H. Elvet Lewis, Elfed

782 A nation becomes great, however small in
numbers, according to its belief in its own
purpose.*

'Y Gogwyddiad Ysprydol yn ein Llenyddiaeth a
Hanes'
in *Y Geninen* (vol. 16, no. 4, Autumn 1898)

Herbert Roberts MP

783 There is no portion of the United
Kingdom which is prouder of the British
Empire than Wales. [In our call for
domestic self-government] there is not a
shadow of desire to impair the supreme
authority of this Parliament or to advance
one single step along the road to
separation.

speech in House of Commons, 1898

Theodore Watts-Dunton

784 Winifred Wynne is meant to be the typical
Welsh girl as I have found her –
affectionate, warm-hearted, self-sacrificing
and brave.

preface
Aylwin (1898)

— 1900 —

Anonymous

785 When you can see the coast of Devon from
Swansea, it's going to rain; when you can't
it's already raining.

traditional weather lore, early 20th cent.

786 Mumbles is a funny place,
    A church without a steeple,
Houses built of old shipwrecks
    And a most peculiar people.

popular rhyme, early 20th cent.

787 The Welsh are the Irish who couldn't swim.

popular saying, early 20th cent.

788 A visitor to homes in Glamorgan is asked to help himself to sugar for his tea; in Carmarthenshire he is asked whether he wants one lump or two; in Cardiganshire he is asked to give the tea another stir.

joke, early 20th cent.

789 Shrewd in the market-place, devout in chapel, and frantic in bed.

traditional description of the ideal Welshwoman, early 20th cent.

790 It is the duty of every true Welshman to work to free his country from the rule of strangers, and so when he has made his country free, to be able to help other people to gain their liberty.

leaflet distributed by the Socialists of Llanelly Hill, Abergavenny, *c.* 1900

Thomas Johns
791 The Welsh rural areas are still the location of 'the Land of the White Gloves' [districts free from serious crime]; only the southern industrial valleys have been corrupted by the influx of English people and their vicious habits.

in *South Wales Press* (5 July 1900)

John John Roberts
792 He talked too much . . . about Wales and Eternity.*

adjudication of poem by Ben Bowen, at Liverpool Eisteddfod, 1900

— **1901** —

Anonymous
793 Every period and age dwindles into insignificance when compared with the nineteenth century . . . [when] Wales at a

bound emerged from the obscurity in which it lay in 1800, so that in this year of grace 1901 it is one of the brightest and most truly civilized spots in the Queen's dominions.

editorial
in *Western Mail* (1 Jan. 1901)

Ben Bowen
794 It is easy enough to follow Christ: the difficulty is in following His followers.*

entry in diary, 2 Dec. 1901

Owen M. Edwards
795 Wales is a land of mountains.

Wales (1901)

796 There are mountains and mountains; there are Welshmen and Welshmen.

A. C. Humphreys Owen
797 Lloyd George [has become] a below-the-gangway English radical – nothing more.

letter to Stuart Rendel, 23 March 1901

— **1902** —

Robert Ambrose Jones, Emrys ap Iwan
798 When a language deteriorates it is ready to die; and when it becomes too poor to be suitable for every occasion, the sooner it dies the better.*

'Gwella Gwallau'
in *Y Geninen* (Jan. 1902)

David Lloyd George MP
799 The Church has over twelve thousand schools in the country, which are mission rooms to educate the children of the poor in the principles of the Church. In eight thousand parishes there are no other schools and the whole machinery of the law is utilized to force Nonconformist children into them.

speech in House of Commons, 8 May 1902

— **1904** —

Anonymous
800 Blessèd be the Western Mail. *

editorial
in *Y Goleuad* (18 Nov. 1904)

Ben Bowen

801 The Wales of the Future must be a Free
Wales.*

'Williams Pantycelyn'
Cofiant a Barddoniaeth (1904)

Herbert Lewis

802 If Lloyd George had gone into the pulpit,
he would have started a new sect.

entry in his diary, 22 Dec. 1904

Sir Walter Raleigh

803 The Welsh are so damned Welsh it sounds
like affectation.

attributed remark

— 1905 —

Anonymous

804 Awake, it is day!*

motto of the city of Cardiff, *c.* 1905

H. H. Asquith MP

805 I would sooner go to hell than to Wales.

speech in House of Commons, 1905

R. J. Derfel

806 During my first years of travelling in
Wales, the commercial rooms were
hotbeds of abuse and ridicule of everything
Welsh. *

in *Llais Llafur* (12 Aug. 1905)

J. A. Morris

807 Of all the nations around us, we in Wales,
in all probability, are among the most
ardent lovers of freedom and the bitterest
haters of bondage and tyranny.

'The Welsh Nation and its Mission'
Welsh Religious Leaders in the Victorian Era (ed. J.
Vyrnwy Morgan, 1905)

Mrs Philip Snowden

808 Wales, a hot-bed of Liberalism and
Nonconformity in the past, [will] become
a hot-bed of Socialism and real religion in
the future.

'Socialism in South Wales'
in *Labour Leader* (27 Oct. 1905)

— 1906 —

Owen M. Edwards

809 Before I went to school there was no
happier child than I anywhere on the hills
and mountains of Wales.*

'Ysgol y Llan'
Clych Atgof (1906)

810 It was believed in the country that a
schoolmaster could not speak Welsh, that
it was an insult to him to believe that he
could.*

811 I knew nothing of the principle of the
thing [the Welsh Not], but my nature
rebelled against this damnable way of
destroying the foundation of a child's
character.*

812 Damnable old system, I give thanks in
recalling that there is hope I shall see the
time when I shall dance on your grave.*

813 [When I went to college] I believed that a
Tory was an odious aspect of the devil and
that a Liberal was the incarnation of
virtue.*

814 A nation's literature depends, to a large
extent, on its nursery rhymes.*

'Hwiangerddi'

815 There is the mighty Aran – if I were a
pagan, that is what I should worship.*

'Y Bala'

816 It is often supposed that a country's wealth
lies in the number of its great towns, where
machines are more important than souls;
but a country's true riches are the small
places that have been home to its teachers
and the cradle of its mind.*

**Robert Ambrose Jones, Emrys ap
Iwan**

817 It is easier for a nation that is free and
independent, and for a nation that lives
quietly in its own country, to find God
than it is for a nation that is suppressed or
conquered.*

'Y Ddysg Newydd'
Homiliau (1906)

818 It is true that God suffers a strong nation
to lord it over a weak nation; but he does
not approve of everything that he suffers.*

819 To destroy a nation is a disaster next to destroying the human race, and to destroy a nation's language is a disaster next to destroying the nation, because a nation ceases to exist, sooner or later, after losing its language.*

820 If you are unfaithful to your country and your language and your nation, how can you be expected to be true to God and mankind?*

821 For inasmuch as God has made you a nation, keep yourselves a nation; because He took thousands of years to fashion a language specially for your purposes, keep that language; for in working together with God in his intentions for you, it will be easier for you to seek and discover Him. Who knows not that God has preserved the Welsh nation thus far for the reason that He has special work to be done through them in the world? Be that as it may, it would do no harm for you to believe as much. There is many a small nation which has grown influential in a short while, and many a mighty nation brought low as it were in a day. Nations, like human beings, have their allotted times. Let not the Welsh be found unready when their time is at hand. *

822 Every oppressed nation is more likely to tell lies than a free, independent nation.*

'Cymru Gelwyddog'

David Lloyd George MP

823 Caernarvon was founded two thousand years ago as the outpost of a great Empire – the greatest Empire that the world had seen. It was the Bulawayo of the Roman Empire, the very extreme of barbarism and savagery, just a fortified camp. The ruins are still there, and little children go to a school close by. They learn a language in that school, a dead language; it is the language of that great Empire. They go out and play amongst the ruins, and they talk a language, a living one; it is the language of the conquered and the savages. Let no man despise Wales, her language or her literature. Her time will come. When the last truckload of coal reaches Cardiff, when the last black diamond is dug out of the earth of Glamorgan, there will be men then digging gems of pure brilliance from the inexhaustible mines of the literature and language of Wales.

speech at St David's Festival dinner, Cardiff, 1906

Theodore Watts-Dunton

824 For what race in Europe has a story so poetic, so romantic, so pathetic as the Welsh?

introduction to George Borrow, *Wild Wales* (1906 edn.)

Eliseus Williams, Eifion Wyn

825 It's worth turning exile now and again
      And from little Wales to go,
   In order to come back to Wales
      And be able to love her more.*

'Y Llanw'

826 Wear a leek in your cap,
   And wear one in your heart.*

'Os wyt Gymro'

— 1907 —

Edward Anwyl

827 There is scarcely a family in Wales that has not some member in England.

'The Welsh Language in relation to Welsh National Life'
in *Wales Today and Tomorrow* (ed. T. Stephens, 1907)

828 Some years ago, Welshmen who knew no Welsh used to make jocular apologies for their ignorance of Welsh, but such apologies are now being rapidly discontinued, as they tend to produce marked coolness.

829 The mistake often made by many people outside Wales who think of the Welsh language is that of supposing that it has no natural spontaneous life and that it is kept alive merely by a process of artificial respiration.

J. Glyn Davies

830 I rejoice that the English Churches in Wales are prospering. In the inevitable recession of Welsh, in the overwhelming inrush of English, it is a matter of joy that the needs of the people are being provided for. This is, after all, the highest patriotism.

'English Churches in Wales'
in *Wales Today and Tomorrow* (ed. T. Stephens, 1907)

831 But still the hard fact remains – the Englishman is upon us.

J. M. Davies

832 If Wales is to take a worthy place among the nations of the world, it is absolutely necessary that she should re-organize her theological studies.

'The Present-day Theology of Wales'
in *Wales Today and Tomorrow* (ed. T. Stephens, 1907)

J. Hugh Edwards

833 Snowdon, the most majestic of our mountains, is hideously disfigured, and its heights have been sacrilegiously converted into a bar for the sale of Bass beers.

'From the Watch-Tower'
in *Wales Today and Tomorrow* (ed. T. Stephens, 1907)

834 I have again and again been exceedingly amazed at the suspicion and distrust with which North Walians and South Walians, among the lower classes, regard each other.

Owen M. Edwards

835 Until such time as our national pride is awakened, until we find self-respect, until we put aside the worship of all things alien, until we pay due respect to our own fathers, we should not dare to deserve respect from the people of other countries.*

'Ty'n-y-Groes'
Tro trwy'r Gogledd (1907)

836 For a district to lose its Welsh is not only a matter of losing a language: the strength of its mind is lost as well.*

'Llanidloes'

837 Our country is something alive, not a dead grave under our feet. Every hill has its story, every district its romance. Every valley is new, every hill wears its own splendour. And for a Welshman, no other country can be like this. *

'Adfyfyrion'

838 As in every land where a love of all things old is to be found, there is in Wales an excessive love of the gentleman.*

'Llanymawddwy'

Alfred Elias

839 The idea of the establishment of an Independent Welsh Party is by no means a new one.

'An Independent Welsh Parliamentary Party'
in *Wales Today and Tomorrow* (ed. T. Stephens, 1907)

Harry Evans

840 There can be no doubt that the victory of Caradog's famous South Wales choir at the Crystal Palace some thirty years ago did much to disturb the equilibrium of Welsh people, inasmuch as they held the belief from that time forth that they had conquered the world, and nothing more was necessary.

'Welsh Choral Singing'
in *Wales Today and Tomorrow* (ed. T. Stephens, 1907)

Rees Evans

841 To speak English and to get drunk were the insignia of a gentleman in the Wales that was.

'Aspects of the Temperance Question'
in *Wales Today and Tomorrow* (ed. T. Stephens, 1907)

W. Eilir Evans

842 The Welsh language is not sufficiently flexible to express the tenth part of the many-sidedness of twentieth century life.

'Newspapers and Magazines of Wales'
in *Wales Today and Tomorrow* (ed. T. Stephens, 1907)

J. Rogues de Fursac

843 I am too embarrassed to reply.*

in seeking to account for the Welsh Religious Revival of 1904–5
Un Mouvement Mystique Contemporain: le Reveil Religieux du Pays de Galles (1907)

G. Penar Davies

844 With a wider knowledge, the Welshman's servility will vanish, and a simple and enlightened strength will take its place. He will be plain and straightforward, without ceasing to be gentlemanly.

'The Career of Wales'
in *Wales Today and Tomorrow* (ed. T. Stephens, 1907)

Keir Hardie MP

845 All Celtic people are, at heart, Communists.

'Socialism and the Celt'
in *Wales Today and Tomorrow* (ed. T. Stephens, 1907)

846 A thousand years of English oppression and inculcation of materialism have not been able to sour the milk of human kindness in the Welsh breast.

847 Socialism means that the land of Wales will again belong to its people.

H. M. Hughes

848 It is only too true that, as soon as English gets a footing in the Welsh home, it sets about, like the cuckoo fledgeling, to oust the old language from its own nest.

'The Bilingual Difficulty'
in *Wales Today and Tomorrow* (ed. T. Stephens, 1907)

849 More powerful and harmful still has been the contempt of all things Welsh, engendered by race hatred, on the part of those who have come to live and pile their wealth among us.

Augustus John

850 Wales must be barbarised!

'Art in Wales'
in *Wales Today and Tomorrow* (ed. T. Stephens, 1907)

Ellis Jones

851 The Welsh Temperance Movement was born in a storm and its first years were spent in the midst of uproar.

'The Welsh Temperance Movement'
in *Wales Today and Tomorrow* (ed. T. Stephens, 1907)

852 Although things are somewhat better in South Wales than they are in North Wales, they are not as good as in England.

T. Lewis

853 Welsh preaching today is not what it was fifty years ago.

'Higher Criticism and Welsh Preaching'
in *Wales Today and Tomorrow* (ed. T. Stephens, 1907)

Sampson Morgan

854 There is immediate room for a million extra workers on the land in Wales at the present time.

'Small Fruit Farms in Wales'
in *Wales Today and Tomorrow* (ed. T. Stephens, 1907)

Sir Lewis Morris

855 Unite, dear land, march on united still
By one consentient and contraining will,
And dare what lofty fate, untried before,
God's purpose holds in store.

epigraph
in *Wales Today and Tomorrow* (ed. T. Stephens, 1907)

John Morris-Jones

856 And yet I sing my country,
   for Wales shall one day be
the happiest and loveliest land,
   a time when we shall see
no violent hand to waste her,
   no coward to betray her,
no quarrelling to weaken her,
   and when Wales will be free.*

'Cymru Fydd'

D. J. Nicholas

857 The Welshwoman who has mastered the mysteries of the broth, and is acquainted with the various ways in which oatmeal may be made palatable and digestible, may be said to have, for her purposes, finished her education in cookery.

'Welsh Home-Life'
in *Wales Today and Tomorrow* (ed. T. Stephens, 1907)

858 Half the Welshmen living might be classified under half a dozen Christian names, and fully half of these were called after their grandfathers.

859 The Welshman is a conservative, who always votes liberal at elections.

860 The Welsh are a brood of singing birds, most of whom touch their sweetest notes singing of their own nest.

861 There is not a parish in Wales without its poet; scarcely a village of half a thousand inhabitants, without its chaired bard.

J. Evans Owen

862 The Wales of today is the product of religious revivals, and the spirit of Liberalism and the Welsh newspaper are her progeny.

'The Welsh Newspaper'
in *Wales Today and Tomorrow* (ed. T. Stephens, 1907)

Richard Jones Owen, Glaslyn

863 The future of Wales is in the ink-bottle.*

in *Cymru* (Jan. 1907)

W. J. Perkins

864 While coal remains the most effective and economical source of power, and the population of the world increases, the position of Wales is assured.

'Coal Trade and Shipping'
in *Wales Today and Tomorrow* (ed. T. Stephens, 1907)

J. Tertius Phillips

865 Cardiff is a much abused and misrepresented city.

'Drunkenness in Cardiff'
in *Wales Today and Tomorrow* (ed. T. Stephens, 1907)

J. S. Popham

866 In the fruits of the Eisteddfod we have the most striking refutation of the argument that the use of Welsh keeps the Welsh people ignorant and narrow-minded.

'Should English People Learn Welsh?'
in *Wales Today and Tomorrow* (ed. T. Stephens, 1907)

J. H. Puleston

867 In almost every part of the civilised world are found Welshmen occupying important positions, and where a number of Welsh people are congregated, patriotic fervour for the old land is always noticeable.

preface
in *Wales Today and Tomorrow* (ed. T. Stephens, 1907)

J. Machreth Rees

868 I am prepared to admit that the Eisteddfod has been of little use; and furthermore, from the bottom of my heart, do I hope that she never will be.

'The Eisteddfod'
in *Wales Today and Tomorrow* (ed. T. Stephens, 1907)

Evan Roberts

869 May God make Wales a victorious people through the victory of the death of Christ. Let us continue praying that the Arm of the Lord be revealed, and that a holy shout of victory shall echo and re-echo throughout the valleys of Wales.

'What Wales Needs – Religiously'
in *Wales Today and Tomorrow* (ed. T. Stephens, 1907)

John M. Saunders

870 The outstanding characteristic of life in Wales during the last quarter is, doubtless, the appearance of the national feeling: the Spirit of Welsh Patriotism has been awakened as never before.

'The True Patriot'
in *Wales Today and Tomorrow* (ed. T. Stephens, 1907)

S. M. Saunders

871 Young women of Wales, are you ready for the fray? The time is coming when you will have to take your stand.

'An Open Letter to the Young Women of Wales'
in *Wales Today and Tomorrow* (ed. T. Stephens, 1907)

Thomas Stephens

872 When any great Imperial question arises, the Welsh recognize no interests apart from those of the whole of the United Kingdom.

introduction
in *Wales Today and Tomorrow* (ed. T. Stephens, 1907)

T. H. Thomas

873 Unless some movement can be made in this direction, of employing artists of Wales upon Welsh work and Welsh themes, Welsh painting and sculpture can only become what Welsh music has become, an echo – a fainter reflex, of the art of our predominant neighbour.

'Art in Wales'
in *Wales Today and Tomorrow* (ed. T. Stephens, 1907)

Iona Williams

874 Wales is as conservative in theology as it is liberal in party-politics.

'Authority and Liberal Theology'
in *Wales Today and Tomorrow* (ed. T. Stephens, 1907)

Mallt Williams

875 Education in modern Wales must be carried out on fresh lines if Welsh women are to ever enter into their heritage.

'Welshwomen's Mission in the Twentieth Century'
in *Wales Today and Tomorrow* (ed. T. Stephens, 1907)

T. Charles Williams

876 We know that some of the greatest heresies have been Welsh.

'The Influence of the Higher Criticism upon Welsh Preaching'
in *Wales Today and Tomorrow* (ed. T. Stephens, 1907)

877 The great questions which occupy the minds of the people of Wales have always been of a religious type.

878 The Welsh prefer philosophy to philology; music and poetry to both.

W. Llewelyn Williams

879 The Church [of England] . . . which today, unrepentant at heart and unchanged in action, sets its face against any national movement and every national aspiration, is not, and cannot be, in any true and real sense, the Church of the Welsh people.

'The Church in Wales'
in *Wales Today and Tomorrow* (ed. T. Stephens, 1907)

880 She [the Church of England] has succeeded in attracting the English resident, the anglicised Welshman, the time-server, the sycophant, the socially ambitious, and the few who are irritated and estranged by the democratic spirit and perfervid emotionalism of Dissent. But she has not touched the heart or the imagination of the people.

— 1908 —

David Davies

881 The Protestant Nonconformity of the Welsh people, as lived and taught by their religious teachers during the last two centuries . . . has preserved them from ignorance, lawlessness and irreligion, and made of them one of the most scripturally enlightened, loyal and religious nations on the surface of the earth.

Echoes from the Welsh Hills (1908)

J. H. Davies

882 Colonel John Jones [the regicide] was the first Welshman to play a prominent and leading part in the political life of Great Britain.*

Gwaith Morgan Llwyd (1908)

W. H. Davies

883 Girls scream,
　Boys shout;
Dogs bark,
　School's out.

'School's Out'

— 1909 —

Anonymous

884 The help of the state is no longer a humiliation; it is a right, and the aged people therefore rejoice.

on the Lloyd George Pension
in *South Wales Press* (6 Jan. 1909)

Ben Bowen

885 Wales has drawn more inspiration into its song from defeat than from victory.*

'Duw yn Ateb'
Rhyddiaith Ben Bowen (ed. David Bowen, 1909)

Robert Ambrose Jones, Emrys ap Iwan

886 God punishes those who neglect the language of their country; because of that the Welsh of Radnorshire and Breconshire and the borders are so much lower in understanding, in morals and in religion than the Welsh of the most Welsh part of the Principality.*

Homiliau (1909)

David Lloyd George MP

887 Five hundred men, ordinary men, chosen accidentally from among the unemployed.

of the House of Lords
speech at Newcastle, 9 Oct. 1909

888 A fully equipped duke costs as much to keep as two Dreadnoughts; and they are just as great a terror and they last longer.

Sir William Watson

889 An ancient folk, speaking an ancient speech,
And cherishing in their bosoms all their past,
Yet in whose fiery love of their own land
No hatred of another finds a place.

'Wales: a Greeting'

— 1910 —

Anonymous

890 For Wales, see England.

cross-reference in early edition of *Encyclopaedia Britannica, c.* 1910

891 When the Welsh language expires, the spirituality and sacredness of religion will expire at the same time.

report of the Royal Commission on the Church and Other Religious Bodies in Wales, 1910

892 It is just the same oppressive atmosphere that one experienced in the streets of Odessa and Sevastopol during the unrest in Russia in the winter of 1904. It is extraordinary to find it here in the British Isles.

of the Tonypandy Riots
in *The Times* (23 Nov. 1910)

893 Every nice girl loves a collier
In the Rhondda Valley war,
Every nice girl loves a striker –
And you know what strikers are;
In Tonypandy they're very handy
With their sticks and stones and boot,
Walking down the street with Jane,
Breaking every window-pane,
That's loot! Pom pom! That's loot!

popular song, parody of 'Every nice girl loves a sailor', 1910

Wilkie Bard

894 I'm porter at a station now called Llangfeckfinngenneck;
The llanguage there would dislocate your chin;
As I've no idea of Welsh it nearly breaks my neck
When I have to shout as all the trains come in –
All change for Llanfairfechan,
Llanrwst, Llandaff and Brecon,
Llandrillo and Llandudno –
The llanguage is so strange!
All change for Llanglamorgan
(It strains my vocal organ),
Llanammarch and Llanamoch,
And Llananeff and Llanadoch,
And Llan-what-else-you-like – All change!

music-hall song, *c.* 1910
'All change for Llanfairfechan!'

W. H. Davies

895 It was the Rainbow gave thee birth,
And left thee all her lovely hues.

'The Kingfisher'

James Elroy Flecker

896 Grace on the golden dales
Of thine old Christian Wales
Shower till they sing.

'God Save the King'

897 Evening on the olden, the golden sea of Wales,
When the first star shivers and the last wave pales.

'The Dying Patriot'

Keir Hardie MP

898 Mr Keir Hardie's election colours are Red, White and Green. Red represents Labour

in revolt, Green represents Nature and Nationalism, Home Rule for Ireland and for Wales. White represents Strength and Purity.

bulletin at General Election, Jan. 1910

Arthur Tyssilio Johnson

899 No people were ever less fitter to call a country their own and themselves a nation than the Welsh.

The Perfidious Welshman (1910)

900 Few people can tell a lie to your face with such perfect composure as a Welshman.

901 It is as a poacher of fish that the Welshman excels.

902 The Welsh police-court is known all over the world as a very hotbed of perjury.

903 Like vultures coming out of the distant blue to congregate around the carcase of the tottering horse or stricken bullock which they have marked for their own, these Welsh men and women flock to the scene of the funeral to fill their insatiable gullets with the carrion of morbid curiosity.

904 Wales has had no great women of good repute.

905 If it should ever be your misfortune to have to spend Sunday in Wales, always get to windward when the chapels are disgorging the faithful.

906 Keep Taffy at arm's length, or he will take liberties, and become familiar; not only that, remember, he spits copiously and dangerously when moved by any slight emotion.

907 It is mainly the bigotry and the revolting ignorance of the dissenting parson which are responsible for the perpetuation of the hoggish manners common to the natives of Wales.

908 The Welsh, though they may sing their mournful hymns in a minor key at street corners, are not in any high sense musicians.

909 The world has never produced a more unscrupulous and self-interested hypocrite than the Welsh Member of Parliament who springs from Nonconformist stock. He has all the wiles of a serpent and the slipperiness of an eel.

910 The visitor to Wales may go into a hundred cottages and find no books except a Bible, some commentaries, and perhaps a volume of sermons by a local preacher.

911 To any one who does not know the shallow transparency of the average Welsh mind, its utter want of ballast and lack of independence, the humbug with which the Welsh Member of Parliament feeds his herd of ignorant voters is almost beyond comprehension.

912 Go where you will in Wales, you cannot fail to be struck by the poverty of her architecture.

Rudyard Kipling

913 The Celt in all his variants from Builth to Ballyhoo,
His mental processes are plain – one knows what he will do,
And can logically predicate his finish from his start.

'The Puzzler'

H. Elvet Lewis, Elfed

914 Not charity for a man – but work!*

'Rhagorfraint y Gweithiwr'

David Lloyd George MP

915 The political power of landlordism in Wales was shattered as effectively as the power of the Druids.

of the General Election of 1868
speech, 1910

916 An aristocracy is like cheese; the older it is, the higher it becomes.

speech at Mile End, London, Dec. 1910

Robert Scourfield Mills, Owen Rhoscomyl

917 No Welsh boy can well read the history of his ancestors – so stirring a record of so stubborn a race, such a good, grim,

fighting race – without feeling that it is good to be a Cymro.

preface
Flame-Bearers of Welsh History (school edn., 1910)

918 Cymru, then, is the right name for our country, meaning the Land of the Cymro . . . Cymro, then, is the right name, and the proud name, for every honourable man of us today.

— 1911 —

Anonymous

919 All that the nation of the Welsh lost [as the result of the fall of Llywelyn ap Gruffudd in 1282] was political independence, the least loss of all losses from a national point of view*

in *Y Beirniad* (1911)

920 Through all the long dark night of years
The people's cry ascendeth,
And earth is wet with blood and tears
But our meek sufferance endeth;
The few shall not for ever sway,
The many toil in sorrow;
The powers of hell are strong today,
Our kingdom comes tomorrow.

manifesto of the Cambrian Strike, 16 June 1911

921 Fellow workers, we need your support in this strenuous struggle and the support of every man and woman who is prepared to make his or her sacrifice to put an end to Capitalist Despotism and to do battle for the cause of Industrial Freedom.

922 It was indeed a veritable pandemonium. . . a case of Tonypandy being outpandied.

of the Llanelli Riots
in *Cambrian Daily Leader* (21 Aug. 1911)

923 Men are born into the world to live, not to be slaughtered and shot at like dogs. Were it not for the importation of troops, Llanelly would be as peaceful as it has always been. We Llanelly men do not want soldiers to teach us how to behave. This afternoon there has been cold-blooded murder, and there will be a heavy reckoning.

worker
reported in *Llanelly Mercury* (24 Aug. 1911)

924 The cottage homes of Gwalia,
How dreadfully they smell,
With phthisis in the thatched roof
And sewage in the well.

parody of Mrs Hemans, 'The Stately Homes of England'
in *South Wales Daily News* (25 Aug. 1911)

W. H. Davies

925 What is this life if, full of care,
We have no time to stand and stare.

'Leisure'

926 Can I forget the sweet days that have been,
When poetry first began to warm my blood;
When from the hills of Gwent I saw the earth
Burned into two by Severn's silver flood.

'Days that have been'

J. Hugh Edwards

927 There is no part of the British Empire where there is a greater diffusion of democratic sentiment than in the Principality of Wales, nor is there a portion of the King's realms where loyalty to the throne is deeper and more fervid. . . The badge of conquest which the first investiture wrought has, under the magic touch of King George, apotheosised into a jewel of Royal favour, to be prized as a priceless legacy by future generations of Welshmen.

Wales (1911)

W. J. Gruffydd

928 Among all forms of literature, drama is the most national.*

'Drama i Gymru'
in *Y Beirniad* (vol. 1, no. 1, March 1911)

Keir Hardie MP

929 Wales is to have an Investiture as a reminder that an English King and his robber barons strove for ages to destroy the Welsh people, and finally succeeded in robbing them of their lands, driving them into the mountain fastnesses of their native land like hunted beasts. . . The ceremony ought to make every Welshman who is patriotic blush with shame.

speech at Tonypandy, 1 May 1911

930 We hear a great deal of Welsh nationalism
and the great need for Welsh nationalism.
John Jones was not a rioter, he did not
throw stones; he went into the garden to
watch what was going on. And John Jones
the Welshman was shot down by English
soldiers. Yet not one of these Welsh
Nationalists has said a single word of
protest. When I hear men talking of Welsh
nationalism and are prepared to shut their
eyes to a crime like that, they do not know
the meaning of nationalism, and simply
use the term to deceive and delude.

during the strike and riots at Llanelli
reported in *South Wales Daily News* (29 Sept.
1911)

931 Men and women of Dowlais: the National
Party I have in mind is this: the people of
Wales fighting to recover possession of the
land of Wales; the working classes
acquiring possession of the mines, the
furnaces, and the railways, of the great
public works generally, and working there
as comrades, not for the benefit of
shareholders, but for the good of every
man, woman and child within your
borders. That is the kind of nationalism
that I want to see brought about. And
when that comes, the Red Dragon will be
emblazoned on the Red Flag of Socialism,
the International Emblem of the working-
class movement of the world.

speech at Dowlais, Merthyr Tydfil, 14 Oct.
1911
The Red Dragon and the Red Flag (1912)

John Edward Lloyd
932 [Giraldus Cambrensis] was always willing
to try his hand at the interpretation of
Welsh place-names, a pursuit as
fascinating to him as for others in our own
day no less slenderly equipped than he
was.

*A History of Wales from the Earliest Times to the
Edwardian Conquest* (1911)

933 The Cistercian abbot was a St David or a
St Teilo brought to life.

934 It was for a far distant generation to see
that the last Prince had not lived in vain,
but by his life-work had helped to build
solidly the enduring fabric of Welsh
nationality.

of Llywelyn ap Gruffudd

G. K. Chesterton
935 In the mountain hamlets clothing
Peaks beyond Caucasian pales,
Where Establishment means nothing
And they never heard of Wales.

'Antichrist, or the Reunion of Christendom: an
Ode'
in answer to F. E. Smith (see 950)

T. W. H. Crosland
936 The traveller in Wales cannot fail to be
struck with two things – namely, the
romantic beauty of the country and the
absolute lack of romance exhibited by the
people.

Taffy was a Welshman (1912)

937 According to all accounts, it was Offa who
built a dyke to separate Wales from
England, and we are inclined to think that
Offa was a man of sense and discernment.

938 In Wales you have periodic outbreaks of
what the faithful call religious revival, and
what may be more correctly described as
religious lunacy, which no honest person
can regard with approval.

939 The population of Wales is two million or
thereabouts, and the Welsh poets, male
and female, but chiefly male with flowing
beards, would appear to include quite a
million and a half.

940 The fact is that Wales is a little land, and
the Welsh are a little people, with little
intellects and little views.

941 There can be no doubt that many regular
attenders at Welsh chapels and meeting-
houses do not appear to carry their
religion with them into the everyday affairs
of life.

942 Considered as a spectacle pure and simple,
an Eisteddfod is a pitiful and almost
squalid affair.

943 The difference between England and
Wales is that England consists of an upper
class, a middle class and a democracy,
while Wales is a democracy pure and
simple.

944 I hope for everybody's sake that Mr Alfred Noyes really is a Welshman.

945 The Welsh resemble the modern Greeks in this respect, that they appear to devour newspapers with the appetite of the cormorant.

946 When it pleases him – and it quite frequently does please him – Mr Lloyd George can be very proud of his Welshness.

947 It is time we remembered that England is our messuage and demesne, and not the backyard of Mr Ellis Griffiths, and that Englishmen were born to rule and not to be ruled, and least of all to be ruled by a bumptious, snuffling, flighty, tiresome, fifth-rate bunch of barbarians like the Welsh.

Robert Ambrose Jones, Emrys ap Iwan

948 If Welsh is killed, it will be killed in the house of its friends.*

quoted by T. Gwynn Joes, *Emrys ap Iwan: Cofiant* (1912)

Thomas Jacob Davies, Sarnicol

949 In their coffins,
    Respect;
In their lifetime,
    A cross.*

'Proffwyd a Sant'

F. E. Smith

950 A Bill which has shocked the conscience of every Christian community in Europe.

of the Welsh Disestablishment Bill, 1912

— 1913 —

J. O. Francis

951 Don't be hard on him, boys, because he doesn't look at things with your eyes. He can't help himself any more than you. He belongs to the old valley. At heart he's of the agricultural class – slow, stolid, and conservative. You, Lewis, you're of a different kind altogether – you've grown up in modern industry, with no roots in the soil. That's why you're a rebel. That's why the men of your time are rebels, too.

Change (1913)

T. Gwynn Jones

952 If it is worth keeping Welsh at all, [it's] worth keeping according to its own rules.*

Cofnodion a Chyfansoddiadau Eisteddfod Genedlaethol 1913

T. E. Nicholas

953 Wales is a land of poets; but it's the poets who say that.*

'Beirdd Cymru'
in *Y Geninen* (vol. 31, no. 3, July 1913)

— 1914 —

Anonymous

954 Stick it, the Welsh!

battle-cry, First World War

955 The South Wales miner is a very real factor in the Nation's fighting strength and his loyalty in this crisis is well nigh indispensable to the State.

editorial
in *The Times* (24 Aug. 1914)

Wil Hay

956 The Welsh collier . . . and the colliers of Europe may presently learn to down tools and arms for the cause of human fellowship.

quoted in *Welsh Outlook* (Sept. 1914)

Granville Barker

957 The greatest service Wales can render to the world is to be herself to the last drop of her blood.

in *Cambrian Daily Leader* (13 June 1914)

W. H. Davies

958 The collier's wife had four tall sons
    Brought from the pit's mouth dead,
    And crushed from foot to head;
When others brought her husband home,
Had five dead bodies in her room.

'The Collier's Wife'

959 Sweet Chance, that led my steps abroad,
    Beyond the town, where wild flowers
        grow –
A rainbow and a cuckoo, Lord,
    How rich and great the times are now!

Know, all ye sheep
And cows, that keep
On staring that I stand so long
In grass that's wet from heavy rain –
A rainbow and a cuckoo's song
May never come together again;
May never come
This side the tomb.

'A Great Time'

David Lloyd George MP

960 God has chosen little nations as the vessels by which He carries the choicest wines to the lips of humanity . . . Ah, the world owes much to the little five-foot nations.

speech at Queen's Hall, Sept. 1914

George Bernard Shaw

961 The next Shakespeare and Goethe may be born in Wales.

'On Welsh Drama'
in *South Wales Daily News* (13 June 1914)

962 Just as the preachers of Wales spend much of their time in telling the Welsh that they are going to Hell, so the Welsh writers of comedy will have to console a good many of them by demonstrating that they are not worth wasting good coal on.

963 Everything that is narrow and ignorant and ridiculous and dishonest in Wales will be castigated ruthlessly in the Welsh national theatre, and the process will not be popular with the narrow, the ignorant, the bigoted and the ridiculous.

— 1915 —

Anonymous

964 Lloyd George knew my father,
Father knew Lloyd George.

popular song, sung to the tune of 'Onward, Christian soldiers', *c.* 1915

Caradoc Evans

965 As is usual, when the state is in real danger, it is the working classes that come to the rescue.

in *Ideas* (30 July 1915)

966 Wales would be brighter and more Christianlike if every chapel were burnt to the ground and a public-house raised on the ashes thereof.

letter
in *Western Mail* (27 Nov. 1915)

Stanley Jevons

967 The South Wales coalfield is in many respects the principal coalfield in the United Kingdom.

The British Coal Trade (1915)

968 The South Wales coalfield is now producing at the rate of nearly 60 million tons per annum, and the rate of production is pretty sure to increase within thirty or forty years to about 100 million tons per annum.

969 The peculiar Welsh temperament, essentially imaginative, intellectual and impatient, manifests itself continually in industrial disputes.

970 The quality of the houses in South Wales, taken as a whole, is probably better now than in any of the other principal coalfields.

K. V. Jones

971 The revival of the Welsh national spirit will lead to a closer union with England.

Life of John Viriamu Jones (1915)

David Lloyd George MP

972 I am only a bit of a Welshman in an office in London.*

speech at National Eisteddfod, Bangor, 1915

Edgar Lee Masters

973 You would not believe, would you,
That I came from good Welsh stock?
That I was purer blooded than the white
trash here?
And of more direct lineage than the New
Englanders
And Virginians of Spoon River?

Indignation Jones
Spoon River (1915)

D. Lleufer Thomas

974 The idea of nationality and of religion would seem in danger of being repudiated in some of the industrial districts in favour

of an illusory idea of a cosmopolitan, and perhaps to some extent, materialistic brotherhood.

speech at National Eisteddfod, 1915

Edward Thomas

975 Make me content
With some sweetness
From Wales
Whose nightingales
Have no wings.

'Words'

— 1916 —

Anonymous

976 Wales is such a particular part of England.*

Papal Encyclical, 1916

977 The Welsh miner is always in the van of Trade Union progress; what he suggests today, his comrades in other coalfields adopt tomorrow.

editorial
in *Welsh Outlook* (July 1916)

978 The young men decide industrial issues; the older men political issues.

(Aug. 1916)

Thomas Davis

979 A million of the Kymri have as good a right to a local senate as the 700,000 Greeks or the half million of Cassel or Mecklenburg have to independence or as each of the states of America has to a local Congress.

quoted in *Welsh Outlook* (March 1916)

Caradoc Evans

980 The Welshman has many vices, and drinking is not one of them.

'The Welsh Miner'
in *New Witness* (7 Dec. 1916)

T. Gwynn Jones

981 The English language is associated in my mind with tyranny.

in *Welsh Outlook* (April 1916)

Bonar Law

982 It would be better to shoot a hundred men in suppressing a strike than to lose thousands in the field as a consequence of it.

of coal strike in South Wales
quoted by Trevor Wilson, *The Political Diaries of C. P. Scott* (1970)

David Lloyd George MP

983 There are no nightingales this side of the Severn . . .We do not need this exquisite songster in Wales; we can provide better. There is a bird in our villages which can beat the best of them. He is called Y Cymro.

speech at National Eisteddfod, Aberystwyth, 17 Aug. 1916

984 Now *The Times* is not exactly the organ of the Welsh peasantry.

985 National ideals without imagination are but the thistles of the wilderness, fit neither for food nor fuel. A nation that depends on them must perish.

Walter Hinds Page

986 The Welshman's truth is more in the nature of a curve than a straight line.

speech, *c.* 1916

J. Arthur Price

987 Wales has the same right as Poland and Bohemia; otherwise the war is waged on false pretences by the Allies.

in *Welsh Outlook* (Oct. 1916)

Edward Thomas

988 Helen of the roads,
The mountain ways of Wales
And the Mabinogion tales
Is one of the true gods.

'Roads'

— 1917 —

Anonymous

989 To fight for the freedom of the Belgian, it is not absolutely necessary to oppress and bully the Welshman.

editorial
in *Welsh Outlook* (Feb. 1917)

990 He was a silent fellow . . . it would appear he could speak but little English, or if he could, he did not.

English officer, of the poet Hedd Wyn, killed at Pilkem Ridge, 1917
quoted by Bethan Phillips, 'A Fine Day's Work', in *Planet* (no. 72, Dec. 1988–Jan. 1989)

991 It is sometimes said that west of Newtown, the spirit of enterprise does not exist.

editorial
in *Welsh Outlook* (May 1917)

992 The 'advanced' men have of late years been advocating a form of Industrial Unionism . . . To [them] political action is of temporary and deluding value.

report of the Commission of Inquiry into Industrial Unrest, 1917

993 No disturbance is likely to occur during the period of the war, although we take a grave view as to the situation that is likely to develop immediately after.

994 Until some fifteen or twenty years ago, the native inhabitants had. . . shown a marked capacity for stamping their own impress on all newcomers . . . Of more recent years the process of assimilation has been unable to keep pace with the continuing influx of immigrants.

W. J. Edwards
995 The antagonism of the workshop must eventually express itself in the ballot box and eventually in our system of education.

in *Welsh Outlook* (June 1917)

Caradoc Evans
996 Not one Welshman has produced fiction which has lived six months after the day of its publication.

letter
in *Western Mail* (23 Jan. 1917)

997 I have no desire to become notorious; no one has. I have no wish for fame. I write because I believe that the cesspools of West Wales should be stirred up, because I want to see my people freed from religious tyranny, because I love my country so much that I would exhibit her sores that they may be healed.

Robert Graves
998 No traveller yet has hit upon
A wilder land than Meirion,
For desolate hills and tumbling stones,
Bogland and melody and old bones.
Fairies and ghosts are here galore,
And poetry most splendid, more
Than can be written with the pen
Or understood by common men.

letter to Siegfried Sassoon from Mametz Wood, 1917

John Harris
999 Workers of the Vale of Amman,
   Echo Russia's mighty thrust;
Strike a blow for Cambria's freedom,
   Bring oppression to the dust,

'Welsh Workers, Arise!'

John M. Jones
1000 Forty years ago, the conviction that the Welsh language was doomed to die was prevalent among prominent Welshmen. No man who is at all competent to judge believes that today.

in *Welsh Outlook* (Feb. 1917)

1001 If Welsh nationalism allows the period after the war to pass without an effort to obtain autonomy . . . there will be a plausible argument for saying that the Welsh people themselves regard their nationalism merely as an amiable sentiment and not as a political matter.

1002 The identification by Welsh Liberal politicians of the whole Welsh church with the Bishops and a few Tory Peers has driven the Welsh Church – clergy and laity – into an unnatural alliance with the Anglicising forces.

— **1918** —

Anonymous
1003 Labour believes in self-government. The Labour Party is pledged to a scheme of statutory legislatures for Scotland, Wales and Ireland, as part of the larger plan which will transform the British Empire into a Commonwealth of self-governing nations.

manifesto of Labour Party at General Election, 1918

Ellis Humphrey Evans, Hedd Wyn

1004 Only the purple moon
     On the bare mountain's rim,
And the sound of the old river Prysor
     Singing in the cwm. *

'Atgo'

Arthur Henderson

1005 Given self-government, Wales might
establish itself as a modern Utopia and
develop its own institutions, its own
culture, its own ideal of democracy in
politics, industry and social life, as an
example and an inspiration to the rest of
the world.

statement by Transport House, June 1918

David Lloyd George MP

1006 What is our task? To make Britain a fit
country for heroes to live in.

speech at Wolverhampton, 24 Nov. 1918

Ramsay Macdonald MP

1007 One of the most important measures of
reconstruction after the war should be
national self-determination within this
kingdom.

speech in House of Commons, 1918

— 1919 —

Anonymous

1008 Since 1868 . . . Wales has not experienced
a more disappointing election from the
national standpoint.

editorial
in *Welsh Outlook* (Jan. 1919)

1009 In days when Bohemia and Poland are
being reconstituted as democratic
republics, Wales cannot accept as a
substitute for self-government a new Court
of the Marches set up in the backroom of
some dingy office in Whitehall.

(March 1919)

1010 It [the Eisteddfod] encourages vulgarity of
mind because it allows . . . the nation's
leaders, from the Prime Minister down, to
be self-complacent and self-congratulatory
and smugly to tell us, year in year out,

what a wonderful little people we really
are.

(Aug. 1919)

1011 It came with a preacher and went with a
preacher . . . Welsh Liberalism that sprang
to life under the writings and oratory of
Henry Richard was whipped to its death
by Mr Towyn Jones.

(Sept. 1919)

1012 Nationalisation ought to be, in principle,
at once determined upon.

interim report of the Royal Commission on the
Coal Industry, 1919

1013 The voice of Welsh Nationalism and Tory
Democracy.

motto of *Western Mail* on occasion of its fiftieth
anniversary, 1919

Stephen Gwynn

1014 You wanted disestablishment not because
you were Nonconformists but because you
were Welshmen . . . In the name of the
Welsh nation, you wanted to disestablish
something. If you are to keep your
nationality, you will have to seek after
establishing something.

in *Welsh Outlook* (Aug. 1919)

J. Tywi Jones

1015 We were simply robbed of our birthright
by a foreign system of education and its
paid servants . . . Our system of education
was moulded to help the few favoured ones
to get on in the world.

(Dec. 1919)

J. Arthur Price

1016 It was to help the poor that Lloyd George
abandoned nationalism.

(March 1919)

F. E. Smith MP

1017 We [the British] have muddled along
tolerably well for ten centuries . . . Why
should the Scots and Welsh give up
governing the Empire to send them back
to the insignificant task of governing their
own country?

, speech in House of Commons, April 1919

Edward Wood MP

1018 The Government . . . should forthwith appoint a parliamentary body to consider and report upon a measure of Federal devolution applicable to England, Scotland and Ireland . . . and upon the extent to which [this is] applicable to Welsh conditions and aspirations.

speech in House of Commons, 1919

— 1920 —

Anonymous

1019 It is no advantage to Wales to have Lloyd George as Prime Minister. It is in truth a danger. It is a danger to our spiritual independence.

editorial
in *Welsh Outlook* (Jan. 1920)

1020 There are thousands of young men and women in Wales today who would gladly attend the Feast of the Slaying of their political fathers with very little regret.

[March 1920]

1021 We are in danger of becoming, like English Nonconformity, the churches of a bourgeoisie.

(April 1920)

1022 From the national standpoint, our railway system is the worst in the world.

(June 1920)

1023 He [Lloyd George] has put a premium on mediocrity in Welsh politics for it is only mediocrity that can serve a political taskmaster slavishly.

(Nov. 1920)

1024 A considerable measure of Devolution on national lines can alone satisfy the national aspirations of Scotland and Wales.

three of the signatories of report of the Speaker's Conference on Devolution, 1920

Hilaire Belloc

1025 The Cambrian Welsh or Mountain sheep
　　Is of the Ovine race;
　His conversation is not deep
　　But there – observe his face!

'The Welsh Mutton'

W. H. Davies

1026 I turned my head and saw the wind,
　　Not far from where I stood,
　Dragging the corn by her golden hair
　　Into a dark and lonely wood.

'The Villain'

Dudley G. Davies

1027 Carmarthen hills are green and low
　And there along the small sheep go
　Whose voices to the valley come
　At eve, when all things else are dumb.

'Carmarthenshire'

John Masefield

1028 One road leads to London,
　　One road runs to Wales,
　My road leads me seawards
　　To the white dipping sails.

'Roadways'

— 1921 —

Anonymous

1029 Few men worth their salt willingly place themselves in the unenviable position of being a charge on the charity of the congregation they serve. Wealthy 'Noncons' [Nonconformists] rear no sons for the ministry.

editorial
in *Welsh Outlook* (March 1921)

1030 Among the most faithful patrons of the Eisteddfod is Jupiter Pluvius.

(Sept. 1921)

1031 He [Lloyd George] may talk proudly . . . of his position as Imperial Prime Minister, but by nature and tradition he will always remain a Joseph in the court of Pharoah.

(Sept. 1921)

1032 It has paralysed scores of hands and chilled scores of minds.

of the reform of Welsh orthography
(Oct. 1921)

Owen M. Edwards

1033 A child born in the country has a quicker and a deeper mind than a child reared in the town. He possesses more words, he knows more about nature, he can see further.*

'Dyddiau Mafon Duon'
Yn y Wlad ac Ysgrifau Eraill (1921)

1034 It is the people who think, and the people who speak, and if literature does not accept the words and style of the people, Welsh literary style will be too archaic and classical, and become unnatural and useless for the purposes of life.*

'Arddull'

1035 The nation's inner tower is safe so far; there are poets there singing odes to one another. But the danger is on the ramparts, and few are they able to fight there.*

'Angen Mwyaf Cymru'

1036 If Wales loses its life as a nation, it will go to the grave a wonderfully rich nation, and not as a poor one.*

1037 Not on the battlefield but in literature a Llywelyn and a Glyndŵr are needed.*

1038 The Welsh are a lively, energetic nation, full of imagination and skill; but, for all their enthusiasm, they are a timid nation when it comes to taking a step forward. They know they can show the way to other nations; but their old cowardly habit is to look for paths already trodden, and often to seek alien leaders to take them on their way.*

'Prifysgol y Gweithwyr'

J. Arthur Price
1039 While the French peasants were demolishing the squire's pew in the parish church, the Welsh peasants were building the *sêt fawr* in the chapel.

in *Welsh Outlook* (Sept. 1921)

— 1922 —

Anonymous
1040 The leaders of Irish nationalism live a great deal of their time in gaol and many of them die on the gallows. In Wales they live in comfort and die with a considerable amount of property to dispose of in their wills.

editorial
in *Welsh Outlook* (Jan. 1922)

1041 I believe that it is Wales that is going to stand between the world and the next war.

(April 1922)

Noah Ablett
1042 Such a man [the collier] is entitled to our sympathy and our respect, but what he frequently gets is abuse.

What we want and why (1922)

Gwilym Davies
1043 Wales is called upon to fit herself for the supreme task of being the moral and spiritual driving force among the nations of the world.

Welsh Outlook (Jan. 1922)

Ifan ab Owen Edwards
1044 I shall be faithful to Wales, to my fellow man, and to Christ.*

motto of Urdd Gobaith Cymru, founded in 1922

Owen M. Edwards
1045 The spirit of Wales is born in the mountain farmhouse, in the cottage by the brook, in the coal-miner's home.*

Er Mwyn Cymru (1922)

1046 Wales has her own language and, without it, she cannot keep her soul. For it is not merely a collection of words . . . Within it are treasured the poetry of life and the hope of a thousand years.*

Ernest Hughes
1047 Resolutions will never achieve Home Rule – resolution will.

in *Welsh Outlook* (May 1922)

Saunders Lewis
1048 An artist has no right to be a man of the people. His heritage is too old.*

'Barddoniaeth Mr R. Williams Parry'
in *Y Llenor* (vol. 1, no. 1, Summer 1922)

1049 It is evident that the 'ordinary man' cannot understand the extraordinary except in the fullness of time; and the extraordinary is the essence of literature.*

'Safonau Beirniadaeth Lenyddol'
(vol. 1, no. 4, Winter 1922)

1050 To forget is to betray.*

Gwaed yr Uchelwyr(1922)

Megan Lloyd George
1051 Whatever happens, Tada will be in power.

of her father, David Lloyd George, after his resignation from the Premiership,
letter to her sister Olwen, 25 Oct. 1922

Arthur Machen
1052 I shall always esteem it as the greatest piece of fortune that has fallen to me that I was born in that noble, fallen Caerleon-on-Usk in the heart of Gwent . . . The older I grow, the more firmly am I convinced that anything I may have accomplished in literature is due to the fact that when my eyes were first opened in early childhood, they had before them the vision of an enchanted land. As soon as I saw anything I saw Twm Barlwm, that mystic tumulus, the memorial of peoples that dwelt in that region before the Celts left the Land of Summer.

Far Off Things (1922)

Griffith John Williams
1053 Unless Wales comes into contact with the Continent, unless she knows what the great world beyond the borders of Wales and England is thinking, in vain will be our hope for a literary renaissance.*

'Cyfres y Werin'
in *Y Llenor* (vol. 1, no. 1, Spring 1922)

1054 When one nation begins to imitate another, it is the lowest and worst things that are usually imitated.*

1055 The Eisteddfod and the Gorsedd have for years been the nursery of quackery, and no institution that nurtures quackery can flourish and bear fruit.*

'Yr Eisteddfod a'r Orsedd'
(vol. 1, no. 2, Summer 1922)

1056 They [the Gorsedd of Bards] are not poets; they are not literary critics; they know little about the history of Wales and still less about its literature . . . They are merely useless members of an institution that was founded on deceit and maintained by arrogance and ignorance.*

— 1923 —

Caradoc Evans
1057 We are what we have been made by our preachers and politicians.

'Do I insult the Welsh?'
in *Sunday Express* (4 March 1923)

1058 Wales is Heaven on earth, and every Welsh capel is a little Heaven; and God has favoured us greatly by choosing to rule over us preachers who are fashioned in His likeness and who are without spot or blemish.

1059 Our God is a big man: a tall man much higher than the highest capel in Wales and broader than the broadest capel.

J. O. Francis
1060 We Welsh people are sadly prone to expend ourselves in vague benediction. In this Drama Movement, we need less oratory and more carpentry. The man with a 'hwyl' is now not so useful as the man with a hammer.

in Transactions of the Honourable Society of Cymmrodorion, 1923–4

Saunders Lewis
1061 It would be a great blessing for Wales if some Welshman did something for his nation that caused him to be put in prison.*

speech at meeting of Cymdeithas y Tair G, Mold, 1923

R. J. Lloyd Price
1062 As to my latter end I go,
To meet my Jubilee,
I bless the good horse Bendigo
Who built this tomb for me.

inscription on tomb at Llanfor, near Bala, commemorating a race-horse which won the Derby on which he had placed a bet

— 1924 —

Anonymous

1063 To the critical mind of the class-conscious worker, our scholarship system only serves as a safety valve for an economically privileged class which thrives on intellectual inequality.

editorial
in *Welsh Outlook* (Jan. 1924)

A. G. Edwards

1064 In many ways the results have been different from what we feared. The Church [in Wales] is poorer in possessions but richer than ever in the generosity of her own children. She has lost whatever prestige there may have been in a state connection. She can regain the hearts of the people.

on the consequences of Disestablishment,
in *Handbook of the Church in Wales* (1924)

Caradoc Evans

1065 You hear better singing and more tuneful music in a third-class revue than at the National Eisteddfod. Like the House of Commons, the eisteddfod does not appeal to genius or ability, if there is any in Wales. It does appeal to our apishness, to our love of playacting . . . The National Eisteddfod is an ill-managed circus.

'A Tilt at the Eisteddfod'
in *Western Mail* (2 June 1924)

J. O. Francis

1066 For my own part, I refuse to yield to this upstart ethnology. What was good enough for our fathers is good enough for me. Not all the British Association in congress assembled will shake my conviction that Welshmen are Welsh and that Englishmen are English.

'Against Measuring Heads'
The Legend of the Welsh (1924)

1067 Amidst the loud claimants for precedence amongst the Welsh counties, we of Glamorgan have been far too modest. We have seen a whiff of smoke in our atmosphere. We have been sensitively aware of a few pit-heads in the Rhondda Valley, and by nature lovers of the beautiful, we have not been able to hide from ourselves the fact that there is a slag-heap or two near Dowlais.

'The Glory of Glamorgan'

1068 In that Martyr's Town in Glamorgan everybody was a bitter politician by the time he had done teething. There were no neutrals among us above six months old.

'Knickerbocker Politics'

1069 [Mabon] was one of the saints in the South Wales calendar. Father Christmas and St David had but one day in the year. Mabon, however, was the patron of Monday once a month.

1070 Thus did Keir Hardie appear among us – bearing a new torch.

1071 Our compatriots in North Wales, where the Iberian strain is now thinnest, view us South Welshmen with a dubious eye, for to them we appear a rather obstreperous community . . . To the Southerner there is in North Wales a restraint which he cannot quite understand and which, to him, seems to border on passivity. Which region has the greater final wisdom the oracles have not yet revealed.

'Mr Hergesheimer's Welshmen'

1072 The course of drama in Wales has been so inconsistent that only the reckless dared assume the mantle of prophecy.

'The Deacon and the Dramatist'

1073 In all the thirteen counties there is still the lingering suspicion that the London Welshman is a prodigal who has left his father's home to go into a far country.

'Wales and the London Welsh'

1074 I realize that Cardiff must be a little weary of being patted on the back for this manifestation of itself in Cathays [the civic centre]. Nevertheless, . . .it is something that Cardiff may set off against its dreadful distinction in Britain as the city with the largest percentage of millionaires.

'The City of Cardiff'

J. Arthur Price

1075 The Welsh educational system has been a more successful device for the destruction of nationality than all the armies of the Habsburgs.

in *Welsh Outlook* (July 1924)

A. G. Prys-Jones

1076 The mountains of Glamorgan
Look down towards the sea,
Their song is clear as any bell
In melodies that sink and swell,
And there they stand to sentinel
A land of mystery.

'The Mountains of Glamorgan'

1077 My son, go kiss your mother, kiss her
    gently, she'll not wake,
For an older mother calls you, though you
    perish for her sake:
The fabled Dragon banner flies once more
    above the Dee
Where the sons of Wales are gathering to
    set our people free
From wrong and dire oppression; pray, my
    son, for strength anew,
For widows will be weeping at the falling
    of the dew.

'A Ballad of Glyndŵr's Rising'

— 1925 —

Anonymous

1078 Wales is an extinct palatinate.

editorial
in *Welsh Outlook* (Oct.1925)

H. Idris Bell

1079 A healthy paganism would heal . . . many
of our maladies

in *Welsh Outlook* (May 1925)

1080 In nine cases out of ten the Welshman who
loses his Welsh will probably not exchange
it for the language of Shakespeare at all.
What he will get in exchange will be . . .
the language of the *Daily Mail*; not the
poetry of Milton or Shelley, but the faded
inanities of the London music-halls; not
the fine flower of cosmopolitan culture, but
the brainless, heartless, hopeless vacuity of
English suburbia.

Welsh Poems in English Verse (1925)

David Davies

1081 That miserable stick [the Welsh Not] was

an outward visable sign of the systematic
effort made not only to teach English, but
also to suppress Welsh, and well I
remember how, even at that age [about
six/seven], I felt the hardship of being
punished for speaking my mother-tongue,
when my command of English was pitiably
limited.

Reminiscences of my Country and People (1925)

St John Ervine

1082 Cardiff is a devil of a place for plays.
Actors come away from it subdued to
silence.

in *Western Mail* (5 Oct. 1925)

Caradoc Evans

1083 In the knowledge that other people are too
polite to say what they think of him, the
Welshman tells other people what he
thinks of himself. So he wears his vanities
like a soldier wears his medals.

'The Publicity Club Address'
in *Western Mail* (10 Feb. 1925)

David Lloyd George MP

1084 Mussolini wants to see me . . . The Fascists
are very friendly to me.

letter to his wife, 27 Dec. 1925

John Morris-Jones

1085 Place-names in Wales . . . are part of the
language and of its poetry.*

Cerdd Dafod (1925)

Hilda Vaughan

1086 I *hate* Wales, I tell you – and the Welsh. I
hate them more than any other place and
people because they are my own whom I
have tried to love.

Rhys Lloyd
The Battle for the Weak (1925)

1087 It's a poor hard soil, no better nor that of
other countries, but 'tis *ours*. Welsh I was
born and Welsh I was bred. I've tried to
make the world my country and all folk
my kin, but 'tis to Wales as I've come
home, and to my first love.

Arnold Lunn

1088 The Architect of the Universe has lavished

beauty on the Alps, but economy is the dominant note of Welsh scenery.

The Mountains of Youth (1925)

— 1926 —

Anonymous

1089 Welsh will live or die, not in the schools, but on the hearths of the people.

editorial
in *Welsh Outlook* (Jan. 1926)

1090 The recent strike proves that for all big questions, the Parliament at Westminster can adequately deal with Wales.

(June 1926)

1091 Thy will be done, in Merthyr as it is in Devon.

prayer of small girl during General Strike, 1926

A. J. Cook

1092 Not a minute on the day, not a penny off the pay!

slogan during General Strike, 1926

W. J. Gruffydd

1093 Ever since it was disestablished . . . the Church in Wales has, as it were, vowed to kill the Welsh language.*

editorial
in *Y Llenor* (vol. 5, no. 1, Spring 1926)

1094 We have had no architecture, hardly any painting, and very little music until quite recently; the culture of Wales has always been a literary culture, and it depends on the Welsh language and the use that is made of it.*

(vol. 5, no. 2, Summer 1926)

1095 The University of Wales is further from the thought and culture of its own nation than any other University in the world.*

1096 1926 will be a black year for Wales. We hardly got used to the loss of Principal Rees, when we heard of the death of Principal J. H. Davies.*

(vol. 5, no. 3, Autumn 1926)

1097 Prose is not possible without a certain amount of national feeling, without some interest in political matters, without some awareness of the wide world, and awareness of the world is not possible without a nation.*

Llenyddiaeth Cymru: Rhyddiaith o 1540 hyd 1660 (1926)

1098 Every man is an exile after the age of forty, and it is with an exile's ear that he listens to the sayings of his youth.*

Saunders Lewis

1099 What then is our nationalism? . . . To fight not for Welsh independence but for the civilization of Wales. To claim for Wales not independence but freedom.*

Egwyddorion Cenedlaetholdeb (1926)

1100 Wales became superficial and materialistic, idolatrous, throne-loving, because she ceased to think in terms of the Sacrament.*

in *Baner ac Amserau Cymru* (8 July 1926)

Sir Alfred Mond

1101 Vales for the Velsh.

attributed, *c.* 1926

— 1927 —

Anonymous

1102 Today, the policy of the BBC is a greater danger to the language than anything else.

Welsh in Education and Life (1927)

Rhys Davies

1103 You Welsh! A race of mystical poets who have gone awry in some way.

The Withered Root (1927)

A. G. Edwards

1104 The Church is everywhere; Nonconformity only somewhere.

Memories (1927)

W. J. Gruffydd

1105 And as for Anglo-Welsh literature, I blush for my country at seeing any of it in print.*

editorial
in *Y Llenor* (vol. 6, no. 1, Spring 1927)

1106 I would not mind if dock-leaves or dandelions were the emblems of my country. I do not need, thanks to my upbringing, to wear anything to show that I am a Welshman.*

1107 I sometimes think that the national struggle is lost, that the fate of the language has been settled, and that Wales by the end of the century will be an insignificant and inarticulate part of England.*

(vol. 6, no. 2, Summer 1927)

1108 Half of our best men and women have gone to England; the other half have become preachers and teachers, a few have joined other professions such as medicine and the law. And on these, the ones who have stayed in Wales, the responsibility for enlightenment and example now rests.*

1109 I am quite convinced that as a nation we suffer badly from the inferiority complex of the peasant, and that it is a fairly recent thing in our history.*

(vol. 6, no. 4, Winter 1927)

David Emrys James, Dewi Emrys
1110 Any fool can be a crown bard of Wales, because genius is low in Wales.

in *The Sunday Express* (25 April 1927)

T. Gwynn Jones
1111 Argoed, Argoed of the secret places . . .
　　Your hills, your sunken glades, where were they,
　　　Your winding glooms and quiet towns?*

'Argoed'

Saunders Lewis
1112 The loss of sin is a loss to literature. Without sin we shall never have anything but lyrical poetry.*

'Llythyr ynghylch Catholigiaeth'
in *Y Llenor* (vol. 6, no. 2, Summer 1927)

1113 The great mistake of Welsh literature in our time is that we have no anti-Christian writers . . . We have only heretics.*

Eliseus Williams, Eifion Wyn
1114 Why, Lord, did you make Cwm Pennant so lovely,

And the life of an old shepherd so short?*

'Cwm Pennant'

— **1928** —

Anonymous
1115 The coal valleys bear the marks, psychological as well as physical, of having been the arena for a scramble by everybody, high and low, for quick money.

in *The Times* (2 April 1928)

W. J. Gruffydd
1116 Wales finds it difficult to learn the simple lesson that no one will take her seriously until we learn a little of the dignity of silence.*

editorial
in *Y Llenor* (vol. 7, no. 4, Winter 1928)

John Edward Lloyd
1117 Without medieval history, the core of Welsh History must vanish; no nation can less afford than ours to be explained in terms of the nineteenth century.

in *Welsh Outlook* (Jan. 1928)

Kate Roberts
1118 As it is impossible to earn a living in Wales by writing novels, they must be written during leisure hours. Only a little can be written during leisure hours, if one does one's other work honestly, and so, as far as I can see, no one will ever be able to write a novel in Wales.*

'Y Nofel Gymraeg'
in *Y Llenor* (vol. 7, no. 4, Winter 1928)

1119 No one can be expected to buy and read Welsh books for patriotic reasons only.*

Evelyn Waugh
1120 From the earliest times the Welsh have been looked upon as an unclean people. It is thus that they have preserved their racial integrity.

Dr Fagan
Decline and Fall (1928)

1121 The Welsh are the only nation in the world that has produced no graphic or

plastic art, no architecture, no drama.
They just sing . . . sing and blow down
wind instruments of plated silver.

— **1929** —

H. Idris Bell
1122 One thing is certain, if the language is to
die, it will die on the field of battle.*

'Tad Awen'
in *Y Llenor* (vol. 8, no. 2, Summer 1929)

Robert Graves
1123 On the hills behind Harlech I found a
personal harmony independent of history
or geography.

Goodbye to All That (1929)

1124 'Welch' referred us somehow to the archaic
North Wales of Henry Tudor and Owen
Glendower and Lord Herbert of
Cherbury, the founder of the regiment; it
dissociated us from the modern North
Wales of chapels, Liberalism, the dairy
and drapery business, slate mines, and the
tourist trade.

1125 These Welshmen are peculiar. They won't
stand being shouted at. They'll do
anything if you explain the reason for it –
do and die, but they have to know their
reason why. The best way to make them
behave is not to give them too much time
to think. Work them off their feet.

Captain Dunn

1126 The chapels held soldiering to be sinful,
and in Merioneth the chapels had the last
word. Prayers were offered for me by the
chapels, not because of the physical
dangers I would run in France, but
because of the moral dangers threatening
me at home.

1127 They began singing. Instead of the usual
music-hall songs they sang Welsh hymns,
each man taking a part. The Welsh always
sang when pretending not to be scared; it
kept them steady. And they never sang out
of tune.

1128 Criccieth's mayor addressed them
First in good Welsh and then in fluent
English,

Twisting his fingers in his chain of
office,
Welcoming the things.

'Welsh Incident'

W. J. Gruffydd
1129 It [Llandovery College] has grown to be
one of the strongest instruments of the
English mission in the Church and in the
country; I doubt whether any other
institution in south Wales has had such a
damning effect on everything that is
valuable in the eyes of the Welshman who
loves his language.*

editorial
in *Y Llenor* (vol. 8, no. 3, Autumn 1929)

1130 Without him [Sir John Morris-Jones] the
Welsh language would not have been
worth keeping by now. He brought back
elegance and reason and pride to Wales,
and recreated a civilization that was to be
a cradle for the most wonderful
renaissance our language has seen.*

editorial
in *Y Llenor* (vol. 8, no. 2, Summer 1929)

1131 There is no room in Wales for small and
snarling prelates.*

in response to A. G. Edwards, the first
Archbishop of Wales, 'There is no room in the
world for small and snarling nations.'

Saunders Lewis
1132 Modern Wales has taken its standards
from the only English class which would
readily give it conversation and friendship,
and that was the English Nonconformists
of the industrial towns. The ideal we have
thus accepted is the quintessence of
bourgeois mediocrity.

in *Welsh Outlook* (Oct. 1929)

1133 Give [Wales] self-government and you will
give her a capital city where her writers
will congregate and meet artists and form
a society. Give her a government and a
capital and she will in time gather an
urban class which will be the basis of a new
Welsh aristocracy.

1134 Welshmen in their chapels do not kneel in
prayer. They bend down, sitting as though
they are vomiting.

Mary Webb

1135 I come from the Cymru, sir, and my home is in the waste; and my lineage is elf-lineage, and for our sign, it is a churn-owl with a kingly crown on his head.

The Armour Wherein he Trusted (1929)

D. J. Williams

1136 The purpose of education is to make men, not money.*

A. E. a Chymru (1929)

1137 A living paganism is much nearer to heaven than a dead religion.*

1138 It is difficult to be moderate where love and hatred are concerned.*

— **1930** —

Anonymous

1139 Did you ever see,
Did you ever see,
Did you ever see,
Such a funny thing before?

'Cosher Bailey's Engine', *c.* 1930

1140 Mr and Mrs Jones . . . are nothing if not modern, but they *do* like to have a little dash of rural serfdom in the kitchen.

editorial
in *Welsh Outlook* (July 1930)

W. H. Auden

1141 　Westward is Wales
Where on clear evenings the retired and
　rich
From the french windows of their sheltered
　mansions
See the Sugarloaf standing, an upright
　sentinel
　Over Abergavenny.

'The Malverns'

1142 　. . . and Glamorgan hid a life
Grim as a tidal rock-pool's in its glove-
　shaped valleys.

'Perhaps'

Caradoc Evans

1143 Better the lumpy mattress of marriage than the feather bed of sin.

Nothing to Pay (1930)

1144 Get English teached you, mister. You're in Cardiff now.

1145 The Welsh in Cardiff take pains to hide their origin.

1146 She meant hwyl, the singing incantation by the means of which the Welsh preacher casts a spell upon his hearers and inflames their spiritual and carnal appetites.

1147 Braggers are the North Welsh and they throat their words like cuckoos.

Ianto

1148 When a man suspects the fidelity of his woman the first thing he denies her is money.

W. J. Gruffydd

1149 Welsh Nationalism should be able to include people of conservative mind as well as people of progressive mind, like the nationalism of every other country.*

editorial
in *Y Llenor* (vol. 9, no. 1, Spring 1930)

Saunders Lewis

1150 To stop lusting is to die.*

Monica (1930)

— **1931** —

Anonymous

1151 As compared with other historic communions in Christendom, Dissent is a whim, a happy whim.

editorial
in *Welsh Outlook* (March 1931)

1152 Where there is civilization, there is Welsh coal.

(April 1931)

W. J. Gruffydd

1153 It is easy to love Wales when you are far away from it making a fortune in England.*

editorial
in *Y Llenor* (vol. 10, no. 1, Spring 1931)

1154 St David's Day . . . the Welsh saturnalia which releases us all from the bonds of patriotism and its responsibilities for a whole year.*

1155 One of the essentials we have been slow to learn in Wales, it seems to me, is that of looking at things as they are.*

(vol. 10, no. 2, Summer 1931)

1156 If the language is of secondary importance to the Nationalist Party, it is every Welshman's duty to do his best to ensure that the Party is not a success.*

(vol. 10, no. 4, Winter 1931)

Saunders Lewis

1157 If a nation that has lost its political machinery becomes content to express its nationality henceforward only in the sphere of literature and the arts, then that literature and those arts will very quickly become provincial and unimportant, mere echoes of the ideas and artistic movements of the neighbouring and dominant nation. This danger is real for Wales today.

The Banned Wireless Talk on Welsh Nationalism (1931)

1158 I do not think the Welsh language will disappear rapidly, even if that should happen. But it will cease to be a language worth cultivating. Its literature will become entirely second-hand and fifth-rate. Believe me, there is something worse and more tedious than the death of a language, and that is its functionless survival.

1159 You cannot artificially encourage the language and literature and arts of a people and at the same time refuse them any economic and political recognition.

1160 What the Welsh today and tomorrow need is a call to heroism. The heroic note has not been heard in Welsh politics. But it is the only note that can save us now.

— 1932 —

Anonymous

1161 All mining camps after a time become worked out. South Wales today presents just such a picture of a worked out mining camp.

editorial
in *Welsh Outlook* (Jan. 1932)

1162 There's no need for Welsh books here: the language is holding its own in these parts.*

Cardiganshire farmer
quoted by Ffransis G. Payne, 'Pacmon yng Ngheredigion',
in *Y Llenor* (vol. 11, no. 2, Summer 1932)

W. J. Gruffydd

1163 If the Eisteddfod, I say, is to live, a lot of changes must be made to it.*

editorial
in *Y Llenor* (vol. 19, no. 2, Summer 1932)

Saunders Lewis

1164 Welsh Nationalism [has become] the spare-time hobby of corpulent and successful men.

editorial
in *The Welsh Nationalist* (Jan. 1932)

— **1933** —

W. H. Davies

1165 Can I forget your coming, like the Moon
　　When, robed in light, alone, without a
　　　　star,
　　She visits ruins; and the peace you
　　　　brought,
　　　　When I with all the world was still at
　　　　　　war.

'Stings'

W. J. Gruffydd

1166 It would be easy for a foreigner to think that the Welsh are the most religious nation in the world, that they are the greatest lovers of poetry and music, and that they have the highest ideal of education. He would think thus mainly because the Welsh think thus about themselves, and make a lot of noise about these three things.*

editorial
in *Y Llenor* (vol. 12, no. 2, Summer 1933)

J. M. Keynes

1167 How can I convey to the reader, who does not know him [Lloyd George], any just impression of this extraordinary figure of our time, this syren, this goat-footed bard, this half-human visitor to our age from the hag-ridden magic and enchanted woods of Celtic antiquity?

Essays and Sketches in Biography (1933)

Saunders Lewis

1168 The certain effect of killing the Welsh language will be the enhancement of the victory of capitalism.*

in *Y Ddraig Goch* (Aug. 1933)

1169 We want to free Wales from the grip of the English. We want to de-Anglicize Wales.*

'Un Iaith i Gymru'

1170 That English is a spoken language in Wales is an evil, an unmixed evil. It must be wiped out from the land of Wales; delenda est Carthago.*

'Deg Pwynt Polisi'

1171 Agriculture should be the principal industry of Wales and the basis of its civilization.*

'Deg Pwynt Polisi'

1172 For the sake of the moral health of Wales and the moral and physical well-being of its population, South Wales must be de-industrialised.*

1173 Shortly after the extinction of the monoglot Welsh, the life of the Welsh language will come to an end.*

Dylan Thomas

1174 It's impossible for me to tell you how much I want to get out of it all, out of the narrowness and dirtiness, out of the eternal ugliness of the Welsh people and all that belongs to them, out of the pettiness of a mother I don't care for and the giggling batch of relatives . . . I shall have to get out soon or there will be no need. I'm sick and this bloody country's killing me.

letter to Pamela Hansford Johnson, Oct. 1933

— **1934** —

Anonymous

1175 You've heard of the Gresford Disaster,
    The terrible price that was paid,
Two hundred and sixty-two colliers were
        lost,
    And three of the rescue brigade . . .

The fireman's reports are all missing,
    The records of forty-two days,
The colliery manager had them destroyed
    To cover his criminal ways.

Down there in the dark they are lying,
    They died for nine shillings a day,
They've worked out their shift and now
        they must lie
    In the darkness until Judgement Day.

The Lord Mayor of London's collecting
    To help our poor children and wives,
The owners have sent some white lilies
    To pay for the poor colliers' lives.

Farewell, our dear wives and our children,
    Farewell to our comrades as well,
Don't send your sons down the dark
        dreary mine,
    They'll be damned like the sinners in
        Hell.

'The Gresford Disaster'

1176 I have come to the clear conclusion that, for an appreciable proportion of the workpeople in parts of the depressed areas, transfer to other districts and other trades is necessary if they wish to gain a living.

report of the Commissioner for Special Areas, 1934

W. J. Gruffydd

1177 First and foremost, speak in platitudes.*

advice to speakers at St David's Day dinners
editorial
in *Y Llenor* (vol. 13, no. 1, Spring 1934)

Jack Jones

1178 Revolutionary and riotous; religious and musical; sporting and artistic, coal-bearing Rhondda.

Rhondda Roundabout (1934)

Saunders Lewis

1179 Wales was Christian and Catholic even before she was Welsh. . . and I see the mark of her Catholic formation upon the whole of her history and culture.*

Catholigiaeth a Chymru (1934)

1180 I have no hesitation in saying that Welsh literature was one of the three great literatures of medieval Europe.*

Dylan Thomas

1181 Man be my metaphor.

'If I were tickled by the rub of love'

D. J. Williams

1182 No man becomes a member of an old rural district unless his grandfather, at least, was born there.*

'Y Tri Llwyth'
Hen Wynebau (1934)

— 1935 —

Anonymous

1183 Merthyr Tydfil has many sites of decaying ironworks, the most modern of which stands like a gaunt memorial to past prosperity on the hillside at Dowlais.

report of the Royal Commission on Merthyr Tydfil, 1935

Llewelyn Wyn Griffith

1184 The two lives, English and Welsh, were growing within me, each in its own direction, and the division was made manifest at this early stage; it was important to me that I should be English in England, and equally necessary that no Welshman should dare to suspect that I was not Welsh.

Spring of Youth (1935)

W. J. Gruffydd

1185 When we are asked why we need self-government, it is impossible to answer without mentioning the preservation of Welsh traditions and the Welsh language.*

editorial
in *Y Llenor* (vol. 14, no. 1, Spring 1935)

T. Gwynn Jones

1186 Thus . . . it always was with literature in Wales . . . when something new arrives, it is stamped upon at first, and then imitated to death.*

'Cymru a'r Drama'
Beirniadaeth a Myfyrdod (1935)

Thomas Jones (of Rhymney)

1187 South Wales should be scheduled as a Grand National Ruin.

in *New Statesman and Nation* (1935)

Eiluned Lewis

1188 We who were born

In country places
Far from cities
And shifting faces,
We have a birthright
No man can sell,
And a secret joy
No man can tell.

'The Birthright'

Alun Llywelyn-Williams

1189 The tendency of the Welsh-speaking Welsh is to refuse to face the artistic problems of our industrial areas and to try to escape from them by considering them as unWelsh phenomena.*

editorial
in *Tir Newydd* (no. 3, Autumn 1935)

T. J. Thomas, Sarnicol

1190 God made the Poet,
    Then took a fistful
Of the rubbish that was left
    And made three critics.*

'Y Bardd a'r Beirniaid'

1191 He sacked his workmen, small and
        great,
    To show how fine a man he was, did
        Jack;
    He's gone now to another pit
    Where no one ever gets the sack.*

'Bos y Pwll'

1192 He scorned his land, his tongue denied;
    Nor Welsh nor English, lived and died
A bastard mule, and made his own
    Each mulish fault save one alone:
Dic somehow got, that prince of fools,
    A vast vile progeny of mules. *

'Dic Siôn Dafydd'

— 1936 —

W. H. Auden

1193 It wasn't always like this?
Perhaps it wasn't, but it is.
Put the car away; when life fails,
What's the good of going to Wales?

'Letter to Lord Byron'

Edward, Prince of Wales

1194 Something must be done. I will do all I can to assist you.

during a visit to the unemployed of Dowlais, Merthyr Tydfil, Nov. 1936

H. A. L. Fisher

1195 It is true indeed that Anglo-Norman civilization, spreading from the great Welsh monasteries, and from the castles of the Marcher Lords, exercised an influence on this race of quarrelsome nightingales [the Welsh].

History of Europe (1936)

Edward Garnett

1196 The Welsh are still an old-fashioned, conservative people, who have never been exploited, in literature at least.

letter to Geraint Goodwin, 24 March 1936

W. J. Gruffydd

1197 Wales is such a small country and we all know one another so well that it becomes more and more difficult as a man grows older, and widens the circle of his acquaintance, to offer a fairly honest opinion on topics of the day.*

editorial
in *Y Llenor* (vol. 15, no. 1, Spring 1936)

1198 No Welshman, whatever his political views may be, can do less than bow his head in shame after hearing about the behaviour of the Welsh hooligans of Pwllheli towards the speakers who went there in an attempt to lead the protest against the bombing school.*

1199 From now on, we shall know, more or less, to which camp in the national struggle our leaders belong.*

after protest meeting at Pwllheli against the Bombing School
editorial
in *Y Llenor* (vol. 15, no. 2, Summer 1936)

1200 Unless a nation is interested in religion or morals or society, and in every other activity which can make its life full and fruitful, its literature cannot flourish.*

'Rhagarweiniad i'r Bedwaredd Ganrif ar Bymtheg'

1201 A black day. It is not easy to write about contemporary events in Wales on the day I hear that three of my friends are to stand trial at Pwllheli.*

(vol. 15, no. 3, Autumn 1936)

1202 The truth is that I have never lived in a community since I left Llanddeiniolen for Cardiff a quarter of a century ago. Here I simply reside – sleeping, working and eating; I do not *live* here . . . No one round me speaks my language or thinks the thoughts I think; they are all rootless people, and none of them will be buried with his fathers . . . But how sad it is that a Welshman should be an exile in Wales, for every Welshman living in Cardiff or its suburbs is an exile.*

Hen Atgofion (1936)

J. E. Jones

1203 Wales will interpret a refusal by you to receive a deputation as an indication that protests from Wales and by Welshmen are regarded as unworthy of consideration.

letter to Stanley Baldwin, 4 June 1936, requesting a meeting to discuss the proposed buiding of a Bombing School in Llŷn

Saunders Lewis

1204 The English Government's behaviour in the matter of the Llŷn bombing range is exactly the behaviour of this new Anti-Christ throughout Europe. And in this assize-court in Caernarfon today we, the accused in this dock, are challenging Anti-Christ. We deny the absolute power of the State-God. Here in Wales, a land that has no tradition except Christian tradition, a land that has never in all its history been pagan or atheist, we stand for the preservation of that Christian tradition and for the supremacy of the moral law over the power of materialist bureaucracy. So that whether you find us guilty or not guilty is of importance today to the future of Christian civilization and Christian liberty and Christian justice in Europe.*

speech from dock, Caernarfon, 13 Oct. 1936

1205 We hold the conviction that our action was in no way criminal, and that it was forced upon us, that it was done in obedience to conscience and to the moral law and that the responsibility for any loss due to our act is the responsibility of the British Government.

Why we Burnt the Bombing School (1936)

1206 When all democratic and peaceful methods of persuasion had failed . . . we were determined that even then we would invoke only the process of law and that a jury from the Welsh people should pronounce on the right and wrong of our behaviour.

1207 It was the realisation of the fundamental connection between the literature and the traditional social life of Wales which drew me from doing literary work only to take up public activities and to found the Welsh Nationalist Party.

David Lloyd George MP

1208 This is the first Government that has tried Wales at the Old Bailey. I wish I were there, and I certainly wish I were forty years younger.

of the decision to move the Bombing School trial letter to his daughter Megan, 1 Dec. 1936

H. A. Marquand

1209 South Wales needs a Plan.

title of book, 1936

Iorwerth C. Peate

1210 Wales is the inheritor of the whole of the European tradition, and it is high time it became aware of the duplicity of the claim that nothing good has come, or will ever come, from the direction of France and Italy – or, in short, from Rome.*

'Traddodiad Ewrop'
in *Y Llenor* (vol. 15, no. 1, Spring 1936)

Kate Roberts

1211 This was the weakness of his own people: they had a heroic capacity for suffering, but it did not extend to acting against the cause of that suffering.*

Traed mewn Cyffion (1936)

Dylan Thomas

1212 The ball I threw while playing in the park
Has not yet reached the ground.

'Should lanterns shine'

1213 Though lovers be lost love shall not;
And death shall have no dominion.

'And death shall have no dominion'

— 1937 —

Anonymous

1214 I only wish I could just eat up a whole penny onion pie, all to myself.

small boy in Rhondda
quoted by Ernest Toller in *Wales* (no. 2, Aug. 1937)

1215 We're . . . fed up with people coming down here looking us over as though we were animals in a zoo.

old miner
quoted by James Hanley, *Grey Children* (1937)

Donald Attwater

1216 The English should love and honour England as their mother . . . but the English should also love and honour Wales as their grandmother.*

quoted in 'Tri Ŵr Penyberth'
in *Heddiw* (Feb. 1937)

Rhys Davies

1217 Wales is a beautiful mother, but she can be a dangerously possessive wife.

My Wales (1937)

1218 Other nations have things the matter with them. Not Wales.

1219 It is well known that Welsh people are vigorously unable to tolerate any criticism of their land from their native writers.

1220 The Welsh are the finest full-time actors in the world. But we have no theatre. We do not need one; life is a large enough stage for us.

1221 Go into any bookshop in Wales and you will be in England.

1222 There is still a primitive shine on Wales; one can smell the old world there still, and it is not a dead aroma.

1223 There is something sadistic about a Sunday in Aberystwyth.

1224 They [the London Welsh] love London like a sin.

1225 The fanatics for the language have a heavy task: which is not to say it will not be achieved.

1226 To me it is a lovely tongue [Welsh] to be cultivated in the same way as some people cultivate orchids, or keep Persian cats: a hobby yielding much private delight and sometimes a prize in an exhibition.

1227 The writing of Welsh is entirely a part-time job, a hobby, undertaken mostly by university professors and ministers of the Gospel.

1228 Such a landscape as the Rhondda today is a spectacle satisfying to the pessimist and the satirist.

1229 There is no decadence in Wales, save that imposed upon it by the diseases of modern industrialisation.

Tommy Farr

1230 Hello, Tonypandy, I done my best!

on BBC radio, after attempting to win the World Heavyweight Boxing Championship in New York, 1937

David Jones

1231 My companions in the war were mostly Londoners with an admixture of Welshmen, so that the mind and folk-life of those differing racial groups are an essential ingredient to my theme. Nothing could be more representative. These came from London. Those from Wales. Together they bore in their bodies the genuine tradition of the Island of Britain, from Bendigeid Vran to Jingle and Marie Lloyd. These were the children of Doll Tearsheet. Those are before Caractacus was. Both speak in parables, the wit of both is quick, both are natural poets; yet no two groups could well be more dissimilar.

preface
In Parenthesis (1937)

1232 No one to care there for Aneirin Lewis
        spilled there
who worshipped his ancestors like a Chink.

1233 This Dai adjusts his slipping shoulder-straps, wraps close his misfit outsize greatcoat – he articulates his English with an alien care.
    My fathers were with the Black Prinse of
        Wales

at the passion of
the blind Bohemian king.
They served in these fields,
it is in the histories that you can read it,
Corporal – boys Gower, they were – it is
    writ down – yes.
        Wot about Methuselum, Taffy?

Idwal Jones

1234 To my friend D. Matthew Williams who believes, as I do, that our little country does not take its humour seriously enough.*

dedication
Cerddi Digri Newydd a Phethau o'r Fath (1937)

1235 When my family sent me to college,
        I looked at those spires tall,
And my head was buzzing with bits of
        advice,
        I couldn't remember them all;
But my uncle's advice I shall never forget,
        More precious than rubies to me:
A supporter or two on a Council
        Is better than any degree.*

'Cyngor i Fyfyriwr Ifanc' (trans. Wynne Roberts)

Saunders Lewis

1236 Garmon, Garmon,
        A vineyard placed in my care is Wales, my
            country,
To deliver unto my children
And my children's children
Intact, an eternal heritage;
And behold, the swine rush on her to rend
        her.
Now will I call on my friends,
Scholars and simple folk,
'Take your place by my side in the breach
That the age-old splendour be kept for
        ages to come.'
And this, my Lord, is the vineyard of your
        beloved, too;
From Llan Fair to Llan Fair, a land where
        the Faith is established.*

Buchedd Garmon (trans. D. M. Lloyd, 1937)

Seosamh Mac Grianna

1237 If you are content with the creation of an Anglo-Welsh literature of value, giving expression to Welsh feelings and experiences, but through the medium of English, then you will have provided an

excellent excuse for those who would
acquiesce in the death of the Welsh
language . . . In the end one might even
see 'Welsh' studies in the University
Colleges of Wales represented by a lecturer
in Anglo-Welsh literature in the English
Department.*

An Breatain Bheag (1937)

Sir Henry Mather-Jackson

1238 Monmouthshire is not in Wales. The State
does not regard it as in Wales, except for
Sunday closing. We are in England, and I
am not going to be added to Wales for any
purpose whatever.

reported in *Western Mail* (7 April 1937)

Keidrych Rhys

1239 Though we write in English, we are rooted
in Wales.

editorial
in *Wales* (no. 1, Summer 1937)

— **1938** —

Idris Davies

1240 My fathers in the mining valleys
Were slaves who bled for beer,
Who had no Saviour to acclaim
And whose God was Fear.

Gwalia Deserta (1938)

1241 O timbers from Norway and muscles from
Wales,
Be ready for another shift and believe in
co-operation,
Though pit-wheels are frowning at old
misfortunes
And girders remember disasters of old;
O what is man that coal should be so
careless of him,
And what is coal that so much blood
should be upon it?

1242 Do you remember 1926? That summer of
soups and speeches,
The sunlight on the idle wheels and the
deserted crossings,
And the laughter and the cursing in the
moonlit streets?
Do you remember 1926? The slogans and
the penny concerts,

The jazz-bands and the moorland picnics,
And the slanderous tongues of famous
cities?
Do you remember 1926? The great dream
and the swift disaster,
The fanatic and the traitor, and more than
all,
The bravery of the simple, faithful folk?
'Ay, ay, we remember 1926,' said Dai and
Shinkin,
As they stood on the kerb in Charing Cross
Road,
'And we shall remember 1926 until our
blood is dry.'

1243 There's a concert in the village to buy us
boots and bread,
There's a service in the chapel to make us
meek and mild.

1244 I stood in the ruins of Dowlais
And sighed for the lovers destroyed
And the landscape of Gwalia stained for all
time
By the bloody hand of progress.

1245 Consider famous men, Dai bach, consider
famous men.

1246 The world has bred no champions for a
long time now,
Except the boxing, tennis, golf, and Fascist
kind,
And the kind that democracy breeds and
feeds for Harringay.
And perhaps the world has grown too
bitter or too wise
To breed a prophet or a poet ever again.

1247 When we walked to Merthyr Tydfil, in the
moonlight long ago,
When the mountain tracks were frozen
and the crests were capped with snow,
We had tales and songs between us, and
souls too young to fret,
And we had hopes and visions which the
heart remembers yet . . .

The moon is still as radiant and the
homely hills remain,
But the magic of those evenings we shall
not meet again,
For we were boyish dreamers in a world
we did not know
When we walked to Merthyr Tydfil in the
moonlight long ago.

1248 In the places of my boyhood
   The pit-wheels turn no more,
Nor any furnace lightens
   The midnight as of yore . . .

Though blighted be the valleys
   Where man meets man with pain,
The things my childhood cherished
   Stand firm, and shall remain.

W. J. Gruffydd
1249 From the South comes every revolution, in religion and literature, but it is in the North that the revolution is fully developed.*

Owen Morgan Edwards: Cofiant (1938)

D. Gwenallt Jones
1250 Why have you given us this misery,
   The pain like leaden weights on flesh
      and blood?
   Your language on our shoulders like a
      sack.
   And your traditions shackles round our
      feet.*

to Wales
'Cymru' (trans. Joseph P. Clancy)

1251 But still, we cannot leave you in the
      filth,
   This generation's butt and laughing-
      stock.*

1252 Woe to us who know the words without
      knowing the Word.*

'Ar Gyfeiliorn'

Alun Lewis
1253 We are a long way from the world in Wales, and there is a kind of apathy about things. The poor accept their lot and the well-to-do their comfort. And the farmers pray only for rain. I would like to wake them up.

letter to Jean Gilbert, 12 May 1938

Saunders Lewis
1254 It is an inability to think that is destroying Wales today.*

Canlyn Arthur (1938)

Hugh MacDiarmid
1255 We can hope for life in poetry wherever the Nationalist sign is hung out, whether the Nationalism be Welsh, Scottish or American.

Voice of Scotland (1938)

Emlyn Williams
1256 The Corn is Green.

title of play, 1938

1257 Anybody in Wales will tell you that the people in this part of the countryside are practically barbarians.

Miss Ronberry
The Corn is Green (1938)

— 1939 —

Anonymous
1258 We deny the right of England to push Wales into war once again. Nobody is threatening Wales, and over the centuries Wales has seen only the worst of England.*

editorial
in *Heddiw* (June 1939)

Edgar Leyshon Chappell
1259 Few sea-ports of the magnitude of Cardiff have been developed in so lopsided a fashion.

History of the Port of Cardiff (1939)

Gwilym Davies
1260 To say that Wales is a nation and not a state is to emphasize that it remains a soul without a body.

'Beyond our Frontiers'
in *The Welsh Review* (vol. 1, no. 2, March 1939)

Pennar Davies
1261 There should be a lively communication between Welsh-language literature and English-language literature in Wales. If it comes to that, a literary society should be formed for the English-speaking Welsh and the Welsh-speaking Welsh.*

letter to editor
in *Tir Newydd* (no. 17, Aug. 1939)

J. Goronwy Edwards
1262 What becomes of these Oxford Welshmen when they go down from Oxford?

'From an Oxford Window'
broadcast on Welsh Home Service, 20 Jan. 1939
in *The Welsh Review* (vol. 1, no. 2, March 1939)

Llewelyn Wyn Griffith

1263 Above all, wisdom: for years are shrinking
into a huddle of days and the world a
    parish
where neighbours bolt their doors and
    lights are dimming.
Soon there will be nothing left for us to
    cherish
but the grave words of the last statesmen
before the battle starts and the air is
    darkened:
fast fall the night upon the frightened
    children
and on the wombs where once they
    quickened.
What towered land of man's endeavour
will first be desert, with all our learning
a burnt page in the dust of error?
Farewell to wisdom and to all
    remembering.

'If there be time'

1264 I have no answer, no rising song
to the young in years who are old
with our arrogance, our failure.
Let it be silence: the world is cold.

'Silver Jubilee 1939'

W. J. Gruffydd

1265 The Land of Mountains is a place for old
people, and for young people come home
to die of tuberculosis.*

editorial
in *Y Llenor* (vol. 18, no. 1, Spring 1939)

1266 The future of Wales depends, for as long as
it is a part of England, on an early change
in the Government's attitude towards the
rural areas of Britain.*

1267 Since I wrote the above notes, everyone
has had cause to think of something else
besides the Eisteddfod and the literature of
Wales, but *Y Llenor*, I hope, will contiinue
to keep the flag flying even in time of war.*

(vol. 18, no. 3, Autumn 1939)

1268 We are now a bilingual nation, and thus
we rely upon English for literature of
courage and magnanimity, and keep the
Welsh language to express things that are
harmless and wishy-washy, poetry and
prose which can be expected some day to

be the set-books of the Central Welsh
Board.*

Y Tro Olaf (1939)

1269 It is better, even for the language, to have
a right-thinking Englishman than a
wrong-headed Welshman.*

Emyr Humphreys

1270 I could be Boswell to the dying Wales.

'A Young Man Considers his Prospects'

1271 Freedom, will you not come back?
Our souls are Hungry!

'1536–1936'

Alice Rees Jones

1272 Forget that it is supposed to be Welsh, and
you will enjoy this novel [*How Green was my
Valley*].

in *The Welsh Review* (vol. 2, no. 4, Nov. 1939)

Artemus Jones

1273 It was very interesting for a Welshman to
see the Red Dragon in the royal procession
at the Coronation.*

'Glyndŵr fel Tyst'
in *Y Llenor* (vol. 18, no. 2, Summer 1939)

Gwyn Jones

1274 Welsh ought to be the first language of all
of us Welshman – but it isn't, and most are
afraid that it never will be.

editorial
in *The Welsh Review* (vol. 1, no. 1, Feb. 1939)

1275 Walking the shore of Harlech, I was told
how when the castle was built the sea
washed the base of the castle rock. In this
corner of Wales the land is gaining on the
sea. Over the way, in England, the sea
gains on the land. Is this the index finger
of Providence?

editorial
in *The Welsh Review* (vol. 2, no. 1, Aug. 1939)

1276 It is Corwen's good fortune to be a
provincial centre of literature.

1277 The Englishman is bad at learning
languages, the Welshman good; the
Englishman in these affairs is thick-

skinned, the Welshman courteous; in a free mingling of the two peoples the English language must triumph.

(vol. 2, no. 4, Nov. 1939)

1278 Has Wales the means of securing alteration? Its Nationalist leaders have scholarship, oratory, devotion, and great faith. Have they political ability? So far they have shown little sign of it, both in their attitude towards the crisis of last September and in some of their pronouncements at the beginning of this war.

Saunders Lewis

1279 It is the writers' task to ensure that literature in the language is sufficiently splendid to justify every sacrifice and effort made to keep the language, which is the instrument of that splendour, sprightly and uncorrupted.*

'Cyflwr ein Llenyddiaeth'
in *Baner ac Amserau Cymru* (24 May 1939)

1280 It is not literature's function to keep a language alive; and it is to prostitute literature to make it do work that a nation ought to be brave enough to do itself.*

1281 From Merthyr to Dowlais the tramway climbs,
A slug's slime-trail over the slag-heaps.
What's nowadays a desert of cinemas,
Rain over disused tips, this once was Wales.*

'Y Dilyw, 1939' (trans. Anthony Conran)

1282 Eyes have been changed to dust, we know not our death,
Were buried with our mothers, had Lethe milk to drink.
We cannot bleed, no, not as former men bled,
Our hands would resemble a hand, if they'd thumbs to go on them.
If a fall shatters our feet, all we do is grovel to a clinic,
Touch our caps to a wooden leg, Mond pension and insurance;
Knowing neither language nor dialect, feeling no insult,
We gave our masterpiece to history in our country's MPs.*

1283 And over the waves comes the sound of tanks gathering.*

1284 There is abundant intellectual ability in Wales, but there is a catastrophic lack of moral courage and decision.

Is there an Anglo-Welsh Literature? (1939)

1285 Mr Dylan Thomas is obviously an equipped writer, but there is nothing hyphenated about him. He belongs to the English.

1286 Whatever culture there has been in the mining valleys of South Wales has been the remnant of the social life of the countryside, and has been Welsh in speech. The extension of English has everywhere accompanied the decay of that culture, the loss of social traditions and of social unity and the debasement of spiritual values. It has produced no richness of idiom, no folk-song, but has battened on the spread of journalese and the mechanised slang of the talkies.

1287 I conclude then that there is not a separate literature that is Anglo-Welsh, and that it is improbable that there ever can be that. You will not take it that I therefore demand abruptly that the Anglo-Welsh writers should shut up.

Richard Llewellyn

1288 I am going to pack my two shirts with my other socks and my best suit in the little blue cloth my mother used to tie around her hair when she did the house, and I am going from the Valley.

Huw Morgan
How Green was my Valley (1939)

1289 Owain Glyndŵr said all there is to be said for this country hundreds of years ago. Wales for the Welsh. More of him and less of Mr Marx, please.

Huw's father

1290 My Valley, O my Valley, within me, I will live in you eternally.

Huw Morgan

1291 How green was my Valley, then, and the Valley of them that have gone.

John Cowper Powys

1292 The point which it behoves all Anglo-Welsh writers to remember is that there would be no Anglo-Welsh literature at all if the Welsh language hadn't been a living language for so long.

'Welsh Culture'
in *The Welsh Review* (vol. 1, no. 5, June 1939)

1293 This source is deeper than culture, more diffused than tradition, wider than language. It is the spirit of the Welsh character. It is the occult secret of the most conservative, the most introverted, the most mysterious nation that has ever existed on the earth outside China.

Llewelyn Powys

1294 The blood in my own veins is so mixed that in spite of my two names I cannot brag of being a Welshman as much as I would like. Let this be as it may, I find that as the years gather, it is to the Welsh manner of approaching life that I am most drawn.

'Welsh and English'
in *The Welsh Review* (vol. 1, no. 3, April 1939)

1295 For generations the heart of the Englishman towards the Welshman has been one of open distrust, and the heart of the Welshman towards the Englishman one of civility and covert contempt.

V. S. Pritchett

1296 The Welsh are a nation of toughs, rogues, and poetic humbugs, vivid in their speech, impulsive in behaviour, riddled with a sly and belligerent tribalism.

in *The New Statesman and Nation* (1939)

Keidrych Rhys

1297 Ever heard of a Welshman making a sacrifice for the sake of Art?

'Notes for a new editor'
in *Wales* (no. 8/9, Aug. 1939)

1298 Any painter who flatters the features of some Welsh Gomez is always well publicized, and sure of making a living afterwards.

1299 The squirearchy in most villages are of the decayed English militarist class, who settle down in Wales on account of the salmon-fishing or because they are fussed over.

A. W. Wade-Evans

1300 The Welsh nation was born in and of the Roman Empire. Rome is our mother.

talk broadcast in Welsh Home Service, 2 Jan. 1939
'What the Welsh Nation has Forgotten'
in *The Welsh Review* (vol. 1, no. 1, Feb. 1939)

1301 The Welsh nation has suffered much at the hands of historians.

Emlyn Williams

1302 He is to Wales what Sean O'Casey is to Ireland.

'Jack Jones'
in *The Welsh Review* (vol. 1, no. 4, May 1939)

J. Ellis Williams

1303 The literary life of Wales suffers from what Pharaoh would call minor plagues.

'Welsh Drama Today'
in *The Welsh Review* (vol. 2, no. 1, Aug. 1939)

— 1940 —

Anonymous

1304 If Wales were half as enthusiastic in the work of putting its own life in order as it is in serving at the tables of foreigners, Wales would be much more like what we have in mind when talking about a Christian country.*

editorial
in *Heddiw* (Sept.–Oct. 1940)

Caradoc Evans

1305 Nonconformity and Liberalism are not a religion; they are a wrangle designed to keep us in subjection.

entry in journal, *c.* 1940

1306 Wales is a land of secret sins.

1307 An honest Welshman is not a miracle; the miracle is how he became honest.

1308 There are more scandals hidden in a Welsh town of five thousand people than there are dealt with during a divorce court sessions.

1309 There has never been a great Welsh criminal. The Welshman at home sells addled eggs and diluted milk; but when he goes abroad he steals money.

1310 The Welshman is afraid of only one thing: poverty. That is why he is kind to tramps.

1311 The Welsh are the only people who are brave enough to tell a lie as if that lie were the truth.

1312 The Welshman is like his scenery, triangular.

1313 Dear me. You talk Welsh. I thought you were a gentleman.

1314 Mary Ty-canol tells me that Hitler was in college in Aberystwyth . . . He liked the old town so much that he gave special orders that though London be razed, Aberystwyth must be saved.

1315 No Welshman talks in Welsh if he knows English.

W. J. Gruffydd

1316 We are all in the soup together . . . No one has been more bitter than I in the past in condemning some aspects of the policy of the British Empire, and I do not wish to take back one syllable of what I said. But we shall lose *everything* that was precious to us in Wales if Hitler goes on adding to the havoc that he has already made; it would not be possible for me or you, my friend, who were reared in the liberal and philanthropic traditions of Wales, to live in any country conquered by him or by cowardly Mussolini or by the zealot Franco.*

editorial
in *Y Llenor* (vol. 19, no. 2, Summer 1940)

Ernest Rhys

1317 Wales England wed, so I was bred.

epigraph to autobiography
Wales England Wed (1940)

T. J. Thomas, Sarnicol

1318 Ignore, my friend, the mockeries
Of all that jealous gang:
Stones are only thrown at trees
Where fruits hang.*

'Na Hidia'

— 1941 —

Ambrose Bebb

1319 The Welshman is not a city-dweller, but a countryman.*

Pererindodau (1941)

H. J. Fleure

1320 Urban but not civic.

of the industrial communities of south Wales
introduction to E. G. Bowen, *Wales, a Study in Geography and History* (1941)

Llewelyn Wyn Griffith

1321 The Welsh people of today are still emerging painfully from the nineteenth century.

Word from Wales (1941)

1322 A country that fears its writers is moribund.

1323 The Welsh novel is in a poor way, and Wales is still waiting for its great novelist.

1324 We are merely asking England to be a good neighbour and to allow us to cultivate our garden in our own fashion.

1325 There is no Society for the Abolition of Welsh: there is no enemy but indifference, the inertia of all administration, the unwillingness to provide for bilingualism. It is so much less trouble to pretend that the other language does not exist.

1326 Wales depends upon England for its daily news, with the exception of a five-minute broadcast in Welsh.

1327 The number of English people who can speak Welsh is microscopically small.

W. J. Gruffydd

1328 If the [German] victors saw fit to give us some semblance of independence from England, as Brittany has been promised, it would not be out of love for Wales but in order to weaken England. And then we would be under the feet of our own Quislings in Wales, with neither Parliament nor Whitehall to raise a finger in favour of the common people. I cannot think of a blacker prospect.*

editorial
in *Y Llenor* (vol. 20, no. 1, Spring 1941)

1329 The prospect for the future of Wales is deteriorating day by day.*

1330 After the war has been won, the people of Wales will face another battle, perhaps the most bitter in their history.*

1331 Since I last wrote, three events have been the subjects of conversation among my friends – Russia's part in the war, the Colwyn Bay Eisteddfod, and the sacking of Dr Iorwerth Peate.*

(vol. 20, no. 3, Autumn 1941)

1332 Welsh life has been ripped apart from top to bottom.*

(vol. 20, no. 4, Winter 1941)

1333 If Wales is lost, there is nothing more, for me, to say about life. Wales was my raison d'être, there is no meaning to the life I have lived up to now, nor to any line that I have written, unless *Welsh* children live in Llanddeiniolen and Pontrhydfendigaid and Llanbrynmair after I have ceased complaining.*

Alun Lewis
1334 The quarry villages like Llanllechid and Bethesda are no different from the mining villages in the South.

letter to Brenda Chamberlain, 21 Feb. 1941

Saunders Lewis
1335 St Michael, who loves the hills, pray for Wales,
St Michael, friend of the sick, remember us.*

'Haf Bach Mihangel' (trans. Joseph P. Clancy)

John Lloyd Williams
1336 If an Englishman happened to notice a tinge of a Welsh accent on the English of a boy or girl, and say 'You are Welsh', he or she would feel as much shame as if caught committing an unforgivable crime.*

Atgofion Tri Chwarter Canrif (1941)

— **1942** —

Anonymous
1337 It is hereby enacted that the Welsh language may be used in any court in Wales by any party or witness who considers that he would otherwise be at any disadvantage by reason of his natural language of communication being Welsh.

Welsh Courts Act, 1942

1338 We are not living in normal times and the Welshman has not lived a normal life for more than four centuries.*

editorial
in *Heddiw* (Dec. 1941–Jan. 1942)

H. Idris Bell
1339 Let Wales take from England, as from elsewhere, whatever she can assimilate; but let her beware of abandoning too hastily her native ways. And I suspect that these are much nearer to French than to English ways.

'The Welsh Poetic Tradition'
in *Wales* (no. 1, July 1942)

R. A. Butler MP
1340 I regard as obscurantist the attitude of the Commission of Inquiry a hundred years ago which went to Wales and took the view that to keep alive a knowledge of this beautiful tongue was tantamount to crippling Welsh initiative and penalising Welsh endeavour. I wish now to make amends.

speech in House of Commons, 1942

Alun Lewis
1341 Blue necklace left
On a charred chair
Tells that Beauty
Was startled there.

'Raiders' Dawn'

1342 If I should go away,
Beloved, do not say
'He has forgotten me.'
For you abide,
A singing rib within my dreaming side;
You always stay.

'Post-script: for Gweno'

1343 I have begun to die
And the guns' implacable silence
Is my black interim, my youth and age,
In the flower of fury, the folded poppy
Night.

'The Sentry'

1344 I watch the clouded years
Rune the rough foreheads of these moody
hills,
This wet evening, in a lost age.

'The Mountain over Aberdare'

Saunders Lewis
1345 On a handy lamp-post, the hag [Wales]
hanged herself with her rope.
We saw her legs turning in the rain,
And we knew by her white gloves and
their smell of camphor
That she sprang from the old land.
She was buried non-denominationally by
the BBC
On the imperial wave-length.*

'Golygfa mewn Caffe' (trans. Joseph P. Clancy)

Iorwerth C. Peate
1346 On the survival of the Welsh language –
the strong link that connects us with our
heritage – the personality of Wales
depends.*

Diwylliant Gwerin Cymru (1942)

Keidrych Rhys
1347   Lightning
Is different in Wales.

'Youth'

1348 I know no love for disembodied principles,
improbable tales.
The strength of the common man was
always the strength of Wales.

'Tragic Guilt'

— 1943 —

Winston Churchill MP
1349 I prefer to be a little backward on that
matter.

on appointing a Secretary of State for Wales
speech in House of Commons, 1943

Idris Davies
1350 What will you do with your shovel, Dai,
And your pick and your sledge and your
spike,
And what will you do with your leisure,
man,
Now that you're out on strike?

The Angry Summer (1943)

1351 Mrs Evans fach, you want butter again.
How will you pay for it now, little woman,
With your husband out on strike, and full
Of the fiery language?

1352 High summer on the mountains
And on the clover leas,
And on the local sidings,
And on the rhubarb leaves.

Brass bands in all the valleys
Blaring defiant tunes,
Crowds, acclaiming carnival,
Prize pigs and wooden spoons.

1353 O the lands of Usk are dear
And all the woods of Wye,
And the magic shores of Dyfed
Beneath the summer sky.

But the blackened slopes of Rhymney
I saw with childhood's eye,
These shall be dearer, dearer,
When I must turn to die.

1354 In the square brown chapel below the hill
Dai's frail mother is deep in prayer,
A broken old mother who bears no ill
To anyone anywhere.

1355 And here we come tramping and singing
Out of the valleys of strife,
Into the sunlit cornlands
Begging the bread of life.

1356 In the Admiral Nelson the lads are
together,
And Lizzie the barmaid is rippling with
fun,
And on Saturday night the beer is good.

1357 Let's go to Barry Island, Maggie fach,
And give all the kids one day by the sea.

1358 Who loves not the land of his birth
Should hide himself in the earth.
Who loves not these derelict vales
Is no true son of eternal Wales.

1359 Send out your homing pigeons, Dai,
Your blue-grey pigeons, hard as nails. . .

Go out, pigeons bach, and do what Dai
tells you.

1360 You men of Gwent and Gwalia
From Neath to Ebbw Vale,

Sing us a song of triumph
Out of a Celtic tale . . .

You tenors from Treorchy,
Basses from Abercwmboi,
Sing to the hills and valleys,
Rouse all the people to joy.

Rhys Davies

1361 A man is greater than his country.
Therefore, I do not exist for Wales, but
Wales exists for me.

'From my Notebook'
in *Wales* (no. 2, Oct. 1943)

1362 Amateurs are the curse of art in Wales.

1363 Beware of Welsh sentimentality. It is of the
worst kind, but seductive.

1364 Directly a man becomes self-conscious
about being Welsh, he ceases to be a
Welshman.

1365 A Welshman's horse is always descended
from the beast ridden by Llywelyn the
Great.

1366 There is only one abiding classic: Wales.

Gwynfor Evans

1367 For every minute the present Parliament
gives Wales, the Welsh Parliament would
give a month.

'Rebuild from the Foundations'
in *Wales* (no. 2, Oct. 1943)

1368 Wales shares with Estonia the inestimable
advantage of being small enough to be
properly governed.

1369 The truth is that Wales will have to fight
long and furiously for any kind of
decentralisation.

James Griffiths MP

1370 The decentralisation from Whitehall
should be canalised into the creation of a
Welsh Office, with a Secretary of State of
Cabinet rank. It is along these lines that
real hope lies for the largest measure of
effective self-government in Wales.

'Wales, after the War'
in *Wales* (no. 1, July 1943)

1371 Wales must not beg for bread. It must
claim the right to live.

Llewelyn Wyn Griffith

1372 Over a great part of Wales, but not
everywhere, there are places which have
ceased to be Welsh and have not become
English.

'A Note on "Anglo-Welsh" '
in *Wales* (no. 1, July 1943)

D. Gwenallt Jones

1373 Years later, my father's body came home
after he had been burnt to death by
molten metal, and that unnecessarily.
When in the funeral service, the minister
said that it was God's will, I cursed his
sermon and his God with all the haulier's
swear-words I knew, and when they sang
the hymn at the graveside, I sang in my
heart *The Red Flag.**

in *Credaf* (ed. J. E. Meredith, 1943)

Glyn Jones

1374 The path of the Anglo-Welsh writer is a
hard one, poor dab.

review of Idris Davies, *The Angry Summer*
in *Wales* (no. 1, July 1943)

Alun Lewis

1375 The world is much larger than England,
isn't it? I'll never be just English or just
Welsh again.

letter to his parents, 7 April 1943

1376 When I come back I shall always tackle
my writing through Welsh life and ways of
thought: it's my only way.

letter to his parents, 23 Nov. 1943

1377 If I could live my life over again one of the
things I'd do would be to learn Welsh; to
do an English degree at Oxford or
London; a third, to work underground for
a year; and fourth, of course, to marry
Gweno again.

Keidrych Rhys

1378 For Wales the permanent medium of
literature should always be Welsh. Our
separate identity ceases for us when the
language ceases. Then what is the purpose
of Anglo-Welsh literature? One purpose is

this: it is not that we want to show the English in a small country way that we can beat them at their own language (that attitude is responsible largely for the growing gulf between the Welsh and Anglo-Welsh); but that we want to make them aware of Welsh differences and ventures, and that English is the only medium in which this can be done. A zealous group of Anglo-Welsh writers, properly co-ordinated, should be valuable agents in securing sympathy in the better English minds for Welsh cultural ideals and aims. For we are going to need sympathy, even if we haven't any today.

editorial
in *Wales* (no. 2, Oct. 1943)

Ben Bowen Thomas

1379 When E. T. John stood up in Parliament on 14 March 1914 to propose a measure of self-government for Wales, the few who were present listened to his voice as that of one who had risen from the dead.*

'Agwedd ar Wleidyddiaeth Cymru 1900–14'
in *Y Llenor* (vol. 22, nos. 3 and 4, Autumn–Winter 1943)

1380 He [Lloyd George] was the embodiment of the radical spirit for the Welsh people and the success of his career became synonymous for them with the progress of their nation.

Dylan Thomas

1381 This sea town was my world; outside, a *strange* Wales, coal-pitted, mountained, river-run, full, so far as I knew, of choirs and football teams and sheep and story-book tall black hats, and red flannel petticoats, moved about its business which was none of mine.

'Reminiscences of Childhood'
broadcast 15 Feb. 1943
Quite Early One Morning (1954)

Clough Williams-Ellis

1382 It is the history, folk-lore, and legend attached to a place that interests the Welshman far more than the place itself. After the green hillock named in honour of some fabled princess has been crowned with a café, he will sing about the lady's

exploits just as melodiously and movingly as before the outrage was committed.

'Building in Welsh'
in *Wales* (no. 2, Oct. 1943)

1383 At the moment I can recall no country town in the whole Principality in which one single native building put up during my own lifetime, looks as though it were the legitimate offspring of the architect.

1384 The gross and heartless way in which our lovely old buildings have been subjected to every kind of indignity and our virgin countryside crudely outraged by exhibitionist obscenities, would make one believe that the Welsh were a peculiarly brutal race much addicted to rape and sadistic cruelty, when in fact these horrid results spring merely from ignorance strangely coupled with a spirituality that must surely be not a little warped and ailing.

— **1944** —

John Betjeman

1385 The interesting fact about all Celtic countries to us who live in England is how each country has put up with the English.

review of Rhys Davies, *The Story of Wales*
in *Wales* (no. 3, Jan. 1944)

Aneurin Bevan MP

1386 My colleagues, all of them members of the Miners' Federation of Great Britain, have no special solution for the Welsh coal industry which is not a solution for the whole of the mining industry of Great Britain. There is no Welsh problem.

speech in House of Commons, 17 Oct. 1944

E. C. Cobb MP

1387 When I talk about England, I always include the suburbs, Wales and Scotland.

speech in House of Commons, 20 July 1944

Huw T. Edwards

1388 I want self-government for Wales, but I want it for rather different reasons from the Welsh Nationalist Party.

'What I Want for Wales'
in *Wales* (no. 3, Jan. 1944)

1389 I want to see my Nation ridding itself of the cant and hypocrisy associated with its religious life, and I want to see at least seventy-five per cent of the places of worship in Wales pulled down or used in a more effective way.

1390 I say again that if we had the courage to forget our Party tags and labels and got together to hammer out a progressive policy for Wales, that the matters which keep us apart today would melt away.

1391 I want to see at least twenty-five per cent of the people of the Rhondda Valleys compulsorily removed to new localities.

Caradoc Evans
1392 Cant and humbug and hypocrisy and capel belong to Wales and no one writing about Wales can dodge them.

'Self-Portrait'
in *Wales* (no. 3, Jan. 1944)

1393 I do not think my stuff has done Wales any good. It is not in me to do that. It is not in anyone.

1394 Somehow I came to read Genesis again and when I was about the middle of it, 'Jiw-Jiw, this is English writing,' I said to me. On a Saturday night I went to the Hammersmith Palace and there I saw Marie Lloyd, and 'Jiw-Jiw', I said to me, 'she tells a story not by what she says but by what she does not.' I kept up Genesis and Marie Lloyd.

Nigel Heseltine
1395 The absence of a native tradition of drama in Wales and Ireland left the colonizers a clear field.

'The National Theatre'
in *Wales* (no. 5, Autumn 1944)

T. Rowland Hughes
1396 Keep your bloody chips!*

the eponymous hero of *William Jones* (1944)

Glyn Jones
1397 Here I stand, a middle-aged master.
When my heart went to stone and my
    world to disaster
I repaired my glasses with surgical plaster.

'The Dream of Jake Hopkins'

John Cowper Powys
1398 The Welsh are certainly the most emotional race I have ever lived among.

'Wales and America'
in *Wales* (no. 4, June 1944)

Keidrych Rhys
1399 When it comes to Art we are, as a nation, a hundred years behind the times.

editorial
in *Wales* (no. 3, Jan. 1944)

Robert Richards MP
1400 Wales is a nation and a community which in its tradition, history, language and literature is quite distinct from England. There are many people in Wales who are more concerned about the future of Welsh culture than about the economic life of Wales.

speech in House of Commons, 1944

George Santayana
1401 On landing, an ungainly ridiculous side of this world, and especially of Britain, became suddenly present: we had plumped on a Sunday into a British Nonconformist industrial town [Cardiff]. Ugliness and desolation could not be more constitutional.

on calling at Cardiff, while emigrating from Spain to the USA, 1872
Persons and Places (1944)

Lord Howard de Walden
1402 There seems to be some demand for a National Theatre in Wales. I wonder why?

'Towards a Welsh Theatre'
in *Wales* (no. 4, June 1944)

D. J. Williams
1403 Nationalism is a terrific spiritual force, for good or bad.*

'Y Ddau Genedlaetholdeb yng Nghymru'
in *Y Llenor* (vol. 23, nos. 3 and 4, Autumn/ Winter 1944)

1404 Having lived for four hundred years on a foreign diet, the people have lost their health and their taste for the natural sustenance of their own country.*

1405 The only thing of real importance to Wales is – is she of real importance to herself?*

George Woodcock

1406 Certainly, let us have a free Wales, but let it be populated by free Welsh. Let us have Wales for the Welsh, but not for Welsh politicians, Welsh owners, or the Welsh old men who still govern mental life through the chapels, the schools, and the universities.

letter to editor
in *Wales* (no. 5, Autumn 1944)

— 1945 —

Anonymous

1407 Wales is a small nation which, through increasing difficulties, has preserved her language and cultural life through the centuries. The true freedom of Wales depends not only on political control of her own life, but on economic control as well. True freedom for Wales would be the result and product of a Socialist Britain and only under such conditions could self-government in Wales be an effective and secure guardian of the life of the nation.

manifesto of the Labour Party at General Election, 1945

Winston Churchill MP

1408 As a man of action, resource, and creative energy, he [Lloyd George] stood, when at his zenith, without a rival. His name is a household word throughout our Commonwealth of Nations. He was the greatest Welshman which that unconquerable race has produced since the age of the Tudors. Much of his work abides, some of it will grow greatly in the future, and those who come after us will find the pillars of his life's toil upstanding, massive and indestructible.

speech in House of Commons, 1945

Idris Davies

1409 I lost my native language
For the one the Saxon spake
By going to school by order
For education's sake.

'I was Born in Rhymney'

1410 Poets are dangerous men to have in chapel,

And it is bad enough in chapel as it is
With all the quarrelling over the organ
and the deacons.

'The Lay Preacher Ponders'

1411 O singers, singers in a thousand years to be . . .
Remember a little of Dai and Tonypandy,
Dai and his Martha and his fireside,
Dai and his lamp in the depths of the earth,
Dai and his careless lilting tongue,
Dai and his heart of gold.

'Tonypandy'

Gwyn Jones

1412 Welsh Region [of the BBC] has lacked someone willing and able to thump his fist on the table and say that they just won't stand for it.

editorial
in *The Welsh Review* (vol. 4, no. 3, Sept. 1945)

Alun Lewis

1413 So we must say Goodbye, my darling,
And go, as lovers go, for ever;
Tonight remains, to pack and fix on labels
And make an end of lying down together.

'Goodbye'

Saunders Lewis

1414 None but a nationalist can interpret the history of a nation.*

'Cyfnod y Tuduriaid'
Ysgrifau Dydd Mercher (1945)

Thomas Parry

1415 One might suggest, perhaps with some qualms, that it would not have been wholly undesirable had the supple language of free verse been used when translating the Bible. There would be today less of a gulf between the literary and the spoken language and it would perhaps be easier to write dialogue in plays and novels.*

Hanes Llenyddiaeth Gymraeg hyd 1900 (1945)

John Frederick Rees

1416 The Welsh can claim, not indeed to be the original inhabitants of Britain, but to have invaded it six or seven centuries before the English did.

'Address to Convocation of the University of Ceylon'
in *The Welsh Review* (vol. 4, no. 4, Dec. 1945)

Howard Thomas

1417 What broadcasting has failed to do up to now has been to let the ordinary Welsh people be themselves on the radio.

'The Welsh Voice'
in *The Welsh Review* (vol. 4, no. 2, June 1945)

1418 The Welsh voice, curiously enough for tones of such musical repute, has never yet made an impression with broadcasting listeners. On the radio the Welsh voice has some cold, reedy quality which fails to engender intimacy between speaker and hearer. In twenty and more years of broadcasting there has been no Welsh voice which has won the deep friendship and goodwill of the English.

1419 In radio drama, as in theatre and cinema, the most mystic side of the Welsh character has come in for emphasis. A jovial Welshman never roams into a play about the Welsh, and a listener who forms his impression of the Welsh from the radio continues to believe that Wales is a nation of broody, temperamental and slightly unbalanced people.

R. S. Thomas

1420 The land is sacred and the people who live close to it belong there and must be kept there, and some who have left must be induced to return. It is useless to settle strangers there.

'The Depopulation of the Welsh Hill Couuntry'
in *Wales* (no. 7, Summer 1945)

— 1946 —

Anonymous

1421 For all his sincerity and singleness of purpose, his personality forbids that he [Saunders Lewis] shall ever be a leader of the people. His intellectual pride, his icy contempt for those who do not walk beside, or behind, him, his lack of the common touch, and the authoritarian taint in politics and religion now associated with his name, these have set

him aside from modern, democratic Wales. The personal tragedy of the man is that while earnestly desiring to unite Welshmen, he succeeds only in exacerbating and sundering them. He would give his life for Wales, but cannot give Welshmen his charity: he has become the single greatest obstacle to his party's chance of becoming a party of the Welsh people. Yet history will find him his place, as a pioneer spirit and a patriot who never flinched from private hurt or public odium. Rejected by his people as their political leader, he may be after all the apostle of their new awakening.

in *The Welsh Review* (vol. 5, no. 4, Winter 1946)

Aneurin Bevan MP

1422 There has been too great a tendency to identify Welsh culture with Welsh speaking . . . What some of us are afraid of is that, if this psychosis is developed too far, we shall see in some of the English-speaking parts of Wales a vast majority tyrannised over by a few Welsh-speaking people in Cardiganshire . . . The whole of the Civil Service of Wales would be eventually provided from those small pockets of Welsh-speaking, Welsh-writing zealots and the vast majority of Welshmen would be denied participation in the government of their own country.

speech in House of Commons, 28 Oct. 1946

James Cameron

1423 If the working-man is the salt of the earth, the Welsh working-man is that salt ground to a sharp, astringent powder. He is born to a tradition of the hardest of grim punishing labour. He has the fortune, too, to be born to a kind of tradition of the spirit. Even at his lowest economic ebb, he has that thing which takes him through to much of his choir-practice and debating clubs, that gives him the impetus to read.

in *The Daily Express* (14 Nov. 1946)

W. J. Gruffydd

1424 We are by now well used to hearing the word 'national' coming from the lips of men who have never been over-energetic on behalf of Welsh nationalism in any other way.*

editorial
in *Y Llenor* (vol. 25, nos. 1 and 2, Spring–
Summer 1946)

Griffith Hartwell Jones

1425 Some professors have forgotten that the
University was created to serve Wales, not
Wales to serve the University, and many of
our University authorities have seemed to
be unduly anxious to turn Welshmen into
Englishmen.

A Celt Looks at the World (1946)

Gwyn Jones

1426 The Welsh members would get up and say
their pieces, and the Hon. Gent. from
Ebbw Vale [Aneurin Bevan] would get up
and say his piece, the House would not
divide, and that would be that . . . The
great day was over, and the Red Dragon
stabled for another twelve months, and not
one drop of blood on its nail-less claws.

of Welsh Day at Westminster
editorial
in *The Welsh Review* (vol. 5, no. 4, Winter 1946)

1427 To our nostrils Conservative and Labour
complacency about Wales have much the
same smell.

Thomas Jones (of Rhymney)

1428 We have today a large measure of self-
government in our own hands. Why are
we not better governed? Mainly because
we are indifferent or incompetent, not
because we are under the heel of England.
That is the fact, and because it is
unpleasant we don't want to look at it. We
want to dodge it, we want to find a
scapegoat.

The Native Never Returns (1946)

1429 It is no good trying to preserve the
language and the Welsh tradition by a
political device like Dominion status. It
will certainly antagonise as many as it
conciliates. The past cannot be effaced and
Wales will never be able to return to the
narrow enclosed life it led of old. We shall
not see in the lifetime of anyone now living
the Welsh language as widely spoken in
Monmouthshire and Glamorgan as it is
today in Cardiganshire.

1430 For dear as Wales is to many of us there
are some things that are dearer to us,

dearer to us than the preservation of its
language, dearer to us than Dominion
status, dearer to us than a return to the
Middle Ages.

Dylan Thomas

1431 The position – if poets must have positions,
other than upright – of the poet born in
Wales or of Welsh parentage and writing
poems in English, is today made by many
people unnecessarily, and trivially, difficult.

'Welsh Poets'
broadcast 5 Jan. 1946
Quite Early One Morning (1954)

1432 Not for the proud man apart
From the raging moon I write
On these spindrift pages
Nor for the towering dead
With their nightingales and psalms
But for the lovers, their arms
Round the griefs of the ages,
Who pay no praise or wages
Nor heed my craft or art.

'In my Craft or Sullen Art'

1433 It was my thirtieth year to heaven.

'Poem in October'

1434 O may my heart's truth
Still be sung
On this high hill in a year's turning.

1435 After the first death, there is no other.

'A refusal to mourn the death, by fire, of a child
in London'

1436 Now as I was young and easy under the
apple boughs
About the lilting house and happy as the
grass was green,
The night above the dingle starry,
Time let me hail and climb
Golden in the heydays of his eyes,
And honoured among wagons I was prince
of the apple towns
And once below a time I lordly had the
trees and leaves
Trail with daisies and barley
Down the rivers of the windfall light.

'Fern Hill'

1437 Oh as I was young and easy in the mercy
of his means,

Time held me green and dying
Though I sang in my chains like the sea.

R. S. Thomas

1438 We have to face the possibility not, I think,
of the disappearance of Welsh, but of its
inadequacy as a medium for expressing the
complex phantasmagoria of modern life.

'Some Contemporary Scottish Writing'
in *Wales* (vol. 6, no. 3, 1946)

1439 It is true that the Welsh have a good
reputation as a democratic people, but in
my opinion they show all the weaknesses
that belong to democracy.*

'Arian a Swydd'
in *Y Fflam* (vol. 1, no. 1, 1946)

1440 As long as there is food and drink,
greyhounds and cinemas, the majority of
our people do not care what government is
in power.*

1441 To the artist, then, a sense of Welsh
Nationhood should be consistent with a
very definite attitude to life and affairs,
namely the constant realization that he
lives in or belongs to a country of great
age, that by geography and tradition has
developed an individual way of life, and
that his chief duty as an artist is to
beautify, to purify and to enlarge that way
of life.

reply to questionnaire
in *Wales*(no. 23, Autumn 1946)

1442 There is something frightening in the
vacancy of his mind.

'A Peasant'

1443 Yet this is your prototype, who, season by
season
Against siege of rain and the wind's
attrition,
Preserves his stock, an impregnable fortress
Not to be stormed even in death's
confusion.
Remember him, then, for he, too, is a
winner of wars,
Enduring like a tree under the curious
stars.

1444 Don't be taken in
By stinking garments or an aimless grin;

He also is human, and the same small star,
That lights you homeward, has inflamed
his mind
With the old hunger, born of his kind.

'Affinity'

A. W. Wade-Evans

1445 Not since Glyndŵr has Wales produced a
political leader except such as proved
duds, whom to blame is easy but a
mistake, for the onus always lies on the
nation itself.

'Anglo-Welsh'
in *Wales* (no. 23, Autumn 1946)

Vernon Watkins

1446 I think Wales should be proud of being the
humblest country in the world.

reply to questionnaire
in *Wales* (no. 23, Autumn 1946)

— **1947** —

B. L. Coombes

1447 Many a working-class writer has been
ruined by going away from the only life he
has known anything about, and trying to
live on his mental capital. You won't catch
me leaving my valley.

radio talk, 1947
in *Wales on the Wireless* (ed. Patrick Hannan,
1986)

Arthur Horner

1448 I am a Welshman with an international
accent.

attributed
in anonymous profile
in *The Welsh Review* (vol. 6, no. 1, Spring 1947)

T. Gwynn Jones

1449 Blessed is a world that sings,
Gentle are its songs.*

in programme of Llangollen International
Eisteddfod, 1947

Jack Jones

1450 In bed I am and in bed I shall be now. I
am not getting up any more. Satisfied I
am. Now the world is yours. I am not
flinging it at you or spitting it in your eye

or anything like that. In the best spirit I
am leaving it for you to try and make it
better than we were able to make it. It is a
grand world and to have known a little of
it I shall regard as a great privilege for as
long as I can breathe and remember . . .
Yes, friends, the world is yours now.

Off to Philadelphia in the Morning (1947)

William Jones
1451 Young fellow from Llŷn, who's the girl of
    your heart,
    You who wander so late in the evening
    apart?*

'Y Llanc Ifanc o Lŷn' (trans. Harri Webb)

Rhys Lewis
1452 So the coal mines now belong to the
    nation.

'Report on Wales'
in *The Welsh Review* (vol. 6, no. 1, Spring 1947)

Herbert Morrison MP
1453 The device of political expediency has
    served the Labour Party well in Wales.

speech in House of Commons, 1947

John Cowper Powys
1454 One cannot help suspecting that a race as
    ancient as this – whose ways and customs
    still retain memories of the golden age
    when Saturn, or some megalithic
    philosopher under that name, ruled in
    Crete, and the Great Mother was
    worshipped without the shedding of blood
    – must have some secret clues to the
    mystery of life, some magical ways of
    taking life, simply from having lived so
    long in the same hills and valleys, such as
    have not been revealed, and could not be
    revealed, to more recently arrived peoples.

Obstinate Cymric (1947)

1455 The Welsh National spirit has had to bank
    itself up in the Welsh language for want of
    being able to express itself politically.

A. G. Prys-Jones
1456 This is the way the Romans came
    Steadily, steadily over the hill,
    This is the way the Romans came
    And if you listen, you'll hear them still.

'Roman Road'

Dylan Thomas
1457 Above medium height for Wales, I mean,
    he's five foot six and a half.

'Return Journey'
broadcast 15 June 1947
Quite Early One Morning (1954)

Gwyn Thomas
1458 Women, to me, never seemed to be more
    than just me over again. A bit quicker to
    become mothers, I being a man, and a bit
    slower to use the vote, but with no more
    difference than that.

The Alone to the Alone (1947)

Vernon Watkins
1459 When I was born on Amman hill
    A dark bird crossed the sun.
    Sharp on the floor the shadow fell;
    I was the youngest son.

    And when I went to the County School
    I worked in a shaft of light.
    In the wood of the desk I cut my name:
    Dai for Dynamite.

'The Collier'

— 1948 —

Aneurin Bevan MP
1460 No amount of cajolery, and no attempts at
    ethical and social seduction, can eradicate
    from my heart a deep burning hatred for
    the Tory Party . . . So far as I am
    concerned, they are lower than vermin.

speech at Manchester, 4 July 1948

T. S. Eliot
1461 It would be no gain whatever for English
    culture, for the Welsh, Scots and Irish to
    become indistinguishable from Englishmen
    – what *would* happen, of course, is that we
    should all become indistinguishable
    featureless 'Britons', at a lower level of
    culture than any of the separate regions.
    On the contrary, it is of great advantage
    for English culture to be constantly
    influenced from Scotland, Ireland and
    Wales.

'Unity and Diversity: the Region'
Notes Towards the Definition of Culture (1948)

1462 [Welsh] must continue to be a literary
    language. If it is no longer cultivated . . .

the Welsh will be less Welsh; and their poets will cease to have any contribution to make to English literature beyond their individual genius.

Storm Jameson

1463 Wales is easy to reach and not easy to know.

foreword to Kate Roberts, *A Summer Day* (1948)

A. G. Prys-Jones

1464 The road to old St David's
Is the white road of the blest,
The roving road which gave the vales
The pilgrims' songs, the palmers' tales,
When all the wandering roads of Wales
Went winding to the west.

'A Song of the Pilgrim Road'

R. S. Thomas

1465 Towns are not typical of Wales, they are a manifestation of alien influences and the sooner they are scattered, the better.*

'Dau Gapel'
in *Y Fflam* (May 1948)

— 1949 —

Martin Charlesworth

1466 The history of an organised Welsh people begins with an act of recognition by this Spanish-born governor, Magnus Maximus [Macsen Wledig].

The Lost Province (1949)

S. O. Davies MP

1467 Unemployment was the evil that drove nearly half-a-million of our people from Wales between the two wars. It is the evil that breaks up our homes and our Welsh communities, and destroys our culture and our sense of nationhood.

radio talk, 1949
in *Wales on the Wireless* (ed. Patrick Hannan, 1986)

W. J. Gruffydd MP

1468 I was elected to the House as a Liberal, which means, as things are at present, that I can be eclectic in my politics.

'Wales in Parliament'
in *The Welsh Anvil* (vol. 1, no. 1, April 1949)

1469 There is hardly a member of the present Government or of the Opposition who does not regard any insistence on the special claims and problems of Wales as an intolerable nuisance.

T. Gwynn Jones

1470 A pacifist with the accent on the *fist*.*

of his own pacifism
quoted by E. Tegla Davies in 'Atgofion'
in *Y Llenor* (vol. 28, no. 2, Summer 1949)

1471 A people who have neither the sense of craftsmanship nor the honour nor the backbone nor courage enough to sin at all bravely.*

of the Welsh
quoted by John Eilian Jones

Lyn Joshua and James Harper

1472 We'll keep a welcome in the hillsides,
We'll keep a welcome in the vales,
This land you knew will still be singing
When you come home again to Wales.

This land of song will keep a welcome
And with a love that never fails,
We'll kiss away each hour of hiraeth
When you come home again to Wales.

'We'll Keep a Welcome in the Hillsides'

Saunders Lewis

1473 Patriotism is a splendid thing. The man without it is less than a man.*

'Yr Angen am fod yn Siriol'
in *Baner ac Amserau Cymru* (23 March 1949)

1474 A delicacy, a luxury, something to enjoy in leisure hours, social entertainment, that is what religion is in Nonconformist Wales today. And in so far as the Welsh language and Welsh culture and Welsh traditions are all tied in with this religious life, and in so far as they have no other foundation, they will die with the religion that is dying.*

in *Baner ac Amserau Cymru* (8 June 1949)

T. H. Parry-Williams

1475 Why should I give a hang about Wales?
    It's by a mere fluke of fate
That I live in its patch. On a map it does
    not rate

Higher than a scrap of earth in a back
    corner,
And a bit of a bother to those who believe
    in order.

And who is it lives in this spot, tell me that,
Who but the dregs of society? Please, cut it
    out,

This endless clatter of oneness and country
    and race:
You can get plenty of these, without
    Wales, any place.

I've long since had it with listening to the
    croon
Of the Cymry, indeed, forever moaning
    their tune.*

'Hon' (trans. Joseph P. Clancy)

1476 Here's Snowdon and its crew; here's the
    land, bleak and bare,
Here's the lake and river and crag, and
    look, over there,

The house where I was born. But see,
    between the earth and the heavens,
All through the place there are voices and
    apparitions.

I begin to totter somewhat, and I confess,
There comes over me, so it seems, a sort of
    faintness;

And I feel the claws of Wales tear at my
    heart.
God help me, I can't get away from this
    spot.*

John Frederick Rees
1477 Those who seek flame-bearers of Welsh
nationhood are apt to burn their fingers.

'The Problem of Wales'
in *The Nineteenth Century and After* (April 1949)

John Reith
1478 Welsh nationalists were impervious to
reason or fact where broadcasting was
concerned.

Into the Wind (1949)

Sir Donald Somerville
1479 England includes Wales, but does not
include Scotland.

statement in House of Commons, 27 Jan. 1949

Dylan Thomas
1480 I know in London a Welsh hairdresser
who has striven so vehemently to abolish

his accent that he sounds like a man
speaking with the Elgin Marbles in his
mouth.

'Wales and the Artist'
broadcast 24 Oct. 1949
Quite Early One Morning (1954)

— 1950 —

Dannie Abse
1481 A man with no roots is lost
like the darkness in the forest.

'Roots'

Anonymous
1482 Our aim will be to steel the will of our
people for the reconquest of Wales, for a
free and independent Welsh People, for the
establishment of the Sovereign
Independent Democratic Republic of
Wales.

editorial
in *The Welsh Republican* (vol. 1, no. 1, Aug. 1950)

1483 If there is one modern country in Europe
where the so-called 'common people' form
the genuine life of the people, that country
is Wales.

editorial
in *The Welsh Republican* (vol. 1, no. 2, Oct.–Nov.
1950)

1484 It is an insult to every Welshman to have
flown in his country the flag of the 'Union'
effected by England, enforced by England
and maintained by England, for England's
gain, and Wales's extinction.

'What is the Union Jack?'
in *The Welsh Republican* (vol. 1, no. 2, Oct.–Nov.
1950)

Ifor Davies MP
1485 Commercially the Welsh language is dead
and worthless.

reported in *Western Mail* (5 Jan. 1950)

Ithel Davies
1486 We serve neither King nor Kremlin.

'Korea'
in *The Welsh Republican* (vol. 1, no. 1, Aug. 1950)

Llewelyn Wyn Griffith
1487 I feel very strongly that if in the next ten

years we do not make it possible for Welsh painters to live and paint in Wales, our claim to full dignity of stature in the world of culture cannot be maintained.

'The Visual Arts in Wales'
in *The Welsh Anvil* (no. 2, Aug. 1950)

1488 The Welsh eye needs to be educated.

The Welsh (1950)

1489 What Wales needs now, above all else, is a greater measure of responsibility for its own future.

1490 However numerous their faults and shortcomings, let it always be remembered of the Welsh that the most widely popular event of the year in Wales is a festival devoted to the Arts, and that in it the highest form of tribute is reserved for poets. There is nothing quite like it anywhere else in the world.

Richard Hughes
1491 There has been a distinct shift in Wales from *being* a peculiar nation to *saying* that we are a peculiar nation. Instead of talking Welsh as a matter of course, we now talk about being Welsh.

radio talk, 1950
in *Wales on the Wireless* (ed. Patrick Hannan, 1986)

Saunders Lewis
1492 In destroying a society industrialism must of necessity destroy a language.*

'Dyfodol Llenyddiaeth'
in *Baner ac Amserau Cymru* (7 June 1950)

Kate Roberts
1493 The influence of the BBC on the children of Wales is baneful.*

in *Baner ac Amserau Cymru* (28 March 1950)

A. W. Wade-Evans
1494 The inauguration of Welsh national history towards the end of the fourth century was attended by an ebullition of Roman feeling which persisted among the Britons of Wales for centuries.

'Prolegomena to a Study of Early Welsh History'
in *The Historical Basis of Welsh Nationalism* (ed. D. M. Lloyd, 1950)

— **1951** —
Anonymous
1495 Before the career of Thomas Jones, criticism is respectfully dumb.

'Guilty Men'
in *The Welsh Republican* (vol. 1, no. 4, Feb.–March 1951)

1496 Dear Sir, Your postcard complaining about the omission of the Welsh news on Sundays has been passed to us. It has been decided that there is not sufficient purely Welsh news available on Sundays to justify broadcasting a bulletin.

letter from the Welsh Home Service of the BBC quoted in *The Welsh Republican* (vol. 1, no. 5, April–May 1951)

1497 For a Welsh army there can be only one possible enemy.

'England Exposed!'
in *The Welsh Republican* (vol. 1, no. 6, June–July 1951)

1498 To discuss the Conservative Party in relation to Welsh affairs is normally something of an extravagance.

editorial
in *The Welsh Republican* (vol. 2, no. 3, Dec. 1951–Jan. 1952)

1499 A bookless people is a rootless people, doomed to lose its identity and its power of contributing to the common fund of civilization . . . If the published language goes, the language itself as a cultural medium will soon follow; and if Welsh goes, a bastardized vernacular will take its place.

The Ready Report on Publishing in Wales (1951)

David Bell
1500 Parochialism has been at least as much an evil in Wales as Anglicization, and local boy worship is an evil everywhere.

'Contemporary Welsh Painting'
in *The Welsh Anvil* (no. 3, July 1951)

1501 Wales has never had a wealthy, urban civilization, and it is unprofitable to suppose by claiming a few painters of Welsh birth and parentage as Welsh that there has ever been such a thing as Welsh painting.

Cliff Bere

1502 Our exhortation to the people of Wales is to make use of every means they can to precipitate the crisis of England. In that crisis is the dawn of the new day that awaits the Welsh Nation.

'The Way Forward'
in *The Welsh Republican* (vol. 2, no. 2, Oct.–Nov. 1951)

Raymond Garlick

1503 Genuine English culture is rare in Wales, and rarest of all in the English-speaking areas.

editorial
in *Dock Leaves* (Michaelmas 1951)

W. J. Gruffydd

1504 Well, the harm has been done and I think it useless for Caernarfon and Aberystwyth to protest.*

on the elevation of Cardiff to the status of capital of Wales
editorial
in *Y Llenor* (vol. 3, no. 2, Summer 1951)

Cledwyn Hughes MP

1505 If there were six hundred angels in Westminster, they would be English angels, and they would be unable to understand how Wales thinks.*

in speech at Parliament for Wales meeting at Caernarfon
reported in *Y Cymro* (16 March 1951)

D. Gwenallt Jones

1506 On the land of Esgeir-ceir and the fields of Tir-bach,
They have planted the saplings to be trees of the third war.*

'Rhydcymerau' (trans. Anthony Conran)

1507 And by now nothing is there but trees,
Their impudent roots sucking the ancient soil:
Trees where neighbourhood was,
A forest where once there were farms,
The debased English tongue of the South where once
Men made poems and talked theology,

Foxes barking where once were the cries of children and lambs.
And in the dark at the heart of it
Is the den of the English Minotaur;
And on branches, as if on crosses,
Skeletons of bards, deacons, ministers, Sunday School teachers,
Whitening in the sun,
And washed by the rain and dried by the wind.*

1508 The span of the Cross is greater by far
Than their Puritanism and their Socialism,
And the fist of Karl Marx has a place in his Church:
Farm and furnace are one together in his estate,
The humanity of the pit, the piety of the country:
Tawe and Tywi, Canaan and Wales, earth and heaven.*

'Sir Forgannwg a Sir Gaerfyrddin' (trans. Ned Thomas and B. S. Johnson)

1509 With his fiftieth birthday behind him, a man sees with fair clarity
The people and surroundings that made him what he is,
And the steel ropes that tether me strongest to these things
In a village of the South, are the graves in two cemeteries.*

'Y Meirwon' (trans. Anthony Conran)

1510 Our Utopia vanished from the top of Gellionnen,
Our abstract humanity's classless, defrontiered reign,
And today nothing is left at the deep root of the mind
Save family and neighbourhood, man's sacrifice and pain.*

1511 Idleness a sour dog on every street corner,
Workers tramp shadowless from place to place;
There has come to the town's Eldorado this finish:
Neighbourhood scuttled, and break-up of village,
Roots of the South, a culture, a civilized grace.*

'Y Dirwasgiad' (trans. Anthony Conran)

Thomas Jones (of Rhymney)

1512 We are intemperate and inflammable, but neither boycotters nor moonlighters; neither cruel nor murderous, but slanderous within the bounds of the law and compromisers in the gate.

Welsh Broth (1951)

1513 I was able as a Welshman to assess to some measure the magnitude of Anglo-Saxon blunders in dealing with Ireland.

1514 In North Wales the social structure was better balanced than [in the industrial south]. Everybody enjoyed more elbow-room. It had rarely been necessary to order troops into the area to quell or shoot a turbulent mob.

1515 The home of Gwendoline and Margaret Davies [at Gregynog] is unique among country houses in Wales and I know of no parallel in England.

1516 We are witnessing the funeral of a culture which no longer commands allegiance.

radio talk, 1951
in *Wales on the Wireless* (ed. Patrick Hannan, 1986)

Mair Saunders Lewis

1517 The prevalence of Pacifism in Wales is but another manifestation of a slave mentality.

in *The Welsh Republican* (Aug.–Sept. 1951)

1518 Only too often has a Welshman's patriotism been a simmering stew of pacifism, sectarianism, teetotalism and chronic respectability.

Saunders Lewis

1519 Everyone will agree with this principle: safeguarding and ensuring the well-being of the Welsh language is more important for the nation of the Welsh than the winning of a Parliament for Wales . . . For the language can ensure the continuance of the nation; a Parliament cannot do that without the language.*

in *Baner ac Amserau Cymru* (20 June 1951)

1520 Enmity towards the Welsh language . . . as an official language is far more ferocious than enmity towards a measure of self-government for Wales.*

A. G. Prys-Jones

1521 Some of us still believe that the great interpreter of Wales in English . . . will yet come from the ranks of those who are fully within the mystery of our mother tongue.

'Anglo-Welsh Poetry Today'
in *The British Weekly* (22 Feb. 1951)

John Frederick Rees

1522 A cynic might ask whether the Welsh have an historical sense. They were painfully weaned from the twelfth-century fabrications of Geoffrey of Monmouth to fall victims of the eighteenth-century inventions of Iolo Morganwg.

'Of Welsh Nationality and Historians'
broadcast in the Welsh Home Service, 2 Jan. 1951
The Problem of Wales and other Essays (1963)

1523 In Wales, history has played a minor part in fostering the idea of nationality.

Richard Vaughan

1524 We were moulded in earth, soil-bound to the farm.

Moulded in Earth (1951)

D. J. Williams

1525 There is in the Welsh language raw material as lasting in the true craftsman's hands as were the marble-quarries of Greece and Italy in times gone by.*

in adjudication at the National Eisteddfod, Aug. 1951

— **1952** —

Anonymous

1526 Swansea man weds Swansea woman in Swansea.

headline
in *The South Wales Evening Post* (1952)

1527 It is for the eternal honour of Wales that today, four centuries after the framing of the Act of Union, there are more Welshmen than ever prepared to sacrifice all in the glorious cause of Welsh freedom.

editorial
in *The Welsh Republican* (vol. 3, no. 2, Oct.–Nov. 1952)

Cliff Bere

1528 Toryism is the enemy which is murdering Wales. Our answer must be to rise and destroy it in Wales. We will make Wales an untenable position for it under whatever camouflage it tries to remain; we will drive it back into its own land from every entrenchment it has made in our country and in our minds; we will show that Wales belongs not to England, but to the world.

The Welsh Republic (n.d., *c.* 1952)

John Betjeman

1529 In Wales, the chapel architecture of the nineteenth century is not denominational but racial.

First and Last Loves (1952)

Aneurin Bevan MP

1530 A young miner in a South Wales colliery, my concern was with the one practical question, where does power lie in this particular State of Great Britain and how can it be attained by the workers?

In Place of Fear (1952)

1531 Tredegar Workmen's Library was unusually well stocked with books of all kinds . . . The relevance of what we were reading to our own industrial and political experience had all the impact of a divine revelation. Everything fell into place.

1532 There is a universal and justifiable conviction that the lot of the ordinary man and woman is much worse than it need be.

1533 How can wealth persuade poverty to use its political power to keep wealth in power? Here lies the whole art of Conservative politics in the twentieth century.

1534 People live in the present, not in the past.

1535 Political parties, like individuals, can have split personalities. In fact, all political parties in time develop schizophrenia.

1536 With the collapse of the General Strike in 1926, the workers of Britain seemed to

have exhausted the possibility of mass industrial action . . . The trade union leaders were theoretically unprepared for the implications involved. They had forged a revolutionary weapon without having a revolutionary intention.

J. Kitchener Davies

1537 I wanted to save the Rhondda Valley for the nation
and the nation itself as a fertile garden.*

'Sŵn y Gwynt sy'n Chwythu'

1538 . . . the cancer of Englishness that is twisting through Wales.*

A. H. Dodd

1539 The history of Wales in the seventeenth century is necessarily, in the main, the history of a class.

Studies in Stuart Wales (1952)

Islwyn Ffowc Elis

1540 The English can write as much as they like about the Welsh, and the Welsh about the Welsh, but let the Welshman beware who puts the Englishman into black and white.*

'Y Sais'
Cyn Oeri'r Gwaed (1952)

Raymond Garlick

1541 One of the great advantages of living in a small country, as we in Wales know, is that nearly everybody knows everybody else – or at least his cousin.

editorial
in *Dock Leaves* (vol. 3, no. 9, Winter 1952)

Robert Graves

1542 Yet since the first edition appeared four years ago, no expert in ancient Irish or Welsh has offered me the least help in refining my argument, or pointed out any errors which are bound to have crept into the text, or even acknowledged my letters. I am disappointed, though not really surprised.

foreword to the third edition
The White Goddess (1952)

Roland Mathias

1543 This is the boundary: different burrs

Stick, stones make darker scars
On the road down: nightingales
Struggle with thorn-trees for the gate of
    Wales.

'Craswall'

Harold Nicolson

1544 I have no doubt at all that this [Bodnant]
is the richest garden I have ever seen.
Knowledge and taste are combined with
enormous expenditure to render it one of
the wonders of the world.

entry for 18 Aug. 1952
in *Diaries*

J. P. Sankey-Barker

1545 O God, our King and Saviour,
    Whose succour never fails,
Lord, strengthen our endeavours,
    Build Thou again dear Wales.

'National Hymn'

Dylan Thomas

1546 These poems, with all their crudities,
doubts, and confusions, are written for the
love of Man and in praise of God, and I'd
be a damn' fool if they weren't.

note to
Collected Poems 1934–1952 (1952)

1547 Do not go gentle into that good night.

'Do not go gentle into that good night'

Gwyn Thomas

1548 Laughter in the heart is a matter of choice,
not chemistry.

Now Lead us Home (1952)

R. S. Thomas

1549 We were a people bred on legends,
Warming our hands at the red past.

'Welsh History'

1550 We were a people wasting ourselves
In fruitless battles for our masters,
In lands to which we had no claim,
With men for whom we felt no hatred.

1551 We were a people, and are so yet.
When we have finished quarrelling for
    crumbs
Under the table, or gnawing the bones

Of a dead culture, we will arise,
Armed, but not in the old way.

1552 There is no present in Wales,
And no future;
There is only the past,
Brittle with relics,
Wind-bitten towers and castles
With sham ghosts;
Mouldering quarries and mines;
And an impotent people,
Sick with inbreeding,
Worrying the carcase of an old song.

'Welsh Landscape'

1553 Too far, too far to see
The set of his eyes and the slow phthisis
Wasting his frame under the ripped coat,
There's a man still farming at Ty'n-y-
    Fawnog,
Contributing grimly to the accepted
    pattern,
The embryo music dead in his throat.

'The Welsh Hill Country'

1554 I am the farmer, stripped of love
And thought and grace by the land's
    hardness;
But what I am saying over the fields'
Desolate acres, rough with dew,
Is, Listen, listen, I am a man like you.

'The Hill Farmer Speaks'

Robert Williams Parry

1555 To green Nature, not the world, the poet
    belongs;
    He has no truck with it: to make his
      mark
Does not climb pulpits singing fashionable
    songs
    Nor stands his box in the grass of
      Hothead Park.*

'Propaganda'r Prydydd' (trans. Anthony
Conran)

1556 Death does not die. This is woe.*

'Ymson ynghylch Amser'

— 1953 —

Sir Thomas Beecham

1557 I have no opinion of Wales. No one has an
opinion of Wales. It is a blank, a vacuum.

after a visit to Swansea,
reported in *Western Mail* (20 Oct. 1953)

Aneurin Bevan MP

1558 Although those of us who have been
brought up in Monmouth and Glamorgan
are not Welsh-speaking, Welsh-writing
Welshmen, nevertheless we are all aware of
the fact that there exists in Wales, and
especially in the rural areas, a culture
which is unique in the world. And we are
not prepared to see it die.

speech in House of Commons during Welsh Day
debate, 12 Dec. 1953

R. P. Boore

1559 The nation-wide bilingualism advocated
by many Welsh educational experts is an
unattainable ideal. While two languages
are spoken in the same place, one either
has, or gains, greater influence and the
other is extinguished.

'The Cymricisation of Wales'
in *Western Mail* (11 Sept. 1953)

Aneirin Talfan Davies

1560 The role of the Anglo-Welsh writer is the
translator's role. He lives on his
grandmother's memories, and attempts to
translate them into a language which she
knew not. We are allowed the luxury of
the 'Anglo' because some people remain
stubbornly Welsh.

'A Question of Language'
in *The Welsh Anvil* (no. 5, July 1953)

1561 The Anglo-Welsh writer looks at Wales –
and here I do not mean the material Wales
only but the 'Wales' which is the sum total
of all that makes us what we are,
geography, history, language, tradition –
in other words, Welsh culture, which is the
synthesis of all these things – he looks at
Wales through the refracting windows of a
foreign language.

1562 There is this to be said for the term Anglo-
Welsh: it does in some way convey
something of the dilemma which faces
these writers.

Francis Wynn Jones

1563 Welsh names were given to most of the
cows, but horses were given English names

and doubtless the distinction was caused
by the fact that cows were older in the
land.*

Godre'r Berwyn (1953)

D. J. Davies

1564 Wales must have a King.*

title of article
in *Baner ac Amserau Cymru* (29 July 1953)

Idris Davies

1565 There's holy holy people
They are in capel bach –
They don't like surpliced choirs,
They don't like Sospan Fach.

They don't like Sunday concerts,
Or women playing ball,
They don't like Williams Parry much
Or Shakespeare at all.

They don't like beer or bishops,
Or pictures without texts,
They don't like any other
Of the nonconformist sects.

And when they go to Heaven,
They won't like that too well,
For the music will be sweeter
Than the music played in Hell.

'Capel Calvin'

1566 When Christmastide to Rhymney came
   And I was six or seven,
I thought the stars in the eastern sky
   Were the brightest stars in heaven.

I chose the star that glittered most
   To the east of Rhymney town
To be the star above the byre
   Where Mary's babe lay down.

And nineteen hundred years would meet
   Beneath a magic light,
And Rhymney share with Bethlehem
   A star on Christmas night.

'A Star in the East'

1567 O Lord God, save us from tinned donkey,
   From Soviet scientific magazines,
   From the Scottish Sabbath, from
      American war films,
   From the demagogues of Aberdare and
      Abadan,
   And above all, O Lord God, save us from
      the Pentecostals.

'Come to our Revival Meeting'

1568 Pay a penny for my singing torch,
O my sisters, my brothers of the land of my
mothers,
The land of our fathers, our troubles, our
dreams,
The land of Llewellyn and Shoni bach
Shinkin,
The land of the sermons that pebble the
streams,
The land of the englyn and Crawshay's old
engine,
The land that is sometimes as proud as she
seems.

'Land of my Mothers'

Sir Emrys Evans
1569 The University is by far the most effective
instrument we have in Wales for bringing
the different parts of the country together
and healing the divisions between North
and South which the geography of Wales,
powerfully allied with British Railways
and our road system, have done so much
to create.

speech to the Court of the University College of
North Wales, Bangor, Nov. 1953

Thomas Firbank
1570 There is in Wales no equivalent to the
English yokel who is traditionally played
on his own national stage by a man in a
billycock hat with straw in his hair, who
grunts to converse.

A Country of Memorable Honour (1953)

1571 To say merely that the Welsh tongue has
survived is to give a wrong emphasis. An
Assyrian clay tablet may survive, but it
survives only to be a museum piece. It
would convey the fact better to say that
the tongue has continued to flourish. It is
no petrified tree dug from the bogs of time
but a flowering shrub.

Raymond Garlick
1572 The obvious answer to those who attack
the National Eisteddfod because Anglo-
Welsh writers cannot participate is that all
these objectors should start a festival of
their own. There is no reason at all why
they should not: all that is required is the
initiative and the capital – which, one
trusts, the newspapers which attack the all-
Welsh rule would readily provide.

editorial
in *Dock Leaves* (vol. 4, no. 12, Winter 1953)

Bobi Jones
1573 The Anglo-Welsh have had no major
literary critic, nor even a responsible
second-rate critic of talent. There have
been bootless discussions of whether they
were Anglo or Welsh . . . and frequent
mutual back-scratching. But the main
problem, their function as a bulwark of
civilization against suburban conformity,
and their relationship to the community
which had reared them, and its traditions,
have been only superficially dealt with.

'The Anglo-Welsh'
in *Dock Leaves* (vol. 3, no. 10, Spring 1953)

R. Tudur Jones
1574 If any system of justice is to be respected in
Wales it must deal with us as men with the
right to the administration of justice in our
own tongue, and not as rascals who will
ere long, by the grace of further education
and government, attain the status of
civilized, monoglot Englishmen.

editorial
in *Welsh Nation* (June 1953)

T. H. Jones
1575 I am tongue-tied, having not gratitude
enough
To speak in my own language or to hold
my peace.

'The Anglo-Welsh'

Saunders Lewis
1576 Only once did I have the opportunity of
speaking to Dylan Thomas. I found him
quiet, shy and completely unpretentious,
as if he was unaware of his fame
throughout two continents.

tribute to the poet
broadcast in the Welsh Home Service, 10 Nov.
1953

1577 We have lost the most splendid English-
speaking child Wales has produced for
centuries, and at a time when he had an
abundance of plans for the future. Let
perpetual light shine upon him.

of Dylan Thomas

Louis MacNeice
1578 To Wales once more, though not on
holiday now.

'Autumn Sequel'

1579 Thus Wales with her moodiness, madness,
     shrewdness, lewdness, feyness,
    Daily demands a different colour of praise.

1580   We close the door
    On Wales and backwards, eastwards, from
     the source
    Of such clear water, leave that altered
     shore
    Of gulls and psalms, of green and gold
     largesse.

L. Russell Muirhead
1581 Except in the largest towns . . . and the
better resorts, good restaurants are
practically non-existent in Wales.

The Blue Guide to Wales (1953)

J. Parry Lewis
1582 A land of great religious density that is
deplorably short of baths and hairdressers.

'The Condition of the Welsh People'
in *Dock Leaves* (vol. 4, no. 12, Winter 1953)

1583 Welsh is a language of old men.

1584 For every 21 men there are 22 women.

Goronwy Rees
1585 What is surprising is the permanence and
persistence of the Welsh way of life and
belief, an intense cultural and intellectual
conservatism which shows itself sometimes
in an almost Chinese reverence for what is
established and sanctified by custom, a
strange form of ancestor worship which is
all the stranger because, as an articulate
body of thought and belief, it is not more
than a hundred and fifty years old.

radio talk, 1953
in *Wales on the Wireless* (ed. Patrick Hannan,
1986)

Gwyn Thomas
1586 In those days we bathed also in the black
waters of the Taff, a typhoidal deathtrap,
the only river so dark the fish have to get
out every now and then and walk a while
along the bank to get their bearings and
their breath back.

'Rhondda Return'
broadcast in the Welsh Home Service, 1953

1587 The trouble with Mr Rawlins is that he
has been against the Welsh accent ever

since he attended a series of weekend
schools with the Drama League. As far as
Mr Rawlins is concerned, the League has
carried on from where Edward the First
left off.

A Frost on my Frolic (1953)

R. S. Thomas
1588 Is there no passion in Wales?

'The Minister'

1589 Protestantism – the adroit castrator
    Of art; the bitter negation
    Of song and dance and the heart's
     innocent joy –
    You have botched our flesh and left us only
     the soul's
    Terrible impotence in a warm world.

D. J. Williams
1590 A language and a nation are never killed
except by their own people.*

Yr Hen Dŷ Fferm (1953; trans. Waldo Williams)

1591 If it may be said that there is a divine right
to anything on earth, the right over the
land of Wales belongs to the Welsh nation,
and not to any alien, whoever he may be.*

1592 To me the patriotism of these
broadminded 'internationalists' that we
have in our nation, zealous for the rights of
every nation except their own, is but
superficial and meaningless rigmarole,
paper patriotism to be carried on the
strongest wind blowing at the time,
whether from London or Moscow, or any
other centre of wind.*

G. O. Williams
1593 Fundamentally, asking for our own
parliament for our own affairs is a simple
matter of self-respect, not one of throwing
our might about and clamouring for
preferential treatment. It is for us to
decide, one way or another, whether
Wales is to become extinct. A parliament
of its own won't in itself guarantee the
future, but we shall at least have the means
to settle our own affairs. The question to
which we must await an answer is whether
sufficient of us want a Wales with a future
to it.

'Why demand a Parliament?'
in *Dock Leaves* (vol. 4, no. 12, Winter 1953)

1594 There are those who put their finger on an infinitesimal part of the whole and say, That is *my* Wales, the *true* Wales; so expelling the rest to a limbo beyond concern.

1595 We know that to be Welsh is to be something real, whatever it is.

Waldo Williams

1596 They [Anglo-Welsh writers] thrive on a predicament.

'Anglo-Welsh and Welsh'
in *Dock Leaves* (vol. 4, no. 12, Winter 1953)

1597 One hears the wind moaning through the ruins of a noble habitation when one hears a Welsh place-name on the tongues of people to whom it means nothing.

Alfred E. Zimmern

1598 The Wales of today is not a unity. There is not one Wales; there are three Wales. There is Welsh Wales; there is industrial, or as I sometimes think of it, American Wales; and there is upper-class or English Wales. These three represent different types and different traditions. They are moving in different directions, and if they all three survive, they are not likely to re-unite. Welsh civilization has come unduly under the influence and prestige of England.

My Impressions of Wales (1953)

— 1954 —

Anonymous

1599 To call the Eisteddfod's leaders fanatical is not to their discredit; a fanatical desire to enhance the culture of Wales is no subject for disapproval.

editorial
in *Western Mail* (8 April 1954)

Samuel Barnes

1600 Welsh, although it is no more than a domestic language, acts as a means of propagating Welsh Nationalism . . . All the culture they teach in these schools is that Madoc discovered America and that Owain Glyndŵr hung Englishmen from their bedroom windows.

reported in *The Cambrian News* (22 Jan. 1954)

Aneurin Bevan MP

1601 I know that the right kind of political leader for the Labour Party is a dessicated calculating machine.

speech to the Tribune Group, 29 Sept. 1954

Sir Reginald Coupland

1602 A nation is not a state. There is a Welsh and a Scottish nation. There is no Welsh or Scottish state.

Welsh and Scottish Nationalism: a Study (1954)

Raymond Fletcher

1603 To ascribe present Welsh cultural deficiencies to capitalism is empty sloganising at its worst. The Labour Party dominates Welsh politics and controls most of its local authorities. But, except in Swansea, it seems to care about little except parochial, bread-and-butter problems.

in *Tribune* (10 Dec.1954)

James Griffiths MP

1604 We share the deep concern that is felt by the Welsh people for the preservation of our language and the heritage of our cultural life. We shall strive to assist every effort to preserve this precious heritage. The Labour members of Parliament for Wales have been reared in the best traditions of our country. We are inheritors of the social democracy which is the characteristic of the valleys and the countryside. We are determined that we shall play our part in sustaining the heritage which has come down to us.

statement after conference at Llanelli, 15 March 1954

Glyn Jones

1605 Lord, when they kill me, let the job be
    thorough
And carried out *inside* that county borough
Known as Merthyr, in Glamorganshire,
A town easy enough to cast a slur
Upon, I grant.

'Merthyr'

A. G. Prys-Jones

1606 Within the whispering gallery of St Paul's
The merest whisper travels round the
    walls;

But in the parts where I was born and
    bred
Folk hear things long before they're even
    said.

'Quite so'

R. M. Rosser
1607 We realise that the Church in Wales has to
deal with the problem of bilingualism, but
that cannot justify choosing the easier
course and neglecting the language of the
nation it is called to serve.

speech in St Paul's Cathedral, London
during the National Welsh Festival, 25 Feb.
1954

Dylan Thomas
1608 To begin at the beginning.
It is spring, moonless night in the small
town, starless and bible-black, the
cobblestreets silent and the hunched,
courters'-and-rabbits' wood limping
invisible down to the sloeblack, slow,
black, crowblack, fishingboat-bobbing sea.

First Voice,
Under Milk Wood (1954)

1609 Time passes. Listen. Time passes.

1610 Too late, cock, too late.

Captain Cat

1611 Nothing grows in our garden, only
washing. And babies.

Polly Garter

1612 Johann Sebastian mighty Bach. Oh, Bach
fach.

Organ Morgan

1613 I'm *fast*. I'm a bad lot. God will strike me
dead. I'm seventeen. I'll go to hell. . . Just
you wait. I'll sin till I blow up!

Mae Rose Cottage

1614 Lie down, lie easy.
Let me shipwreck in your thighs.

Captain Cat

1615 Oh, beautiful beautiful Gossamer B, I wish
I wish that you were for me. I wish you
were not so educated.

Sinbad Sailors

1616 O Tom Dick and Harry were three fine
men
And I'll never have such loving again
But little Willy Wee who took me on his
    knee
Little Willy Wee was the man for me.

Polly Garter

1617 I love you until Death do us part and then
we shall be together for ever and ever.

Mr Mog Edwards to Myfanwy Price

1618 Oh, what can I do? I'll *never* be refined if I
twitch.

Gossamer Beynon

1619 Men are brutes on the quiet.

Fourth Woman

1620 And then I got you into bed and you
snored all night like a brewery.

Mrs Cherry Owen to her husband

1621 Oh, isn't life a terrible thing, thank God?

Polly Garter

1622 You'll be sorry for this in the morning.

Voice to P. C. Attila Rees

1623 And before you let the sun in, mind it
wipes its shoes.

Mrs Ogmore Pritchard

1624 I must put my pyjamas in the drawer
marked pyjamas.

Mr Ogmore

1625 Oh, what'll the neighbours say, what'll the
neighbours . . .

Mother

1626 Ach y fi!
Ach y fi!

Jack Black

1627 I will lie by your side like the Sunday
roast.

Mr Mog Edwards

1628 I am a draper, mad with love.

1629 Praise the Lord! We are a musical nation.

Revd Eli Jenkins

1630 I'm Jonah Jarvis, come to a bad end, very enjoyable.

Jonah Jarvis

1631 Oh, I'm a martyr to music.

Mrs Organ Morgan

1632 I don't know who's up there and I don't care.

Nogood Boyo

1633 We are not wholly bad or good
Who live our lives under Milk Wood,
And Thou, I know, wilt be the first
To see our best side, not our worst.

Revd Eli Jenkins

Gwyn Thomas

1634 In every situation someone is waiting to be offended. Being offended is the only creative gesture left to nine people in ten. That is why life so often gives the hellish suggestion of being in a tantrum.

The Stranger at my Side (1954)

Mrs Williams Doo

1635 I must regretfully believe that our Welsh language, having fulfilled its purpose and controlled by inexorable laws of the universe, must in this technological age just fade away.

in *Liverpool Daily Post* (15 Feb. 1954)

— 1955 —

Kingsley Amis

1636 He sounded like an actor pretending, with fair success on the whole, to be Owain Glyndŵr in a play on the Welsh Children's Hour.

That Uncertain Feeling (1955)

1637 It was a play by a Welshman about Wales and performed by Welshmen in Wales and therefore redolent of the spirit of Wales.

1638 What a disgrace it was, what a reproach to all Welshmen, that so many of the articulate parts of their culture should be invalidated by awful sentimental lying. All those phoney novels and stories about the wry rhetorical wisdom of poetical miners, all those boring myths about the wonder and the glory and the terror of life in the valley towns, all those canonizations of literary dead-beats, charlatans and flops – all this in a part of the world where there was enough material to keep a hundred honest poets and novelists chained to the typewriter.

1639 It's standard practice, of course, with writers of Probert's allegiance, to pretend to be wild valley babblers, woaded with pit-dirt and sheep-shit, thinking in Welsh the whole time and obsessed with terrible beauty etc. but in fact they tend to come from comfortable middle-class homes, have a good urban education, never go near a lay-preacher and couldn't even order a pint in Welsh.

1640 I seldom get asked for books in Welsh. People want to read stuff about Everest and the Kon-Tiki expedition and escapes from prison-camps and so on. They might still want to if the stuff was translated into Welsh and the English copies burnt. It's difficult to be sure.

John Lewis

1641 It was still one of his chief claims to importance that when, ten years or so ago, a task force of Welsh Nationalists had torn down and burnt the 'English' flag at Treherbert aerodrome, he'd only just not been among them.

1642 Beynon, a very broad man of fifty-odd who'd already demonstrated the fact that he was almost the same height standing up as sitting down (a not all that rare type of physique in Wales), put his great hands on his great knees and cleared his throat.

Anonymous

1643 The Wales Gas Board is the only segment of any nationalised industry which acts for Wales as a nation.

'A Good Example'
in *The Welsh Republican* (vol. 6, no 2, Oct.–Nov. 1955)

1644 We hope the Welsh language can be saved but the historical processes seem to be too strong for it.

editorial
in *Western Mail* (6 July 1955)

1645 We respect and will safeguard the distinctive national cultures of these countries.

Labour Party Manifesto, 1955

Ambrose Bebb

1646 The man with shallow roots endangers the life of all around him.*

'Diweddglo'
Yr Argyfwng (1955)

1647 Wales is our share of the human crisis.*

'Hwyl ac An-hwyl'

Pennar Davies

1648 The use of the term 'Welsh' to describe the Anglo-Welsh is new and springs from ignorance.

'The Poet's Predicament'
in *The Welsh Anvil* (no. 7, Dec. 1955)

Bobi Jones

1649 It has become a psychological necessity for those Welsh intellectuals who frequent meretricious billiard rooms to stimulate our sensibility intermittently with pedantic pleas for detective stories and love romances in the Welsh language.

'Imitations in Death'
in *The Welsh Anvil* (no. 7, Dec. 1955)

Saunders Lewis

1650 After all, between you and me, I am not all that much a better dramatist than Sophocles.*

'Tranc yr Iaith'
in *Empire News* (23 Jan. 1955)

H. Morris Jones

1651 Monoglot Welshmen are proscribed in their own country.

Doctor in the Whip's Room (1955)

1652 The nearest in appearance to a village squire was a retired army officer . . . Some

of the children took off their hats to him, for he spoke no Welsh.

1653 The late Sir Robert Jones, the famous Liverpool surgeon, told me that he thought his surname had delayed his world-wide recognition by many years.

Reginald Pound

1654 [The Welsh are] a race of top-heavy men in black soft felt hats and black buttoned-up overcoats who look as if they are using our civilization only because they have mislaid their own.

quoted in 'Peter Parson's Log'
in *The British Weekly* (1 Dec. 1955)

J. B. Priestley

1655 Most people tell me that the Indians cannot hold out much longer. Another generation at the most, they say. I am not so sure. There is in the world today some spirit rising against the huge forces of uniformity. Who, a century ago, would have imagined the revival of self-consciousness among the Welsh, the renewal of the language and their desire for self-determination?

Journey down a Rainbow (with Jacquetta Hawkes, 1955)

Love Pritchard

1656 *All* sorts come from Cardiff.

comment by 'King of Bardsey' quoted by Mortimer Wheeler, *Still Digging* (1955)

Ioan Bowen Rees

1657 The essential genius of Wales is social. Welsh warmth and comradeship could make nationalisation and the welfare state something more than bureaucracy and turn code-numbers back into human beings.

quoted in *News Chronicle* (21 Dec. 1955)

Dylan Thomas

1658 One: I am a Welshman; two: I am a drunkard; three: I am a lover of the human race, especially of women.

attributed by Geoffrey Moore,
'Dylan Thomas'
in *The Kenyon Review* (Spring 1955)

1659 I hold a beast, an angel, and a madman in me, and my enquiry is as to their working, and my problem is their subjugation and victory, downthrow and upheaval, and my effort is their self-expression.

1660 Land of my Fathers. My fathers can keep it.

attributed by Suzanne Roussillat
in *Adam* (23 Dec. 1955)

J. R. R. Tolkien
1661 Welsh is of this soil, this island, the senior language of the men of Britain; and Welsh is beautiful.

The O'Donnell Lecture (1955)

Mortimer Wheeler
1662 Apart from a handsome civic centre, the streets of Cardiff seemed unbearably mean and dingy, the people in them unbelievably foreign and barbaric.

Still Digging (1955)

1663 The intense local patriotisms of a mountain divided country with indifferent communications were (and are) natural and proper. Wales, save when united in opposition to England, was an aggregate of parish pumps rather than a nation.

David Williams
1664 Her Majesty [Queen Victoria] was always disdainful where the Principality was concerned.

The Rebecca Riots (1955)

— 1956 —

Islwyn Ffowc Elis
1665 If there is one penalty worse than most that a woman can suffer, it is being a minister's wife.*

Yn ôl i Leifior (1956)

Rolfe Humphries
1666 What we know of the Welsh seems mighty little, compared with what we think we know of the Scotch or Irish. An invidious nursery rhyme; some lampooning, not without rough admiration, in Shakespeare; what else? A contumacious people, they seem to have been, the Cymri, confederates never any longer than they

had to be, fighting with, and beaten by Romans, Saxons, Normans, Danes, Irish, turning around, as often as not, and mauling their oppressors, coming home victorious, to betray their leaders and fall to feuding, repeating the cycle.

Green Armor on Green Ground (1956)

1667 Wales, which I have never seen,
Is gloomy, mountainous, and green.

'For my Ancestors'

1668 They dig in mines, they care for sheep,
Some kinds of promises they keep.

1669 They practise magic out of season,
They hate the English with good reason,
Nor do they trust the Irish more,
And find the Scots an utter bore.

R. T. Jenkins
1670 Many years have passed, and behold, I have lived long enough to see the Age of Committees.*

'Symffoni: Amwythig'
Casglu Ffyrdd (1956)

Gwyn Thomas
1671 We go forward because there is a boot behind us.

A Point of Order (1956)

1672 I believe in banning something from time to time. It gives a quizzical look to life's face to have a thing with-held by a group of serious-looking voters and it gives an extra tingle of vitality to the things that are left on view.

Waldo Williams
1673 The day will come when the small ones shall be great,
The day will come when the great shall be no more.*

'Plentyn y Ddaear'

1674 Here are the mountains. One language can lift them
And set them in their freedom against a sky of song.*

'Cymru a Chymraeg' (trans. Joseph P. Clancy)

1675 We didn't notice her. She was the light, without colour.*

of the Welsh language,
'Yr Heniaith' (trans. Joseph P. Clancy)

1676 Let us guard the wall from the beast, keep
    the well-spring free of filth.*

'Preseli' (trans. Joseph P. Clancy)

1677 My Wales, brotherhood's country, my cry,
    my creed,
    Only balm to the world, its mission, its
    challenge.*

1678 In me Wales is one.*

'Cymru'n Un'

1679 Welshmen, were you a nation, great would
    be the glory
    These would have in your story.*

'Y Merthyron Catholig' (trans. Anthony
Conran)

1680 What is being a nation? A talent
    Springing in the heart.
    And love of country? Keeping house
    Among a cloud of witnesses.*

'Pa Beth yw Dyn?' (trans. Emyr Humphreys)

— 1957 —

Dannie Abse

1681 Stranger, he is laid to rest
    not in the nightingale dark nor in the
        canary light.
    At the dear last, the yolk broke in his
        head,
    blood of his soul's egg in a splash of
        bright
    voices and now he is dead.

'Elegy for Dylan Thomas'

1682 The coin is spun. Here all is simplified,
    and we are partisan who cheer the Good,
    hiss at passing Evil. Was Lucifer offside?
    A wing falls down when cherubs howl for
        blood.
    Demons have agents: the Referee is bribed.

'The Game'

David Bell

1683 It has always been an evil in Wales that
    second-rate work, perhaps from an
    Eisteddfod competition, has a tendency to
    get displayed as a masterpiece, and great
    harm can be done to values by calling the
    second-rate first-rate.

The Artist in Wales (1957)

Aneurin Bevan MP

1684 If you carry this resolution . . . you will
    send a Foreign Secretary, whoever he may
    be, naked into the Conference Chamber.

attacking proposal that Britain should abandon
an independent nuclear deterrent
speech at Labour Party Conference, 2 Oct. 1957

Euros Bowen

1685 He harvested the fruit of poetry's acre
        Till his lips were red,
        Doting on the grapes, till
        Drunken, he fell, widowed the wine.*

'Dylan Thomas'

Raymond Garlick

1686 Poised among peaks, we find our dignity.

'Blaenau Observed'

Bobi Jones

1687 Death, you are afraid of me.*

'Y Gân Gyntaf'

David Jones

1688 Whether there can be any continued co-
    existence between the old culture-patterns
    and the new technological schematization
    is, *in itself* just as problematical in England
    as it is in Wales, but in the latter country
    the situation is much exacerbated because
    the specific heritage of the Welsh people is
    caught in the crossfire of this conflict: that
    is to say, the oldest living tradition in
    Britain is intricated very adversely in our
    general dichotomy.

letter in *The Manchester Guardian* (Sept. 1957)
Epoch and Artist (1959)

Gwyn Jones

1689 When you have a considerable number of
    authors working in different literary kinds,
    working in different ways and at different
    levels, and towards different ends, you
    have a literature. If you have less than this,
    you have a 'school', a movement, a group.
    The Anglo-Welsh now have a literature.

The First Forty Years (1957)

1690 The Anglo-Welsh, though they are a
    danger to the Welsh language, must never
    be its enemy; and the Welsh Welsh, even if
    they are the true dancers before our tribal

ark, will be unwise to try to impose an irresistible logic upon an immovable fact; they must accept that they cannot speak for, or even to, half their fellow-countrymen, while to the great world outside they may not speak at all.

1691 Perhaps we are doomed always to be a People of the Short Puff, stricken with the trembles beyond a middle distance, and with gripes, grunts and staggers after the vital sixth round. Deft assemblers of the house of one night, but lacking the architectonics for castles or cathedrals.

1692 'Anglo-Welsh', after all, is just a tag, a literary label, a device for avoiding circumlocution.

1693 I believe the Anglo-Welsh [writers] to be the strongest bulwark Wales has in the linguistically eroded parts of the country.

1694 The majority of the Anglo-Welsh have been quite painfully modest and deferential in face of native Welsh criticism: we would no more talk back to a proper Cymro than we would cheek our mother.

1695 But with Caradoc Evans the war-horn was blown, the gauntlet thrown down, the gates of the temple shattered. Or in homelier metaphor, it was as though some new-style yahoo had flung a bucket of dung through the Welsh parlour-window, and in case anyone was genteel or well-meaning enough not to notice anything amiss, had flung the bucket in after, with a long-reverberating clangor.

T. H. Jones
1696 I took her to the golden gorse,
  We made a gold to-do,
No deacon sighed with such content
  As we, when we were through.

'Gorse Idyll'

John Osborne
1697 You're just a sexy little Welshman and you know it.

Jimmy Porter to Cliff Lewis
Look Back in Anger (1957)

— **1958** —

Elwyn Davies
1698 Welsh is a brave language and cannot be

spoken mincingly or through immobile lips.

A Gazetteer of Welsh Place-names (1958)

1699 The history of Anglo-Welsh relations has been such that the correct pronunciation of Welsh place-names has never acquired the status attached to the proper pronunciation of French, Italian or Spanish names.

David Jones
1700 [The] survival of something which has an unbroken tradition in this island since the end of the sixth century, and which embodies deposits far older still, cannot be regarded as a matter of indifference by any person claiming to care for the things of this island. It is by no means a matter for the Welsh only, but concerns all, because the complex and involved heritage of Britain is a shared inheritance which can, in very devious ways, enrich us all.

letter in *The Times* (11 June 1958)
Epoch and Artist (1959)

James Morris
1701 Plaid Cymru has its trappings of crankiness.

'Welshness in Wales'
in *Wales* (Sept. 1958)

1702 Today almost everyone, from Queen to comic, acknowledges the nationhood (if not the statehood) of Wales.

1703 Few Welshmen, it must be admitted, actually suffer from the English presence; and many thousands benefit.

1704 The stranger in Wales, however warm his sympathies for things Welsh, must walk a precarious conversational path.

1705 A foreigner could spend a week in Cardiff or Penarth and think himself still in England.

1706 For centuries it has been the sad but noble duty of the Welsh to protect their national identity under alien rule. Sometimes they defended their heritage by force of arms; generally by the resilience of their culture; always by the exertion of peculiar racial characteristics and the cherishing of their old patriotism.

1707 When an Englishman has a pint too many, he wants to fight, or make love, or subside into the womb of smutty anecdote; but when the Welshman stands beside the bar he, apparently, wants to sing.

Lord Raglan
1708 In general, therefore, Welsh is the language of the illiterate Welsh, English of the literate Welsh.

'I take my Stand'
in *Wales* (Oct. 1958)

1709 It will be a happy day for Wales when that language [Welsh] finally takes its proper place – on the bookshelves of the scholars.

1710 Ebbw Vale is in England.

on refusing to attend the National Eisteddfod, 1958

Gwyn Thomas
1711 There are still parts of Wales where the only concession to gaiety is a striped shroud.

in *Punch* (18 June 1958)

Iori Thomas MP
1712 Land is land.

speech in House of Commons, 1958

R. S. Thomas
1713 For centuries now
We have been leaving
The hills and the high moors
For the jewelled pavements
Easing our veins of their dark peat
By slow transfusions.

'Expatriates'

Mrs Williams Doo
1714 We who desire peace and goodwill before all else in life must deeply deplore this modern obsession with our language. We believe it to be on the side of those forces that lead to war.

in *Western Mail* (24 Oct. 1958)

Raymond Williams
1715 Culture is ordinary, that is where we must start.

'Culture is ordinary'
Convictions (ed. Norman MacKenzie, 1958)

— 1959 —

Anthony Conran
1716 Most Englishmen, if they thought about the subject at all, would consider that to be born and bred in Wales, apart from the chance of imbibing a little local colour from the hymns and sabbaths, is almost identical with being born in England.

'The English Poet in Wales'
in *The Anglo-Welsh Review* (vol. 10, no. 25, 1959)

Walter Dowding
1717 When I am listening to the sweet tuneful airs of my country,
Sung by fresh and young voices that love them,
In the language so strong and beautiful,
That has grown out of the ageless mountains and the deep, deep valleys,
I am fulfilled as I am in no otherwise fulfilled.

Then I am caught up into a realm of natural being
And am at one with my fathers,
And with them that shall come after me,
And with those who yet, in these so unregenerate days,
Do speak that marvellous speech of wondrous beauty
That our fathers wrought.

'I'r Hen Iaith a'i Chaneuon'

Gareth Lloyd Evans
1718 There is no more noble sight than that of a Welshman and an Englishman facing one another across a pint of simple beer, each aware of the other's failings – laying their cards on the table with that cool intellectuality which so characterizes the relationship between the two races; smilingly tolerant, so glad that a common frontier, with no passport difficulties, has made them, with all their differences, so understanding of one another.

'How to Live in England'
in *Wales* (no. 40, May 1959)

Gwynfor Evans
1719 The ideas of our professional politicians as to what can be done for Wales are vague, obscure and tentative. Their views upon

what cannot be done for her are clear and strong.

'Wales as an Economic Entity'
in *Wales* (nos. 42/44, Sept. 1959)

Sir Ifor Evans

1720 The worst dragon is the one that believes that life should be a way of gloominess and not a way of enjoyment. Let us hope that this one is not the dragon of Wales.

'Prospects for a Ministry of Fine Arts'
broadcast in the Welsh Home Service, 29 Jan. 1959

1721 The idea of the State or, indeed, of any authority being involved in the arts and in culture, is hostile to Welsh opinion.

Emlyn Hooson MP

1722 The greatest tragedy which has happened in Wales in the twentieth century has been the establishment of the Welsh Nationalist Party.

speech in House of Commons, 23 May 1959

Albert Evans-Jones, Cynan

1723 When I am old and honoured,
     With silver in my purse,
All criticism over,
     All men singing my praise,
I shall buy a lonely cottage
     With nothing beyond its door
But the rocks of Aberdaron
     And the wild waves of the shore.*

'Aberdaron'

Bobi Jones

1724 If it's true that Madog discovered America, it is much more true that O. M. Edwards discovered Wales.*

'O. M. Edwards'
Pr Arch: dau o bob Rhyw (1959)

David Jones

1725 It would seem to me that by all the accidents of history and every attendant circumstance, the placeless cosmopolis of the technocrats which more and more conditions us all, whoever and wherever we are, hits the things of Wales where it most hurts.

'A London Artist looks at Contemporary Wales'
in *Wales* (no. 40, May 1959)

1726 We know now that even the loveliness of lovely Gwynedd will avail her nothing and that Mona Insula, whose grain-yield has since the earliest times made her proverbial as the mother and nourisher of Wales, must now be thought of as best fitted for industrial sites necessitating an influx from the English Midlands.

D. Gwenallt Jones

1727 Let us celebrate him for his diligence, his
          daring, and his holiness,
     And for helping to keep alive the
          learned language of the nation,
Conferring dignity on Welsh and giving it
     the highest honour
     By converting it to one of the dialects of
          God's Revelation.*

of William Morgan, translator of the Bible into Welsh,
'Yr Esgob William Morgan' (trans. Joseph P. Clancy)

Ernest Jones

1728 [Freud's] first remark was to say that from my appearance I couldn't be English; was I not Welsh? This greatly surprised me. . . since I was getting accustomed to the total ignorance of my native land on the Continent.

recalling his first meeting with Freud in 1908
Free Associations (1959)
a footnote states, 'Only recently have I learned that Jung had already told him.'

1729 I must confess to have never entirely succeeded in achieving a detached attitude towards the callous English acquiescence in assaults on the Celtic languages and culture.

1730 All the masters were from English public schools and they never let us forget their opinion of our native inferiority, from which our only hope of redemption was through emulating the *Herrenvolk* whose outposts they were.

of Llandovery College

Wyn Roberts

1731 We have always lived under an oligarchy as far as art is concerned; let's hope the day of cultural democracy is now at hand.

'Television in Wales'
in *Wales* (nos. 42/44, Sept. 1959)

Vernon Watkins

1732   So, in these Welsh hills,
I marvel, waking from a dream of stone,
That such a peace surrounds me, while the
    city
For which all long has never yet been
    built.

'Peace in the Welsh Hills'

Harri Webb

1733   A Welshman writing in English only
acquires significance when he is seen
to be inextricably committed to and
involved in the predicament of his
country.

review
in *Wales* (no. 46, Nov. 1959)

D. J. Williams

1734   Wales is England's breast-pocket.*

Yn Chwech ar Hugain Oed (1959)

— **1960** —

Dannie Abse

1735   I don't think there is such a thing as a
specifically Anglo-Welsh style or tone, and
that the Welshness of an English poem
simply depends on what the poem is
about.

radio talk, 1960
in *Wales on the Wireless* (ed. Patrick Hannan,
1986)

Anonymous

1736   Remember Tryweryn!*

slogan painted on walls in 1960s
the Tryweryn valley was drowned to make a
reservoir for Liverpool

Anthony Conran

1737   Wales has had enough inspired
ignoramuses to last her till Doomsday;
what we need is a drop of the old culture,
with its grace that is only gained by a great
deal of hard work.

'The English Poet in Wales'
in *The Anglo-Welsh Review* (vol. 10, no. 26, 1960)

1738   The Arts Council mentality
Minces in teashops, talks glibly of

Striking a blow for Wales – five more
    minutes
In Welsh on the Welsh BBC.

'An Invocation of Angels'

1739   A Welshman at twenty
Is either an awkward edition of fifty
Or else he's gone English.

1740   Even today the Welsh male is arrogant,
Secretly arrogant, under his subservience.

Arthur Horner

1741   The exposure of the inability of privately
owned industry to maintain any standards
for the workers employed made our claims
for nationalisation inevitable.

Incorrigible Rebel (1960)

Alun Owen

1742   All this play-acting about Wales doesn't
matter, boy. Wales is just another country
like any other.

Captain John Roberts to Dave and Morgan
After the Funeral (1960)

1743   My family always spoke Welsh at home.
My father was Sir Tom Lloyd-Thomas . . .
He was knighted for his service to the
Welsh language.

Ailwen to Vera

Oh, well, in that case you'd have to speak
Welsh. You'd look a bit soft if you didn't,
wouldn't you?

Vera to Ailwen

1744   In my experience of funerals in Wales,
everybody wants something. Death's a
great time for grabbing the left-overs, my
boy. An acre, a sow, an old engagement
ring.

Captain John Roberts to Morgan

David Verey

1745   Llanwrtyd Wells was once a spa, but is
now dead.

The Shell Guide to Mid-Wales (1960)

Raymond Williams

1746   The shape of Wales: pig-headed Wales,
you say, to remember to draw it.

Border Country (1960)

— 1961 —

Gwynfor Evans

1747 No language can be restored by a
language movement. It can be restored
only by a movement which reaches down
to the deep sources of a people's will. The
Welsh language can be saved by only a
great national revival directed to securing
full nationhood for Wales.

in *Celtic Voice* (vol. 1, 1961)

David Jones

1748 Queen of the differentiated sites,
administratrix of the demarcations, let our
cry come unto you . . . When they
proscribe the diverse uses and impose the
rootless uniformities, pray for us.

The Tutelar of the Place (1961)

D. Gwenallt Jones

1749 Some writers have seen the need for a
Literary Society, a national Literary
Society: a Society where they can consort
with one another and discuss Welsh
literature.*

editorial
in *Taliesin* (no. 1, 1961)

1750 The writer in Wales is a lonely creature.*

Saunders Lewis

1751 Immerse yourself in the literature of your
language. Give yourself up to it as far as
you are able. Everything else is of
secondary importance. To be in the
fashion and to follow the fashions of
London or Paris are wholly secondary in
comparison with knowing your Welsh
tradition.*

advice to a young writer
in conversation with Aneirin Talfan Davies
broadcast by the BBC, 19 May 1960,
in *Taliesin* (no. 2, Christmas 1961)

1752 I find it painful to write plays I know no
one can act.*

1753 I had a desire, no small desire, a great
desire to change the history of Wales. To
change the entire course of Wales, and
make Welsh Wales something alive,
strong, powerful, belonging to the modern
world. And I failed utterly.*

1754 You say we're for the dark, that our
language is doomed? Alright my bonny, be
it so, and how long is your own expectancy
of life? At any rate, we here in Wales will
make it the end of a lovely party.

radio talk, 1961
in *Wales on the Wireless* (ed. Patrick Hannan,
1986)

Hugh MacDiarmid

1755 A poetry the quality of which
Is a stand against intellectual apathy,
Its material founded, like Gray's, on
    difficult knowledge,
And its metres those of a poet
Who has studied Pindar and Welsh poetry.

'The Kind of Poetry I want'

John Morgan

1756 Other countries may, from time to time,
defeat us at football, but these are merely
the triumphs of brute strength over talent.

radio talk, 1961
in *Wales on the Wireless* (ed. Patrick Hannan,
1986)

Alun Owen

1757 They can be pretty rough, them Taffies, if
they put their mind to it.

Ted to Tom
Lena, Oh my Lena (1961)

R. S. Thomas

1758 Even God had a Welsh name:
We spoke to him in the old language;
He was to have a peculiar care
For the Welsh people.

'A Welsh Testament'

1759 I have looked long at this land,
Trying to understand
My place in it – why,
With each fertile country
So free of its room,
This was the cramped womb
At last took me in
From the void of unbeing.

'Those Others'

1760   I find
This hate's for my own kind,
For men of the Welsh race

Who brood with dark face
Over their thin navel
To learn what to sell.

1761 It is too late to start
For destinations not of the heart.
I must stay here with my hurt.

'Here'

1762 What to do? Stay green.
Never mind the machine,
Whose fuel is human souls.
Live large, man, and dream small.

'Lore'

Vernon Watkins

1763 I like to think of Swansea as a place with
no sophistication, no cultural props, no
reputation of any kind. A hidden place.

radio talk, 1961
in *Wales on the Wireless* (ed. Patrick Hannan,
1986)

Emlyn Williams

1764 Rural Wales is where I belong, but I don't
want to live in it, I want to have it to go
back to.

George (1961)

— 1962 —

Dannie Abse

1765 Unable to communicate, I'm easily
betrayed.

'Return to Cardiff'

Kingsley Amis

1766 The journal of some bunch of architects
Named this the worst town centre they
could find;
But how disparage what so well reflects
Permanent tendencies of heart and mind?

'Aberdarcy: the Main Square'

1767 There's more to local life today,
I know, than what I've found to say:
But when you start recording it
You've got to tone it down a bit.

postscript to *The Evans Country* (1962)

Brenda Chamberlain

1768 You who are in the traffic of the world: can
you guess the thoughts of an islander?

Tide-Race (1962)

Saunders Lewis

1769 It will be nothing less than a revolution to
restore the Welsh language in Wales
today. Success is only possible through
revolutionary methods. Perhaps the
language would bring self-government in
its wake – I don't know. The language is
more important than self-government.*

Tynged yr Iaith (1962)

1770 I predict that Welsh as a living language
will cease to be, if present trends continue,
about the beginning of the twenty-first
century, supposing that there are still men
alive in Britain then.*

1771 In Wales all can be forgiven except being
serious about the language.*

1772 In my opinion, if any kind of self-
government for Wales were obtained
before the Welsh language was
acknowledged and used as an official
language in local authority and state
administration in the Welsh-speaking parts
of our country, then the language would
never achieve official status at all, and its
demise would be quicker than it will be
under English rule.*

Philip O'Connor

1773 Too much Welsh talent is condemned to
scholarship.

Living in Croesor (1962)

1774 Wales may be Chapel-ridden, but there is
a powerful horse beneath this rider: he will
never be subdued, because he will never be
killed.

1775 Gloom is subjective; the Welsh mountains
are not gloomy, can manage well enough
without any of our little anthropo-
morphisms.

Kate Roberts

1776 It is a novelist's privilege to be unfaithful
to the society to which he belongs.

Tywyll Heno (1962)

Meic Stephens

1777 O were you at Trefechan Bridge
In Aberystwyth town,
Among the demonstrators
Who on the road sat down?

We wanted summonses in Welsh
And created quite a fuss
When we stopped a hundred motor-cars
And one Penparcau bus.

'The Ballad of Trefechan Bridge'

Brinley Thomas

1778 Instead of bemoaning the rural exodus, the
Welsh patriot should sing the praises of
industrial development . . . The
uprighteous Mammon in opening up the
coalfields at such a pace unwittingly gave
the Welsh language a new lease of life and
Welsh Nonconformity a glorious high
noon.

The Welsh Economy (1962)

Gwyn Thomas

1779 Laugharne was the town of Dylan
Thomas, the Welsh poet who in his short
days on earth was as much a wizard as
Merlin, a man who climbed a unique
throne of love and laughter, and died from
the sheer height of it . . . At his worst, he
traversed some most peculiar valleys of
disgrace. At his best, he lit up a whole new
sky of delight, put to shame some of the
darker absurdities of our serge-bound
consciences and added to the Anglo-Welsh
tongue a new dimension of lovely sound.

in *TV Times* (14 Sept. 1962)

1780 Poverty, said Jehoidah Knight, is a bigger
tree than even the Fabians have made it
out to be, and harlotry is one of its
branches.

Loud Organs (1962)

Harri Webb

1781 Come all valiant Welshmen, I'll tell you a
tale
Of the boozing of beer and the swilling
of ale,
'Twas in the Cross Foxes, the pride of fair
Rhos,
We drank all they had and the pub had
to close.

'The Cross Foxes'

1782 Three acres and a Welsh-speaking cow.

attributed, of Plaid Cymru's economic policies
(based on smallholders' slogan of 1880s)

— 1963 —

Huw T. Edwards

1783 The story of Tryweryn remains like a scar
on the consciousness of every Welshman
worthy of the name.*

Troi'r Drol (1963)

Peter Gruffydd

1784 No blood suffices and we attend
The slow funeral of a small nation:
In the end there will be silence;
Now, even the withered heart rages.

'The Small Nation'

Cledwyn Hughes MP

1785 The future of Wales depends on young
people who have the ability to draft a good
amendment, not on those who can handle
high explosives.

'The Importance of Welsh Water'
in *The Liverpool Daily Post* (26 April 1963)

T. H. Jones

1786 Always I feel the cold and cutting blast
Of winds that blow about my native hills,
And know that I can never be content
In this or any other continent
Until with my frosty fathers I am at last
Back in the old country that kills and sings.

'Land of my Fathers'

1787 Exile, like love, is a word not to be lightly
said.

'Mr Jones as the Transported Poet'

Saunders Lewis

1788 The Welsh language is the only weapon
which can supplant English government in
Wales.*

in *Barn* (March 1963)

Kenneth O. Morgan

1789 The national movement in Wales remains
an essential and significant aspect of the
political development of modern Britain
. . . Its major consequence today is that the
existence of Welsh nationality is rarely in
dispute. Wales it seems is unlikely now to
degenerate into the status of a mere region:
it can no more be compared with
Yorkshire or Cornwall than the Province
of Quebec with Ontario.

Wales in British Politics 1868–1922 (1963)

Meic Stephens

1790 There is only one true patriotism: that which sees the homeland as it really is and loves it nevertheless.

'The Matter with Wales'
in *The Nationalist* (vol. 1, no. 1, June 1963)

1791 I hope that it will not be long before the people of Wales realise that, although the dead are always with us, the walking dead can sometimes be avoided.

1792 If we all keep saying 'After you' for much longer, there will be no Wales after us.

1793 The cleverness of Welsh undergraduates has nothing to bite on except the national grievance.

1794 It can be heart-breaking business to fight the lethargy of our own people, their disillusionment and their smugness.

1795 Wales at the moment is a rag-and-bottle shop of superseded ideas and there is a formidable vested interest in our huge national stock of junk.

1796 It may be that many of the institutions which we are proud to regard as uniquely Welsh are only so because others see no sense in imitating them . . . Customs which contribute something of value to the world rarely remain unique.

1797 The Welsh are too fond of waving rhetorical flags of defiance while preparing for the expected defeat.

1798 I am a London Welshman, for Wales I am on fire.
    When I have made my fortune to Wales I shall retire,
Or I shall give my money, like good Sir David James,
    To help more London Welshmen play patriotic games.

'The Exile's Song'

1799 Let's be kind to Anglo-Saxons,
    To our neighbours let's be nice,
Welshmen, put aside all hatred,
    Learn to love the bloody Sais!

'Our English Friends'

1800 There once was a man called Dr Price
    Who lived on lettuce, nuts and rice,
His idols were the moon and sun
    And he walked the hills with nothing on
        Singing, 'I don't care a bugger
        What anyone thinks of me!'

'The Ballad of Dr Price'

Gwyn Thomas

1801 Of romance in the conventional sense, wild passion or moony devotion, I know little. In the place and time of my upbringing, the golden rule was an emotional decorum.

'Did you hear that?'
in *The Listener* (14 Nov. 1963)

1802 Ever since I can remember the price of bread has been rising like a lark and wages have ruptured themselves trying to catch its tail.

Jackie the Jumper (1963)

1803 I tried to interpret the dreams of a people who didn't know they were asleep.

R. S. Thomas

1804   Seeing how Wales fares
Now, I will attend rather
To things as they are; to green grass
That is not ours; to visitors
Buying us up. Thousands of mouths
Are emptying their waste speech
About us, and an Elsan culture
Threatens us.

'Looking at Sheep'

J. R. R. Tolkien

1805 In modern England the usage [of 'British'] has become disastrously confused by the maleficient interference of the Government with the usual object of Governments: uniformity. The misuse of 'British' begins after the union of the crowns of England and Scotland, when in a quite unnecessary desire for a common name the English were officially deprived of their Englishry and the Welsh of their claim to be the chief inheritors of the title British.

'English and Welsh'
in *Angles and Britons* (1963)

1806 Welsh at least is still a spoken language, and it may well be true that its intimate heart cannot be reached by those who come to it as aliens, however sympathetic. But a man should look over the fences of neighbouring farm or garden – a piece of the country which he himself inhabits and tills – even if he does not presume to offer advice. There is much to learn short of the inner secrets.

Harri Webb

1807 Queen of the rains and sorrows,
Of the steep and broken ways,
Lady of our tomorrows,
Redeem your yesterdays.

'A Loyal Address'

1808 Come back and sing to us, we have waited
    too long,
For too long have not been worth singing
    for.

'The Nightingales'

1809 We started drinking at seven
And went out for a breather at ten,
And all the stars in heaven
Said, Go back and drink again.

'Big Night'

1810 Cold water, Dewi,
Is not for our palate,
We keep your festival
With foolish mirth,
Self-praise and self-pity,
Dragons and flagons,
But none who will suffer
For Wales in her dearth.

'Ty Ddewi'

D. J. Williams

1811 Wales is older than the British Empire, and she will live long after it, too.*

A. E. a Chymru (1963)

William Wynn

1812 Speak no Welsh to any that can speak English, no, not to your bed-fellows, and thereby you may freely speak the English tongue perfectly. I had rather that you should keep company with studious honest Englishmen than with many of your countrymen, who are more prone to be idle and riotous than the English.

advice to his son, a student at Oxford
quoted in Geraint Dyfnallt Owen, *Elizabethan Wales* (1963)

Richard Crossman

1813 Another idiotic creation is the Department for Wales, a completely new office for Jim Griffiths and his two parliamentary secretaries, all the result of a silly election pledge.

entry in diary

Gwynfor Evans

1814 The highest value is not the nation, but the human personality.*

Rhagom i Ryddid (1964)

Raymond Garlick

1815 To imagine this:
A people at grips
With genesis
Not apocalypse;

'Note on the Iliad'

Goronwy Rees

1816 It may well be that by accepting and assimilating, instead of rejecting, the revolutionary changes of the present age, the Welsh can again succeed in creating a new and living culture in their own form and image.

'Have the Welsh a Future?'
in *Encounter* (March 1964)

1817 Wales is a small country and the Welsh are a small people.

1818 The Welsh are a peace-loving people with a profound respect for established authority. It is not likely that Welsh Gandhis or Welsh gunmen will ever set the hearts of their countrymen aflame.

1819 The Welsh answer to a problem is nearly always to appoint a committee.

1820 The Welsh love fairy tales; what they cannot face is the reality out of which fairy tales are produced, and for that reason they cannot create genuine fairy tales any longer.

1821 Wales until today has lived so long upon its past that it has offered very little to the young imagination, handcuffed and fettered in the narrow world of the chapel and the Eisteddfod.

1822 The Nonconformist chapels which have exerted so decisive an influence on every aspect of Welsh life are today empty or emptying; faith has ebbed away from them, and in Wales as elsewhere, television now has more influence than religion.

1823 It is a mark of the sterility of the official version of Welsh culture that it has never succeeded in giving any adequate expression to the kind of society which flourished in the South Wales valleys.

Gwyn Thomas

1824 We were not, in terms of nationality, a homogenous people. Into the valleys had poured as many Englishmen as indigenous Welsh. The only binding things were indignity and deprivation. The Welsh language stood in the way of our fuller union and we made ruthless haste to destroy it. We nearly did.

A Welsh Eye (1964)

1825 Women have grown so used to seeing men as the supreme intolerable joke that their capacity for jests is limited. By the time they have adjusted themselves to the fact that, by their standards, the average male is an irresponsible and amoral buffoon, their reserves of laughter are drained.

'Women and Humour'
in *Western Mail* (2 June 1964)

Jeremy Thorpe MP

1826 Roll on independence for St Helena and Wales.

letter to Cledwyn Hughes, 1964

Rhydwen Williams

1827 The corpus of our respectable poetry,
    The flowers and the bloody hearse,
All lie in that dignified cemetery –
    *The Oxford Book of Welsh Verse.**

'Y Gerdd Sbeitlyd'

— **1965** —

Anonymous

1828 The trouble with the people of this town is that to your face they're all behind you,

but behind your back they're at your throat.

old man in Merthyr Tydfil to Meic Stephens

1829 Even if he didn't – he did.

old man in Rhondda to Meic Stephens, as to whether Winston Churchill sent troops to Tonypandy in 1910

Lord Arran

1830 Bad teeth.

when asked what the word Wales meant to him

George Brown MP

1831 The price of a pound of beef is more important than your bloody language.

speech in Bangor

Harold Carter

1832 Nothing more sadly epitomises the fact that urban living was not really of Wales than this extremely interesting but remote and forlorn imitation of the piazzas and grandes places of Europe.

of Alban Square, Aberaeron
The Towns of Wales (1965)

Islwyn Ffowc Elis

1833 The plain truth is this: the majority of Welsh-speakers will never ask for forms and documents in their own language . . . It will take two generations to teach the Welsh-speaking Welsh to use their language in oral and written form without shame and fear.*

editorial
in *Taliesin* (vol. 11, Dec. 1965)

Bobi Jones

1834 In the back-kitchen of his house he keeps a nation.*

of the English-speaking Welshman
'Cymro Di-Gymraeg'

Rhiannon Davies Jones

1835 A nation can raise its head twice, but not men.*

Lleian Llan Llŷr (1965)

1836 It occurred to me that fate had given Wales not one dream but many, the one smothering the other.*

1837 It is strange how a man can weep for his ancestors without ever having seen them.*

Saunders Lewis

1838 Alas, there is one sad difference between the Welsh Nationalist Party of the 1960s and the Welsh methodists of the 1760s. The methodists in their day aroused hate, violence, persecution, prison. That is why they triumphed.

'Welsh Literature and Nationalism'
in *Western Mail* (13 March 1965)

1839 Civilization must be more than an abstraction. It must have 'a local habitation and a name'. Here, its name is Wales.

Gwyn Thomas

1840 I never wished to be a headmaster, having never failed to see something grotesque about authority, something insane in the domination and conceit inherent in all leadership.

'No Head for Heights'
A Hatful of Humours (1965)

1841 We are all gossips of more or less ability. Also most of us are cursed with a sense that our lives lack change and movement. That is why we have, through the centuries, leaned so heavily on the witch-doctors of literature – the professional liars, the novelists, the storytellers.

'Not so Deep-laid'

1842 Rugby, as played by the Welsh, is not a game. It is a tribal mystery.

'Padded up for Action'

Wynford Vaughan-Thomas

1843 Lord, let thy glaciers come again:
Out from Snowdonia's fastness flow
Thy rivers of avenging ice,
Remote, remorseless, cold and slow,
To crush in one supreme moraine
Our godless cities of the plain.

'A Malediction on all Developers'

Herbert Williams

1844 If people want to sing, dance, become crowned bards and dress up in night-shirts, why not? It's just that it means so much to

some people and so little to others. In my particular neck of the woods, it falls far short of 'Come Dancing' and the International Horse Show in terms of appeal.

in the *South Wales Echo*

— 1966 —

Tom Earley

1845 So now I'll leave the politics to others
And not be an outsider any more.
I'll go back to the valley, to my mother's,
And never set my foot outside the door;

Except to go to chapel on Bryn Sion
And maybe join the Cwmbach Male
Voice Choir,
I'll sit at home and watch the television
And talk about the rugby by the fire.

'Rebel's Progress'

Raymond Garlick

1846 In any discussion of Welsh poetry there is always a sense of its context in a whole literature, a sense of perspective; in almost any discussion of Anglo-Welsh poetry this is quite absent. Because of the gross failure of the University Departments of English in this respect, and the Training Colleges, and thus the schools, there are only about three people who have any thorough, detailed, scholarly, authoritative, critical knowledge of the four centuries of Anglo-Welsh poetry, of the hundred or so names involved.

letter to Meic Stephens
in *Poetry Wales* (vol. 2, no. 2, Summer 1966)

T. H. Jones

1847 Anguish is my country.

'My Country, my Grief'

1848 Of course I'd go back if somebody'd pay
me
To live in my own country
Like a bloody Englishman.

'Back?'

Lord Ogmore

1849 I am as keen as anyone on the due preservation of the language but many of these fanatics are dancing around the language like a lot of old-time Cherokee Indians around a totem-pole. In fact, they are making a laughing-stock of the language in the rest of the United Kingdom.

reported in *Western Mail* (14 Dec. 1966)

Gwyn Thomas

1850 There can be few parts of Britain where enthusiasm for the arts gutters as tremulously as in South Wales.

'Plaster Saints in the Valleys'
in *Twentieth Century* (Winter 1966)

1851 I have never known people set so smugly high an evaluation on their own philistinism.

of the people of Cardiff

1852 Cardiff contains without question the least intelligent part of the Welsh proletariat, for the simple reason that it is in no sense Welsh.

1853 The Welsh Arts Council mounts brilliant skirmishes.

1854 Today a Gregynog book has as high a prestige among a few as a winning pools coupon among many.

1855 Most of the effects of organized religion I have seen in Wales: the sly malignity of interdenominational intrigue; the gross persecution of beauty and delight by diaconates delirious with some phobic sense of guilt.

reply to questionnaire

1856 Like a super-termite, bingo is eating its way through the supports of our society. Every time it opens its jaws, another little cultured outpost falls . . . When bingo can close down an amateur operatic group, especially a Welsh one, I think it is time we took up battle stations.

'UNO should look into Bingo'
in *Western Mail*

1857 All nationalists, all soldiers, all priests, most mothers project a block that hinders the proper functioning of the human mind.

entry in journal

1858 As I age, the physical scope even of my dreams tends to shrink. In sleep I move scarcely more than a few feet away from that awful bloody bridge in Porth.

entry in journal

1859 Before this event we stand breathless.

of the disaster at Aberfan, 21 Oct. 1966
radio broadcast
in *Wales on the Wireless* (ed. Patrick Hannan, 1986)

R. S. Thomas

1860   There is no other sound
In the darkness but the sound of a man
Breathing, testing his faith
On emptiness, nailing his questions
One by one to an untenanted cross.

'In Church'

1861 It was like a church to me,
I entered it on soft foot,
Breath held like a cap in the hand.

'The Moor'

John Tripp

1862 The bad smell at my nostril
    is some odour of myself – a modern who
      reeks of the museum,
    not wanting his own closed yesterday
but the day before that,
    the last day before dignity went,
when all our borders were sealed.

'Diesel to Yesterday'

1863   We have no
monopoly of compassion, but believe
no distance is too excessive
from a cold heart.

'Welcome to Wales'

Justice Widgery

1864 I think it is quite clear that the proper language for court proceedings in Wales is in the English language.

in the Royal Court of Justice, 9 Dec. 1966

Herbert Williams

1865 Give me the insignificant times,
When circulation managers moan,
And no one is asking for sacrifice,
And honour is safely left alone.

'Nothing to Report'

1866 Oh yes, there have been gains.
I merely state
That the language, for us,
Is part of the old, abandoned ways.

And when I hear it, regret
Disturbs me like a requiem.

'The Old Tongue'

— 1967 —

Anonymous

1867 If Welsh dies the loss to the nation would
be incalculable. A language represents the
consciousness of a nation and is a
safeguard of its individual identity. If we
let that die, then perhaps a part of us will
die too.

editorial
in *Western Mail* (8 June 1967)

1868 In any legal proceeding in Wales or
Monmouthshire the Welsh language may
be spoken by any party, witness or other
person who desires to use it, subject in the
case of proceedings in a court other than a
magistrates' court to such prior notice as
may be required by rules of court; and any
necessary provision for interpretation shall
be made accordingly.

The Welsh Language Act, 1967

Aneirin Talfan Davies

1869 Language is man's most important
possession.*

'Canu a'r Ysbryd a'r Deall'
Astudio'r Byd (1967)

1870 Language is the soil around civilization's
roots.*

R. T. Jenkins

1871 Wales was *given* to us, the English *made*
England.*

Clywed yr Hyfrydlais (1967)

Saunders Lewis

1872 I can't become a Communist. Wales has
had more than her bellyful of Puritanism
already. Communism is just Puritanism
without God.*

Dewi
Cymru Fydd (1967)

Anita Loos

1873 Astoundingly enough, D. W. seemed
almost inhuman: he was of Welsh
extraction, and the Welsh are a very
peculiar breed, poetic, unpredictable,
remote and fiercely independent.

of D. W. Griffith, the pioneer of motion pictures
A Girl Like I (1967)

Gerald Morgan

1874 Talking about national issues is the Welsh
equivalent of sore-scratching: it affords
temporary relief from the problems
involved without moving any nearer to a
cure.

'More of the Dragon's Tongue'
in *Welsh Dominion* (no. 1, Summer 1967)

Ioan Bowen Rees

1875 The first task of the new critics will be to
distinguish Welsh Literature in English
from work in the main stream of English
literature which just happens to have been
written by someone qualified by birth,
residence or parentage to play rugby for
Wales, or just happens to have a
background of Welsh place-names.

letter to editor,
in *Poetry Wales* (vol. 3, no. 2, Summer 1967)

Meic Stephens

1876 Anglo-Welsh literature is a recent
phenomenon. It has its roots in newly
disturbed soil – the social and linguistic
upheaval that occurred in Wales during
the inter-war years.

'The Second Flowering'
in *Poetry Wales* (vol. 3, no. 3, Winter 1967–68)

1877 Quite frankly, there seems to me to be
something rather over-compensatory in
seeking to find an Anglo-Welsh tradition
among the tourists, anglicized gentry and
country parsons who dabbled in English
verse from Tudor times on.

1878 The big danger threatening Anglo-Welsh
verse, as I see it, is that it is and may
continue to be peripheral, both in Wales
and in England . . . While so many of us
acquiesce in the anglo-centric organization
of life in Britain today, I think our
literature will remain in the same position

as Scotland's before its renaissance in the nineteen twenties: parochial, disorientated, minor, conservative, dull, and without one poet, or a critic, of Hugh MacDiarmid's stature.

1879 I am not suggesting that all Anglo-Welsh poets should feel obliged to write about Welsh nationhood but I am convinced that before a poet writing in English can fully justify his position as Anglo-Welsh, he needs either to write about Welsh scenes, Welsh people, the Welsh past, life in contemporary Wales, or his own analysis of all these, or else attempt to demonstrate in his verse those more elusive characteristics of style and feeling which are generally regarded as belonging to Welsh poetry. We are in desperate need of a good critic who will define the Welshness of Anglo-Welsh verse; it seems to me that such matters will have to be properly discussed soon if our poets are to receive the critical attention they merit.

1880 Whether we are likely to flourish and create a literature that measures up to European standards is not yet clear. The only alternative, for me, is that, with the Welsh nation denied the rights and responsibilities of full nationhood, a parliament at least, and therefore obliterated by the end of the present century, the Welsh will have lost their separate identity and the Anglo-Welsh will then have nothing to distinguish them from other regional English writers.

1881 The influence of R. S. Thomas is, of course, much in evidence here but his brooding on rural decay and the spineless attitudes of his countrymen may well prove to be an emotional dead-end, however salutary for the time being.

Dylan Thomas

1882 This town [Swansea] has got as many layers as an onion, and each one reduces you to tears.

quoted by Wynford Vaughan-Thomas, *Madly in all Directions* (1967)

R. S. Thomas

1883 There was a high culture in Wales once, and men willing to die for it.

preface to catalogue of an exhibition about Hugh MacDiarmid (1967)

John Stuart Williams

1884 However warm your secret thoughts,
whatever you've been told
by fat psychiatrist or priest,
the feet of the dead are cold.

'Gwynt Traed y Meirw'

— **1968** —

Anonymous

1885 Perhaps the most tranquil and evocative commercial centre in Europe.

the dockland of Cardiff
in *The Guardian* (26 Jan. 1968)

1886 The proposals for speedily equipping incoming English children with a degree of fluency in Welsh will also cheer those who have the interests of the child at heart. Without the language which is the common means of communication in the country, no child could be expected to be integrated fully with his community, both in school and outside.

editorial
in *Western Mail* (2 March 1968)

1887 The survival of the Welsh language is a matter of concern for most Welshmen. It helps to give Wales its distinctiveness; it is the vessel through which the thoughts and feelings of generations of our predecessors have passed; its loss would leave all Wales much poorer.

editorial
in *Western Mail* (15 Oct. 1968)

Raymond Garlick

1888   Cardiff
   swirls about the numb
and calm cube of its castle cliff:
rune of departed power for some
  to others towers a hieroglyph
   of sovereign power to come
         if if.

'Capitals'

1889 I have lived where blood
Had flooded down men's hands.
Though I look for a Wales
Free as the Netherlands,
A freedom hacked out here

Is a freedom without worth,
A terror without beauty.
Here it must come to birth
Not as a pterodactyl
Flailing archaic wings,
But the dove that broods on chaos –
Wise as a thousand springs.

'Matters Arising'

Peter Gruffydd

1890 The English pound makes much the same
snarl in Wales as anywhere else in these
islands and I have not yet happened on
anyone, poet or otherwise, who scorns its
definitive crackle.

'Further to the Second Flowering'
in *Poetry Wales* (vol. 4, no. 1, Summer 1968)

Lord Heycock

1891 I believe that, with the will and the
energy, it is possible by the end of this
century for Wales to become bilingual, the
two cultures living with each other.

speech in House of Lords, 30 Jan. 1968

Eric Hobsbawm

1892 Industrialization, or any other economic
change, was something done to Welshmen
rather than by Welshmen.

Industry and Empire (1968)

Glyn Jones

1893 I would like Anglo-Welsh writers to see
themselves first as Welshmen. The only
English thing about an Anglo-Welsh
writer ought to be his language.

The Dragon has two Tongues (1968)

1894 I, and those Anglo-Welsh writers brought
up in circumstances similar to mine,
certainly did not reject the Welsh
language. On the contrary, the Welsh
language rejected us.

1895 Welsh speech has been a sort of social
solvent, almost a badge of equality, which
has softened and even obliterated the
sharper and more painful asperities of
class. What we have in Wales is not
classlessness but a condition in which class,
like colour in a multi-racial society, is not
of overwhelming importance.

1896 To me, anyone can be a Welshman who
chooses to be so and is prepared to take the
consequences.

Saunders Lewis

1897 I believe that careful, considered, public
violence is often a necessary weapon for
national movements.*

'Treiswyr sy'n ei chipio hi'
in *Barn* (no. 74, Dec. 1968)

1898 In minorities lies the hope of every age.*

1899 I don't think anyone should join any
movement, even a movement to save the
nation, just because they hope – or are sure
– that it will be successful. I should remain
committed to Wales even if I were certain
. that within ten years Wales would be
finished.*

Ioan Bowen Rees

1900 The battle for Wales is the battle for all
small nations, all small communities, all
individuals in the age of genocide.

Celtic Nationalism (1968)

Glyn Simon

1901 It is intolerable that those who do not
speak Welsh should be regarded as second-
class citizens, or less genuine lovers of their
country than their bilingual counterparts.
But it is equally intolerable that in their
own country or Church those who speak or
think in Welsh should be regarded as
eccentric or perverse or expected in
matters governmental or official to be
provided only with forms in a language in
which they are not at home.

reported in *Western Mail* (26 Sept. 1968)

Gwyn Thomas

1902 I was home, at my earth's warm centre.
The scared monkey was back in the
branches of his best-loved tree. I've never
had any truly passionate wish to be
elsewhere.

A Few Selected Exits (1968)

1903 We shall live out this century in a rising
tide of drink, religion and violence.

1904 People singing hymns in a north Welsh
accent assume the shiftiest expressions I
have ever seen. The combination of the
godly and the guttural must set up some
strange mental tensions.

entry in journal

1905 Our Sunday School music-teacher was a cordial nymphomaniac who could make 'From Greenland's Icy Mountains' sound like a tropical rumba.

R. S. Thomas
1906 Come to Wales
To be buried; the undertaker
Will arrange it for you.

'Welcome to Wales'

1907   Let us
Quote you; our terms
Are the lowest, and we offer,
Dirt cheap, a place where
It is lovely to lie.

1908 I have walked the shore
For an hour and seen the English
Scavenging among the remains
Of our culture, covering the sand
Like the tide and, with the roughness
Of the tide, elbowing our language
Into the grave that we have dug for it.

'Reservoirs'

1909 Where can I go, then, from the smell
Of decay, from the putrefying of a dead
Nation?

1910   Prompt me, God;
But not yet. When I speak,
Though it be you who speak
Through me, something is lost.
The meaning is in the waiting.

'Kneeling'

Vernon Watkins
1911 For me neglect and world-wide fame were
    one.
I was concerned with those the world
    forgot,
In the tale's ending saw its life begun;

And I was with them still when time was
    not.

'Fidelities'

D. J. Williams
1912 Please excuse my English. I learned it in Wormwood Scrubs.

at inaugural meeting of the Welsh Academy, Swansea

1913 Somehow or other, I was born a nationalist.*

radio talk, 1968
in *Radio Cymru* (ed. Gwyn Erfyl, 1989)

1914 I wouldn't have anything to do at all with politics if Wales were a healthy little country like other free countries.*

— 1969 —

Anonymous
1915 We call upon Welshmen to organize, train and equip, to arm themselves with guns, bombs, Molotov cocktails, grenades, pikes, bows and arrows, swords, bayonets, clubs . . . eggs filled with sand, flour and smoke bombs, nuts and bolts, sharpened pennies . . . Stock them up and bring them to Caernarfon.

leaflet distributed by the Free Wales Army prior to the investiture of the Prince of Wales, July 1969

1916 Somewhere on Blackrock, between Gilwern and Brynmawr, there should be a notice: Welcome to the birthplace of the modern world: the birthplace of modern industry.

Plaid Cymru, *Economic Plan* (1969)

Charles, Prince of Wales
1917 Having spent so many hours in the language laboratory here I shall certainly never let it [the Welsh language] die without offering stout resistance.

speech at Urdd Eisteddfod
reported in *Western Mail* (2 June 1969)

Anthony Conran
1918 We are respectable fellow-travellers, us Anglo-Welsh.

'Anglo-Welsh Poetry Today'
in *Poetry Wales* (vol. 4, no. 3, Spring 1969)

Rhys Davies
1919 Carmarthen, which I had always thought of as the cows' capital of Wales, still appeared to be prosperously lactic.

Print of a Hare's Foot (1969)

James Griffiths MP
1920 The Federation was not only a trade

union: it was an all-embracing institution in the mining community. . . In the work and life of the community, the Federation was the servant of all.

Pages from Memory (1969)

1921 When I was a student at the Labour College, I studied Marxism and tried very hard to understand it. I could not bring myself to accept the materialist concept of history; my Welsh temperament recoiled against such an arid doctrine.

Robat Gruffudd
1922 It's sweet to be a Welshman
And to paint the world green.*

I'r Chwyldro (1969)

Bobi Jones
1923 Welsh literature is the major achievement of the Welsh nation and the most complete expression of the Welsh mind through the centuries.

Highlights in Welsh Literature (1969)

1924 The young writer in Welsh today is consciously building up the nerve of his community, and slowly healing a deep and ancient wound.

A. G. Prys-Jones
1925 This Wales, this precious and enduring ground.

'For St David's Day'

Glyn Simon
1926 If we are tempted to think that Welsh language extremists are inexcusable, let us remember that the threats to the survival of Welsh have never, either quantitatively or qualitatively, been greater than they are today. A note of desperation in its defenders should surely be understood and excused.

reported in *Western Mail* (1 March 1969)

Meic Stephens
1927 Now that the bulldog's old and gray,
To bark at lesser breeds no longer fit,
Dogs of the world are having their day,
But the corgi's nose is rubbed in grit.

'Crufts '69'

Gwyn Thomas
1928 I could no more look favourably on Nationalism than on gangsterism. Both are myopic, arrogant and shamelessly larcenous.

entry in journal

Ned Thomas
1929 Sometimes I think I would like a spell in prison,
In a humane country, for a political offence,
Somewhere where the library service is efficient,
Or Scandinavia, where wives come in at weekends.

'Supermarket'

R. S. Thomas
1930   In the striped flag
On the tower there is the insolence
Of a poster advertising
A nation for sale.

'Shame'

John Tripp
1931 How can I write impartially of a land that I love?

'Vulnerable's Lament'

Harri Webb
1932 The Green Desert.

title of collection of poems, 1969

1933 The cockerel crows in the morning
    And the lark sings high at noon,
The blackbird whistles the sun down
    And the owl cries out to the moon;

We have to make do with their music
    For the birds of Safaddan are dumb:
They only sing for the rightful Prince
    And he has not yet come.

'A Song for July'

1934 The draught is bitter we must drain
Before the land is whole again.

'A Whisper'

1935 Two lands at last connected
Across the waters wide,
And all the tolls collected
On the English side.

'Ode to the Severn Bridge'

1936 And now, as in the long green ages,
The Dyffryn trees stand full and tall,
As lovely as in exile's memory,
Breathless, a breath before the fall.

'Dyffryn Woods'

1937 We shall not die, I think, of changes in
Diet or dogma or vocabulary.
We are, after all, still here, if only just.

'Ponies, Cyfarthfa'

1938 There are no withdrawals, advances, but,
in this land,
No victory, no defeat.

'The Old Parish Churchyard'

1939 Who will now conquer the wilderness of
Wales?

'Patagonia'

1940 Sing a song of rugby,
Buttocks, booze and blood,
Thirty dirty ruffians
Brawling in the mud.

When the match is over
They're at the bar in throngs,
If you think the game is filthy
You should hear the songs.

'Vive le Sport!'

1941 When Christ was hanged in Cardiff Jail,
Good riddance, said the Western Mail,
But daro, weren't all their faces red
When he came to judge the quick and the
dead.

'Local Boy Makes Good'

1942 This futile bird, it seems to me,
Would make a perfect Welsh MP.

'Our Budgie'

1943 Where now he lies his old routine
Will suffer scant disruption,
For none could say he'd ever been
A stranger to corruption.

'Epitaph on a Public Man'

1944 One day, when Wales is free and
prosperous
And dull, they'll all be wishing they were
us.

'Merlin's Prophecy 1969'

— 1970 —

Anonymous

1945 Never forget your Welsh.

advertisement for beer

1946 Happiness is knowing you are Welsh.

car-sticker

1947 Keep Wales tidy – dump your rubbish in
England.

car-sticker

Euros Bowen

1948 It is poets that light the hall,
they are lamps among us.*

'Lampau'

Sir Goronwy Daniel

1949 We must not forget that the main cause of
the decline in the Welsh language is that
not enough Welsh mothers see value in
bringing up their children as Welsh-
speakers. Acts which tend to associate the
language with law-breaking and
rebelliousness are not, in my view, going to
encourage these mothers. What is needed
is more constructive work directed at
showing that ability to speak Welsh as well
as English is an asset of real cultural and
vocational use.

First Impressions of the University Scene (1970)

E. Tegla Davies

1950 What is needed is not to save Wales, but to
make Wales worth saving.*

quoted in Robin Williams, *Y Tri Bob* (1970)

Ryan Davies

1951 Never in Europe!

catch-phrase

Tom Earley

1952 They smelt the house out when we got
them home
and, when we changed the water, always
died:
clean water killed them.

'Tiddlers'

Emyr Humphreys

1953 The Welsh condition is worth studying

because it is spreading. In the next century it will be endemic not only among national minorities and small nations: the structure of international technology will ensure that it spreads to what used to be called the European Powers, where the sense of community, alas, may well be too weak to offer any effective restraint on personal or mechanical ambition.

'The Welsh Condition'
in *The Spectator* (28 March 1970)

1954 Small nations have always appeared doomed to be absorbed by their greater neighbours and the struggle for survival seems certain to fail . But success and failure are relative terms and the lost cause is certainly the more accurate reflection of the human condition. This is not a fashionable form of despair. To be reconciled to finitude, to accept the prospect of failure, can be the first step to true progress and genuine development.

1955 If ambition and wealth and power are the highest ventures, then obviously he must strike out into a wider world and take the path of Henry Tudor or David Lloyd George. On the other hand, if he wishes to take up a cause, if he feels a deep sense of loyalty to the community which nurtured him, if he wishes to work out his salvation in fear and trembling, if he sets a high price on honour and personal integrity, or if he is just a high-minded humanist, there is more than enough scope for his talents in Wales itself.

1956 The air is still committed to their speech
Their voices live in the air
Like leaves like clouds like rain
Their words call out to be spoken
Until the language dies
Until the ocean changes.

'Ancestor Worship'

1957 This man is a king except
He makes his living emptying caravan bins
And uses English in the shop to avoid
    giving offence
To visitors who do not know
Where they are or who he is.

'Gŵr y Rhos'

Bobi Jones
1958 I write English like a dead language.

'Why I write in Welsh'
in *Planet* (no. 2, Oct. /Nov. 1970)

J. R. Jones
1959 While accepting that . . . economic developments and the pressure of circumstances have hastened the decline of Welsh, yet somewhere at the heart of the whole business there was a will at work. The destruction of our identity was willed by the power which usurped our sovereignty.*

Ac Onide (1970)

1960 We have no existence as a rightful People . . . except through the inter-penetration of our dwelling-place, 'this corner of the earth', with the Welsh language.*

1961 It is said of one experience that it is among the most agonizing of all . . . namely, that of having to leave the soil of your country for ever, of turning your back on your heritage, of being torn away by the roots from your homeland. . . I have not suffered that experience. But I know of another experience which is just as painful, and more irreversible (for you can always return to your home), and that is the experience of knowing, not that you are leaving your country, but that your country is leaving you, is ceasing to exist under your very feet, is being sucked away from you, as if by an insatiable, consuming wind, into the hands and possession of another country and another civilization.*

Gwaedd yng Nghymru (1970)

Neil Kinnock MP
1962 Perhaps I have a suspicious mind, but the south Wales valleys breed suspicious minds.

maiden speech in the House of Commons,
13 July 1970

Emyr Llewelyn
1963 We are not asking for the moon. We are asking for our own radio and television channels.

'The Future of Broadcasting'
in *Planet* (no. 2, Oct./Nov. 1970)

D. Tecwyn Lloyd

1964 In the past, Plaid Cymru has talked a
great deal about culture, moral values,
roots, self-respect, minority rights, and so
on. In a word, the high, classic ideals. The
majority here – Labour, Tories and
Liberals alike – have shown that they
know nothing about what these words
mean. It is not by appealing to such things
that the support of the middle-aged people
of Carmarthenshire is won now, any more
than in ancient Rome before it fell.*

after the General Election
editorial
in *Taliesin* (vol. 20, July 1970)

Bill MacLaren

1965 They'll be singing in the valleys tonight.

catch-phrase, after Welsh rugby victories

Justice Edward Rowley

1966 Welsh? I have never heard such rubbish.

on refusing permission for defendants to speak
Welsh in court
reported in *Western Mail* (12 Dec. 1970)

Ned Thomas

1967 Mr George Thomas spoke of the language
as of a rejected wife – with deliberate
goodwill, no love, and periodic complaints
about what it was costing him.

'The George Thomas Era'
in *Planet* (no. 1, Aug. /Sept. 1970)

1968 In the long term it is the interaction of
socialism and nationalism that will decide
the future of this corner of the world, and
what sort of socialism and what sort of
nationalism, are important questions for
us. Devolution is a subject that can be
phrased either in terms of national rights
or socialist rights. It scarcely matters
which.

Gwyn Thomas

1969 The Welsh language has become in both
senses a club: it is a conspiracy of people
seeking preferment through the speaking of
an arcane tongue; it is an offensive weapon
for use against the British Government.

entry in journal

John Wain

1970 He had come here to learn Welsh.

Philology was his profession, and a
professional man ought to be constantly
broadening his scope. Roger also wished to
broaden the scope of his sexual activities.
He had discovered that the University of
Uppsala had a large department of Celtic
Studies, and he had reason to believe that
if he added Welsh and possibly Irish to his
scholarly armoury, and made a few
contributions to Celtic Philology, he would
land a job at Uppsala. His motive for
going there was that he liked tall, blonde
girls with perfect teeth and knew that in
Uppsala there were a lot of them about.

A Winter in the Hills (1970)

D. J. Williams

1971 The spirit of a nation conquered by force is
as eternal as the spirit of freedom in the
heart of man.*

'Y Tri Hyn'
Y Gaseg Ddu(1970)

1972 A man's strength or weakness is always in
his secret life, and so it is with a nation.*

'Y Gagendor'

— 1971 —

Elizabeth Beasley

1973 The visitor to North Wales should
remember that, in architecture as in other
matters, English standards do not apply.

The Shell Guide to North Wales (1971)

Pennar Davies

1974 Parochialism is of the mind; the Welsh
language is of Europe and of the world.

in *Artists in Wales* (ed. Meic Stephens, 1971)

1975 I find it difficult to accept the genuineness
of any concern for Wales professed by
those who see London as the centre of their
political activities and aspirations. The
first condition of the very survival of our
people is that there should be a
psychological coming home to Wales, in
political and economic matters as in
others, and that those of our countrymen
who call themselves socialists and radicals
and democrats should see in Wales the
proposed centre for the implementation of
their principles.

Peter Finch

1976 To live in Wales
is to love sheep
and to be afraid
of dragons.

'A Welsh Wordscape'

Robert Graves

1977 I know all the rules of Senghenydd.

letter to Meic Stephens, referring to *cynghanedd*

Carwyn James

1978 Get your retaliation in first.

during British Lions rugby tour of New Zealand

John Jenkins

1979 Force is to diplomacy what bullion is to
banknotes.

letter from prison
in *Planet* (no. 5/6, Summer 1971)

1980 I oppose the leaders of Plaid Cymru
because they are prepared to sacrifice their
people, their country and their heritage on
the shrine of their respectability and
pacifism.

1981 She [Wales] is not a beautiful young girl
after whom I lust, or an old duchess whose
money and status I desire; she is old, well
past her best, decrepit, boozy, and has
taken strange bedfellows without the
saving grace of desperation . . . I owe her
my love and loyalty, she is my mother.

Bernard Levin

1982 But a language in which no serious
literature is now written (if the Welsh
extremists really want their beautiful
tongue to be taken seriously they might
bend their efforts to closing down the
annual Eisteddfod, where it is only made
ridiculous) and which nobody needs to
speak or write, cannot be turned by force,
public or private, into a genuine
instrument of communication written or
spoken.

in *The Times* (11 Nov. 1971)

Saunders Lewis

1983 Wales will not be Wales without the Welsh
language. Without the language strongly
rooted in its soil, it would be another
country, and because of this, there is only
one battle worth fighting in the Wales of
today. And that is the language battle, the
battle to bring it back to the *totality* of the
life of Wales.*

in *Barn* (Feb. 1971)

Roland Mathias

1984 Only out of free choice can there be built a
Wales in English which is not England and
which is in touch with the living heart of a
Wales that beats in Welsh.

in *Artists in Wales* (ed. Meic Stephens, 1971)

1985 It is indeed a depressing experience now to
move about the cultural void which is
English-speaking Wales, to discover how
totally ignorant of Welsh history and
tradition its people are and how
superficially unconcerned about it, and to
observe the absence of leadership in the
necessary quantity and quality from
universities and schools.

Alun Richards

1986 As to whether I am Welsh or not, it is a
highly self-conscious question which I have
never felt the need to ask myself. *I am*. It is
enough, and the rest is propaganda.

in *Artists in Wales* (ed. Meic Stephens, 1971)

1987 I left Pontypridd, but it never left me.

1988 People will not understand that a language
which has had no utility in our lives is
unlikely to be of importance to us ever
again.

Tom Richards

1989 There are probably about six hundred
thousand Welsh-speaking people in Wales,
the great majority of whom never think of
the language's future.

in *Artists in Wales* (ed. Meic Stephens, 1971)

George Thomas MP

1990 Nothing irritates English-speaking areas in
Wales more than bilingual forms.

reported in the *Liverpool Daily Post* (20 April
1971)

Gwyn Thomas

1991 I am a Welsh aristocrat. In a good light I

can trace my ancestry all the way back to my father.

entry in journal

1992 I have had more than one motherland. There was Wales and alongside it, Spain, irony, an overtowering sense of the past, and an anxiety neurosis roughly the size of the Eisteddfod Pavilion.

in *Artists in Wales* (ed. Meic Stephens, 1971)

1993 The Welsh have given too much of themselves to teaching.

1994 The Red Dragon, to the bemused ear of the valley-dweller, could as well refer to a beer or a bus as a flag.

Ned Thomas
1995 Cardiff wants to be seen to be a capital; it doesn't want to act like one.

'I will cling to the old Celtic cross'
in *Planet* (no. 7, Oct./Nov. 1971)

1996 The Welsh Extremist.

title of book (1971)

1997 Very soon there will be no quiet, comfortable way left of being a Welsh-speaking Welshman; traditional Welshness seems more and more a sham. We either have to lie down as if dead or do something new.

The Welsh Extremist (1971)

1998 The fields are greener and the sea bluer because of the unseen company of past generations.

G. O. Williams
1999 We hold that to compel Welsh-speaking defendants to submit to trial in English, against their will, before law courts in Wales, is a violation of the rights of man.

letter, also signed by others
in *The Times* (26 October 1971)

Gwyn Williams
2000 I must live out my life with two tongues and try to put sting into both.

in *Artists in Wales* (ed. Meic Stephens, 1971)

2001 I've heard it said that Welsh will live in the home, at the hearth. It's at the hearth it will die if it's not used for all purposes.

Raymond Williams
2002 Who speaks for Wales? Nobody. That is both the problem and the encouragement.

'Who speaks for Wales?
in *The Guardian* (3 June 1971)

— **1972** —

Anonymous
2003 Yet despite these affinities, doom-laden prophecies of another Irish situation in Wales are, thankfully, too remote to gain credence.

editorial
in *Western Mail* (21 Nov. 1972)

2004 I always order Welsh lamb or mutton in restaurants, in the hope that I'll get to the woolly bastard that keeps tipping my dustbin over.

quoted in
Trevor Fishlock, *Wales and the Welsh* (1972)

2005 The Eisteddfod is the occasion when a lot of Welsh people have a very happy time and there is a great feeling of love and patriotism and a few pretty girls, on a purely temporary basis, you understand, relinquish a little of their virginity.

2006 It is true that I love my country but if there is such a thing as reincarnation, I hope I will come back as an Englishman. To be spared the neuroses and hang-ups of Welshmen, to stop worrying about the threats to the nation and the heritage, to stop all this self-analysis, to stop adopting a self-justifying and defensive attitude, would be a release from a burden.

2007 An aarf of daark and a maarmite saarnie.

traditional description of a Splott breakfast

Euros Bowen
2008 The country's art is in the language.*

'Galatea'

Sir Geraint Evans
2009 It is second best all the time. . . and I am fed up with seeing second best in Wales.

quoted in
Trevor Fishlock, *Wales and the Welsh* (1972)

Trevor Fishlock

2010 I think most Welshmen love Wales more than most Englishmen love England.

Wales and the Welsh (1972)

2011 For all their gloomy analysis, and the Welsh are given to self-examination of the pessimistic kind, history shows that, like their character, their culture has a granite core.

2012 There are Welshmen of my acquaintance whose love of their land is uncrushable, who would sing its praises even on the rack.

2013 Wales is a meld of differences and there is a tradition of argument.

2014 A certain thinness of the skin and inferiority complex is one of the well-known marks of a subject people.

2015 Their hospitality is marvellous and they are the fastest people in the world with the tea-pot, bread-saw and cake-knife.

2016 If you fail to be stirred by the Welsh landscape you will never get to heaven, for you have no soul.

2017 The advancement of the Welsh language is an eminently worthwhile cause and I believe that the fight going on for it may have begun just in time.

2018 Wales is a split-level country. There is Welsh Wales and English Wales, or if you prefer, not-so-Welsh Wales.

2019 Wales, though small, cannot be tidily parcelled. Just as you think you have the picture right, somebody gives the kaleidoscope a nudge and moves the bits.

Raymond Garlick

2020 For some of us, you see,
Wales is another word for peace.

'Explanatory Note'

Lord Hailsham

2021 Although they will probably be horrified to hear it, the thing which differentiates them from the baboons of the IRA, who blow the arms and legs off innocent women and children, and break the knees and tar the bodies of pregnant women, and shoot our lads in the streets of Londonderry and Belfast, is basically a question of degree and not kind.

of Cymdeithas yr Iaith Gymraeg
in address to Welsh Conservatives at Llandrindod,
reported in *Western Mail* (24 April 1972)

Edward Heath MP

2022 The Government already gives practical support in numerous ways to the Welsh way of life, including the Welsh language and culture. That support is a continuing process and wherever new opportunities occur for us to add fruitfully to it, we shall do so. I think it is a great pity that some of the campaigners adopt such an aggressive stance, because it is only by tolerance and friendly co-operation that we can safeguard and strengthen those characteristics of which the people of Wales are justly proud.

reported in *Western Mail* (27 Oct. 1972)

David Jones

2023 John Jones wished his son to be at no disadvantage in the great world, so the more the lad had command of English, the better.

of his own father, in letter to Meic Stephens
in *Poetry Wales* (vol. 8, no. 3, Winter 1972)

Saunders Lewis

2024 The art of the possible does not make sense in the present situation in Wales. The impossible is the only practical way.*

in *Barn* (Christmas 1972)

Goronwy Rees

2025 The Welsh fall easily into complacency and flatter themselves interminably, whereas mediocrity is really the chief mark of what comes out of Wales.

interview
in *Western Mail* (9 Feb. 1972)

2026 Wales is still a peasant society in spite of the Industrial Revolution, and they still have the mentality of peasants.

2027 The Welsh admire a victor, but his success always stimulates their secret resentment, and it is the defeated Cato who really wins their hearts.

A Chapter of Accidents (1972)

2028 This fine disregard for legality is something which comes very easily for the Welsh who, having endured an alien rule for so long, regard its laws as something which it is a duty to circumvent rather than obey.

2029 There are things which can be said in Welsh that cannot be said in English, just as there are things which can be said in English that cannot be said in Welsh, and in choosing a vocabulary and a syntax one is not only choosing a vocabulary and a syntax but what one can say with them. Otherwise, the problem of translation would not remain the almost insoluble one that it is.

2030 In choosing the language of my childhood [Welsh], I should have chosen to remain a child for ever, and this is something Welshmen often do.

2031 The trouble was, I suppose, that I wanted to grow up and felt that I could not do it in Welsh.

2032 I had thought of [Wales] as the land of a dying language and culture which could no longer satisfy anyone except the very young and the very old.

2033 [My wife] thought of the Welsh as some primitive tribe which spoke an unintelligible language, practised savage rites and customs, and was in general shiftless, untrustworthy and hostile to strangers.

Dafydd Elis Thomas

2034 I am being critical of a despair-laden view of Wales generated by a historically-motivated nationalism, which because of its very motivation of necessity has to despair of present and future. And I am being critical of it because for my generation it does not correspond with the exciting living reality which we are experiencing now in Wales.

'The Images of Wales in R. S. Thomas's Poetry' in *Poetry Wales* (vol. 7, no. 4, Spring 1972)

George Thomas MP

2035 In all public matters English must be given priority as long as it remains the majority spoken language.

reported in the *South Wales Echo* (2 Dec. 1972)

Peter Thomas MP

2036 I certainly see the need for people in Wales collectively to feel the urge to support the language and I would like to see as many people as possible in Wales joining together in order to further the language.

reported in *Western Mail* (23 Nov. 1972)

R. S. Thomas

2037　Small as he was
He towered, the trigger of his mind
Cocked, ready to let fly with his scorn.

'Saunders Lewis'

2038 Why no! I never thought other than
That God is that great absence
In our lives, the empty silence
Within, the place where we go
Seeking, not in hope to
Arrive or find.

'Via Negativa'

Rhydwen Williams

2039 The way I see it around me today, for whoever would be committed to his craft as a writer in Wales now, there can be no peace. There is only war, bitter, prolonged, even violent, through which we must write the truth in the face of all the rotten lies that entangle our lives. Every writer in Wales today is charged with this great responsibility, whatever his language. I believe that sticking to your task as a writer can be as valid as going to prison for the language.

letter to Meic Stephens
in *Poetry Wales* (vol. 8, no. 2, Autumn 1972)

— **1973** —

Ewart Alexander

2040 He [the native of north Wales] is usually quite devious, talks as if apple-peel is stuck in his throat and still believes in the Old God.

in *Artists in Wales* (ed. Meic Stephens, 1973)

2041 I believe a writer, if he looks at Wales, can only write farce or drown in nostalgia for things which aren't there.

2042 A country can't progress on candle power which keeps on being blown out by puffs of intersecting hot air.

Aneurin Bevan MP
2043 The purpose of getting power is to be able to give it away.

quoted in Michael Foot, *Aneurin Bevan* (vol. 2, 1973)

2044 I have always been puzzled to know why so great a country as Wales should be represented by so miserable a newspaper [as the *Western Mail*].

Geraint Talfan Davies
2045 Despite all the Government assistance that is given to the language in various forms, it cannot be said to be a language policy, any more than the recital of financial incentives to industry can be called a regional policy. Without such a clear lead from Government, which in these days of increasing state intervention must bear a large part of the burden for fostering the language, the gloomy prospect must be for a running battle with one side deciding its attitude to each manifestation of the language issue on an ad hoc basis.

in *Western Mail* (4 July 1973)

Raymond Edwards
2046 The story of the arts in Wales is not particularly encouraging.

in *Artists in Wales* (ed. Meic Stephens, 1973)

John Fuller
2047 Expecting Wales to be like Borrow
Has filled the tourist with deep sorrow
(It will be twice as bad tomorrow).

'To Angus MacIntyre'

Raymond Garlick
2048 For myself, then, being an Anglo-Welsh writer at the present time involves deploying the English language as an instrument of justice on behalf of Welsh, its senior partner in the bilingual situation.

in *Artists in Wales* (ed. Meic Stephens, 1973)

2049 It is because the mystery of language is the most personal manifestation of each man's unique and immortal humanity that I have felt so deeply the recent linguistic injustices in Wales. It is inconceivable to me that a writer, whatever his language, should feel otherwise.

2050 The language with which all Anglo-Welsh writers are primarily concerned is naturally English, the problem language of Wales. For them it is not a provincialising, alienating, London patois, the sleazy dialect of admass, the insolent cant of the courts; for them it is one of the mother-tongues of Wales, a classical language of beauty and precision, used for literary purposes by some Welshmen for many centuries, a part of the double richness of Welsh civilization. The problems are how to make it a language of integration, of reconciliation, of justice.

Emyr Humphreys
2051 In Wales we know from tribal experience, which is the only indispensable knowledge, that a threatened language can also be a life-line that ties in firmly to a human past.

'The Loss of Incantation'
in *Welsh Music* (Winter 1973)

Robert Hunter
2052 I do not consider my not wanting to speak Welsh as a barrier to understanding. I think that I am in sympathy with the Welsh language; I like the sound it makes.

in *Artists in Wales* (ed. Meic Stephens, 1973)

Glynne Jones
2053 It is puzzling that in Wales, the home of sweeping radicalism, we should be so conservative in our music.

in *Artists in Wales* (ed. Meic Stephens, 1973)

Jonah Jones
2054 Hence the internecine dispute over language. The English hardly appear in the argument and do not really understand what the fuss is all about – that is an English prerogative.

in *Artists in Wales* (ed. Meic Stephens, 1973)

2055 It may be too late for Wales as Wales.

T. Gwynn Jones

2056 The imprisoning of a few prominent Welshmen would be more effective than a thousand namby-pamby, deceitful and unprincipled committees in stiffening the backbone of the Welsh-speaking Welsh.*

quoted in David Jenkins, *Thomas Gwynn Jones, Cofiant* (1973)

Alun Llywelyn-Williams

2057 There can be no doubt at all that the Welsh language has always been the core of our national identity. But I cannot now be absolutely convinced that it will or need always be so, though I do believe that even if the language dies it will for centuries to come have to be accounted as the main factor in shaping whatever distinctive role we may as a community have yet to play in the destinies of mankind.

in *Artists in Wales* (ed. Meic Stephens, 1973)

John Ormond

2058 What I ask of a poem is that, first and foremost, it should be a good poem in the English language, and that is to say my use of the English language. If there is a further element of Welshness in a poem, I know that it will look after itself.

in *Artists in Wales* (ed. Meic Stephens, 1973)

2059 Before we can claim to speak a language properly I think one has to be able, for example, to discuss abstract notions and to pun in it. These things I cannot do in Welsh, and I remember this when I fill in a census form.

Alun Richards

2060 Welshness was like a cottonwool fuzz at the back of the mind because Wales was always around the corner where I lived.

Connie
Home to an Empty House (1973)

2061 Bilingualism is all the rage now, everywhere except where money or commerce is concerned.

2062 It was a country of permanent ills, four centuries rolled into one, and if you didn't get away from it now and again you choked in the back-biting and rancour.

'Bowels Jones'
Dai Country (1973)

Meic Stephens

2063 These beasts are our companions, dark presences from the peasant past, these grim valleys our common hendre, exiles all, until the coming thaw.

'Ponies, Twynyrodyn'

Ned Thomas

2064 More and more Welsh signs lead to fewer and fewer Welsh places.

'Six Characters in Search of Tomorrow'
in *The Welsh Language Today* (ed. Meic Stephens, 1973)

R. S. Thomas

2065 Vote Plaid, mun
and be damned for your own sake.

'He has the vote'

Aled Vaughan

2066 Have we in the Welsh language ignored the existence of evil as part of the human condition? This seems to me to be the missing value that could add the missing dimension to Welsh writing. Maybe we have emasculated our society by creating around us a false paradise.

in *Artists in Wales* (ed. Meic Stephens, 1973)

2067 Wales was – is – such a friendly place. There, the pressure is eased off when it begins to hurt. It's why we'll never be truly professional as a people.

2068 My attitude to it is ambiguous: I feel more secure and relaxed within the sound of it, but when I think about it I'm sad, for I believe it's going to die, and any nation that lives through the death of its language lives through an agony of false values, confusion and constricted thinking.

2069 The making of Welsh-language programmes is now a legitimate occupation and not a comic pastime. I hope the same can be said of English-language programmes produced in Wales in a decade from now.

2070 The official line is to be bilingual, but we're a long way from achieving it.

Richard Vaughan

2071 Wales was never so alive as on those

occasions when I would sit drawing in a pub or café in London. When I came back I was somehow too close to things.*

in *Barn* (no. 123, Jan. 1973)

G. O. Williams

2072 In the past the existence of Ireland, Scotland and Wales has been seen as a threat to the unity of the kingdom centred in London, and in all kinds of subtle ways the prestige of Government and Empire has relegated the Celtic nations to a limbo of the quaint and picturesque cultures that are dead but won't lie down. Now England has to recognise that Britain's future will be far happier and more stable if it accepts the other cultures, not grudgingly but with positive action to sustain their growth.

in *Western Mail* (1 March, 1973)

Kyffin Williams

2073 Like every other man in North Wales, I can trace my descent back to Lludd ap Beli Mawr.

Across the Straits (1973)

2074 Wales is a land of ochres and umbers, only occasionally going mad in a riot of colour.

— **1974** —

Max Boyce

2075 Asso asso yogoshi,
Me Welsh-speaking Japanee.

'Asso asso yogoshi'

Gwynfor Evans

2076 I write these words on 26 April 1971. Tonight the census forms which will tell the government how many people can speak and read and write Welsh are being completed; that is, how successful its policies have been in Wales during the last few centuries.

Land of my Fathers (1974)

2077 While I sit here in comfort, over fifty young Welsh people are in prison in England and in Wales – twenty-five of them girls – because of their attachment to their country and language.

David Jones

2078 Does the land wait the sleeping lord
      or is the wasted land
that very lord who sleeps?

The Sleeping Lord (1974)

Neil Kinnock MP

2079 Bedwellty is not Welsh by language, although Welsh by character and temperament. We have all the essentials of Welsh valley life – clubs and choirs and chapels, and a 22,000 Labour majority.

speech in House of Commons, 12 March 1974

2080 We will meet the genuine demands for new democratic developments with an elected Welsh Assembly.

speech, reported in *Western Mail* (21 Feb. 1974)

Peter Levi

2081 David Jones's tradition was Welsh. He is the last innocent witness to the cultural massacre of the Welsh people by the English and by the modern world.

sermon in Westminster Cathedral during a requiem mass for the writer, 13 Dec. 1974

Leslie Norris

2082 What shall we write about, in Wales, where the concentration Camps are a thousand years old, And some of our own making?

'The Green Bridge'

2083 I would not fight for Wales, the great
      battle-cries
Do not arouse me. I keep short boundaries
      holy,
Those my eyes have recognized and my
      heart has known
As welcome. Nor would I fight for her
      language. I spend
My few pence of Welsh to amuse my
      friends, to comment
On the weather. They carry no thought
      that could be mine.
It's the small wars I understand.

'A Small War'

Enoch Powell MP

2084 Power devolved is power retained.

speech at Llwynypia, 1974

Wilbert Lloyd Roberts

2085 We are the only country in the world
where television came before theatre.

in the *Liverpool Daily Post* (1974)

R. S. Thomas

2086 What is a Welshman?

title of a book of verse, 1974

Harri Webb

2087 Taffy has always been a clown and the
talent scouts are always on the look-out for
new turns.

letter to Sam Adams
in *Poetry Wales* (vol. 10, no. 1, Summer 1974)

2088 Sing for Wales or shut your trap,
All the rest's a load of crap.

'Advice to a Young Poet'

2089 Lady, your land's invaded, we have
thrown
Hurried defences up, our soil is raw,
New, shallow, the old crops do not grow
Here where we man the trench.

'A Crown for Branwen'

G. O. Williams

2090 We beseech you to reconsider your
decision to give priority to the English
language on bilingual road-signs in Wales.
We do so because, like you, we long to see
a general disposition in Wales to promote
the good of the Welsh language and to put
an end to dissension and protest . . . The
significance of putting English first will be
to proclaim that English is the most highly
esteemed language in Wales, and the effect
will be to arouse protestors to challenge
the law. Feeling certain as we do that this
would be as distressing to you as to us, we
beg you to change your decision and to
give priority to the Welsh language.

letter also signed by twenty-five others, to the
Secretary of State for Wales, Oct. 1974

— 1975 —

Anonymous

2091 Although the majority no longer speak it,
the language is still a fundamental bond

holding the people of Wales together. It is
also the main link between present-day
Wales and centuries of national history
and communal tradition. If it disappears,
we fear that little by little most of the other
characteristics which are distinctively
Welsh will in turn disappear. In their
place it is likely to acquire not the best
English traditions but a form of regional
sub-culture which would be a sorry
exchange for the unique living culture that
is still ours.

Welsh Language Council Report on Welsh
Nursery Education (1975)

2092 To deprive a Welsh child of his natural
language, and thus cut him off from his
natural heritage, is as much an act of
vandalism as despoiling beautiful scenery.

Max Boyce

2093 'Cos it's hard, Duw it's hard,
It's harder than they will ever know,
And it's they must take the blame,
The price of coal's the same,
But the pit-head baths is a supermarket
now.

'Duw it's hard'

2094 Up and under, here we go,
Are you ready, yes or no?

'The Pontypool Front Row'

Pennar Davies

2095 When the Anglo-Welsh shake off their awe
of the English they may well produce a
Neruda or a Paz.

review
in *Poetry Wales* (vol. 11, no. 1, Summer 1975)

Glyn Jones

2096 How can we, like the bullet-
Spattering Mexican, kneel down and give
a scooped up
Handcupful of Welsh soil Zapata's kiss
of ecstasy?

'Y Ddraig Goch'

Graham Jones

2097 Now they're trying to alter all our
signposts
And make us live in streets we cannot
say;

I don't mind the Pakistanis or the Eyties
But I wish the bleeding Welsh would
stay away.

'I'm proud to be a citizen of Cardiff'

Neil Kinnock MP

2098 I do not think that we are any more or less
in love with social justice or practise it
better or worse than any nation.

speech in House of Commons, 3 Feb. 1975

2099 Devolutionary reform will not provide a
factory, a machine or job, build a school,
train a doctor or put a pound on pensions.

reported in *South Wales Echo* (1 Nov. 1975)

Adrian Mitchell

2100 Poets of Wales, like trees on fire,
Light the black twentieth century.

'Lament for the Welsh Makers'

Gwyn Thomas

2100 Talk of Welsh to some politicians and
county councillors
And they'll instinctively reach for their
consciences.*

'Soniwch am y Gymraeg'

R. S. Thomas

2102   Life is not hurrying
on to a receding future, nor hankering
after
an imagined past. It is the turning
aside like Moses to the miracle
of the lit bush, to a brightness
that seemed as transitory as your youth
once, but is the eternity that awaits you.

'The Bright Field'

Raymond Williams

2103 Depopulation, unemployment,
exploitation, poverty: if these are not part
of Welsh culture we are denying large
parts of our social experience.

'Welsh Culture'
Culture and Politics (1975)

— 1976 —

Anonymous

2104 Ballet? Ballet is just a leg-show for the
nobs!

Swansea councillor.
quoted in Trevor Fishlock, *Talking of Wales*
(1976)

2105 Wales! Whales? D'you mean da fish, or
them singing bastards?

New York taxi-driver

Quentin Bell

2106 They went . . . to Manorbier on the
Pembroke coast, a wild desolate place.

Virginia Woolf (1976)

Max Boyce

2107 Painted green, painted green,
The signs to Heaven were all in Welsh:
Hell's signs were painted green.

'The Devil's marking me'

James Callaghan MP

2108 My political instincts tell me that the
successful implementation of devolution
offers us, as a party, the best way of
keeping the United Kingdom united,
while at the same time enhancing the
vigour of national diversity within these
islands.

speech at Labour Party Annual Conference,
Brighton, 1976

Frank Hennessy

2109 I'm Cardiff born and I'm Cardiff bred,
And when I dies I'll be Cardiff dead.

'The Cardiff Song'

Emanuel Litvinoff

2110 Many were joining the Communist Party
in the hope that it would get busy again
after the Revolution, which had already
nearly happened in Germany and could
start at any minute in the Rhondda.

Journey through a Small Planet(1976)

Emyr Llewelyn

2111 What is Wales? According to the old
nationalism, Wales is the land from
Anglesey to Monmouthshire, the
territorial unit on this side of Offa's Dyke.
But I would deny that. This Wales has
ceased to be Wales in the true sense of the
word. Only an empty name remains
without the substance of society and

neighbourhood. House by house, farm by farm, district by district, what you call Wales has ceased to be a true Wales.*

Adfer a'r Fro Gymraeg (1976)

Ioan Bowen Rees

2112 To think that, in the United Kingdom, there is opposition to something short of cantonal status for Scotland, which is as big as Denmark, and Wales, which is twice as rich as Ireland and over twenty times bigger than the Jura.

'The Jura Question'
in *Planet* (no. 31, March 1976)

Kate Roberts

2113 We in Wales have a talent for praising the wrong things.*

'Mis Medi'
Yr Wylan Deg (1976)

Harri Webb

2114 Wales is marching backwards into independence, everybody desperately pretending that we are going somewhere else.

'Webb's Progress'
in *Planet* (no. 30, Jan. 1976)

2115 The sad fact must be faced that we are even more boring to the English than they are to us, which is saying a great deal.

'The Historical Context of Welsh Translation'
in *Poetry Wales* (vol. 11, no. 3, Winter 1976)

— 1977 —

Bruce Chatwin

2116 Mrs Powell's first cousin had left Patagonia and gone back home to Wales. 'He *has* done well,' she said. 'He's now the Archdruid.'

In Patagonia (1977)

2117 I slept in the Draigoch Guest House. It was owned by Italians who played Neapolitan songs on the juke-box late into the night.

2118 The beach was grey and littered with dead penguins. Half-way along was a concrete

monument in memory of the Welsh. It looked like the entrance to a bunker. Let into its sides were bronze reliefs representing Barbarism and Civilization. Barbarism showed a group of Tehuelche Indians, naked, with slabby back muscles in the Soviet style. The Welsh were on the side of Civilization – greybeards, young men with scythes, and big-breasted girls with babies.

2119 Their grandfather came out from Caernarvon but she couldn't say where that was. Caernarvon wasn't marked on her map of Wales. 'You can't expect much,' she said, 'when it's printed on a tea-towel.'

T. Glynne Davies

2120 We have lived with the language neurosis for too long now . . . We have bred a generation of young people to whom Welsh is not an exciting medium of expression but a problem and a worry and a sack of stones on their backs.

in *Artists in Wales* (ed. Meic Stephens 1977)

Nicholas Edwards MP

2121 The survival of a culture, individuality and language are natural matters for Conservative concern. Welsh people, even those who speak only English, are interested in the survival of Welsh, though they do not want it to be the cause of division and privilege.

speech at Conservative Party conference
reported in *The Times* (13 June 1977)

Trevor Fishlock

2122 The Language Society is still seen by some as a group of hairy Welsh eccentrics, urged on by old men who should know better. But it is more widely regarded as the point of a spear, the personification of a deep actual grievance. It has the support of many writers, academics, teachers and ministers, and there is sympathy for its aims, if not for its methods, from a fairly large section of the Welsh public.

in *The Times* (11 Nov. 1977)

Michael Flanders and Donald Swan

2123 The Welshman's dishonest – he cheats when he can –

And little and dark, more like monkey
than man;
He works underground with a lamp on his
hat
And sings far too loud, far too often, and
flat!
The English, the English, the English
are best!
I wouldn't give tuppence for all of the
rest.

'Song of Patriotic Prejudice'

Gwyn Jones
2124 I do not believe that Welsh will ever again
become the first language of Wales. That
battle has been lost, if it ever took place.

Being and Belonging (1977)

2125 If you can't make the Welsh Fifteen,
translate the Mabinogion.

Sally Jones
2126 We adapt. To the chimneys, the concrete,
The furnace, the smoke, the dead trees.
Our fields are the names of roadways,
Our flocks and language are gone:
But we hold our diminished city in face of
the sun.

'Community'

2127 Lord, let me not be silent till
All earth is grinding in Your mill!

'Ann Griffiths'

Tom Nairn
2128 [Wales] must be the only country where
one regularly hears nationalists
denouncing nationalism.

The Break-up of Britain (1977)

2129 In Wales, Calvinism figures as a creed of
prolonged opposition to the high and
mighty; in Scotland it has mainly been the
creed of the high and mighty.

2130 Few Scots can easily understand or
sympathize with the anguishing dilemmas
of the language-problem; on the other
hand, Welshmen are often puzzled by the
very existence of a nationalist movement
without a language of its own.

2131 The Scot perceives a colossal fuss being
made about nothing; the Welsh nationalist

is intrigued by a country where there
seems nothing to make a fuss about.

Dewi Prys-Thomas
2132 In fact I am a Finn, and Wales is my
Finland. I am a Dane, and Wales is my
Denmark. I am a Matabele, and Wales is
my Zimbabwe.

in *Artists in Wales* (ed. Meic Stephens, 1977)

Ioan Bowen Rees
2133 This region [Gwynedd] is a great
heartland of Welsh and if it is not defended
here of all places it can have no hope of
survival. It is not a question of fanaticism.
In the first place it is a matter of
democracy. A citizen should be able to use
the language of his choice.

in *The Times* (26 July 1977)

Harri Webb
2134 I do not need Shoni Hoi from Cwmscwt or
Dr Hengist Horsa from Hog's Norton to
tell me how to think or what to write.

in *Artists in Wales* (ed. Meic Stephens, 1977)

2135 One of the pervading weaknesses of the
Anglo-Welsh generally is ghastly good
taste.

— **1978** —

Anonymous
2136 If Wales were to be rolled out as flat as
England, it would be the bigger country of
the two.

quoted in Christie Davies, *Welsh Jokes* (1978)

2137 In answer to a written question, the
Secretary of State for Wales told the
House of Commons that there had been
eight cases of fraud in Carmarthenshire,
twelve cases of fraud in Pembrokeshire,
and two cases of attempted fraud in
Cardiganshire.

John Davies
2138 A quick reference to cynghanedd
always goes down well; girls are cariad;
myth is in; exile, defeat, hills . . .
almost anything Welsh and sad.

'How to write Anglo-Welsh Poetry'

Cledwyn Hughes MP

2139 He [Leo Abse] has a strange, inexplicable hostility towards Wales, or perhaps to Welsh-speaking Wales. This seems to be developing into an obsession. Anything outside the Anglicized circle of Cardiff is anathema to him. He talks about a Welsh-speaking élite taking over if the Welsh Bill becomes law. This is just such a flight of fancy that he must be saying it to frighten his constituents.

entry in diary, 1 March 1978

2140 He [Neil Kinnock] has a bee in his bonnet about Wales which is a pity as he is pleasant and gifted.

Emyr Humphreys

2141 The Welsh language is so well supplied with good poems it seems unbelievable that it should be in the slightest danger of extinction.

'Poetry, Prison and Propaganda'
in *Planet* (no. 43, June 1978)

2142 Save Welsh, Cymry, and you may help to save the world.

Goronwy Jones

2143 'You self-righteous bloody culture-vulture bastard!' said Mick. 'You pathetic self-seeking free-state Plaid Cymru craphouse!' said Ben. 'Come on, then, you reactionary Adfer fascist bum!' said Mick. Connolly shouted, 'Right, boys, stop it! . . . This is a Solidarity Rally.'*

Dyddiadur Dyn Dwad (1978)

Neil Kinnock MP

2144 We cannot afford to flatter nationalism.

reported in *South Wales Echo* (25 Feb. 1978)

Peter Elfed Lewis

2145 When are knickers panties and when are
    they briefs?
And how do convictions differ from beliefs?
    Is an inkspot a stain or merely a blot?
    Is a monoglot Welshman Welsh or not?

'A Question of Definition'

Brian Morris

2146 We are a gentle people, given to charity
    and abstinence.

'Dinas Emrys'

R. S. Thomas

2147 An Anglo-Welsh writer is neither one thing nor the other. He keeps going in a no-man's-land between two cultures.

'The Creative Writer's Suicide'
in *Planet* (no. 41, 1978)

2148 In the Wales in which we live, there is no literary answer to the literary problem. The crisis which is disturbing the nation is caused by political pressure; it must therefore be resolved politically.

2149 Let nobody imagine that because there is so much English everywhere in Wales, it is not a foreign language.

2150 Rise up, you Welsh, demand leaders of your own choosing to govern you in your own country, to help you to make a future in keeping with your own best traditions, before it is too late.

review
in *Planet* (no. 41, 1978)

2151 Our wish is to live at peace with the English, to the point of servility. They too want to live at peace with us – on their own terms.

John Tripp

2152 Think. One day this dry
English pen, this arrogant
instrument, will no longer
be required. Then my short
modest task will be done.

'Irony'

2153 I don't belong here
but who can go home again?
They speak another language
there, and where's the night life?

'Rootless in Crockherbtown'

Wynford Vaughan-Thomas

2154 He's written a hymn! He's written a hymn!
Beethoven and Bach have got nothing on
    him!

untitled poem

2155 Sacred alike to boxing and to art,
For who in Wales can tell the two apart?

'Alexander Pope at the National Eisteddfod'

2156 The sight of the English is getting me down.

'Hiraeth in N.W. 3'

Harri Webb

2157 We're looking up England's arsehole, Waiting for the manna to fall.

'Anglo-maniac Anthem'

Gwyn A. Williams

2158 I can still remember the day when I encountered my first Conservative, a shock all the greater in that it coincided with the crisis of puberty.

The Merthyr Rising (1978)

2159 Being Welsh is not merely a predicament, it is as insufferable as it is inescapable.

— **1979** —

Leo Abse MP

2160 Are the English-speaking Welshmen and Welshwomen of Newport, Pontypool and Gwent to become second-class citizens in their own land?

reported in *South Wales Argus* (27 Feb. 1979)

2161 We wage, you know, guerrilla war. We avoid confrontation, we operate by nudge, by conspiracy, by stealth. In Westminster, the Welsh members wrest, out of the English Establishment, if you like, they wrest a lot of prizes, as you know, by calling upon the old cunning which has enabled Wales and its Welshness to survive, unlike many other territories.

'Talking about Devolution'
in *Planet* (no. 47, Feb. 1979)

Anonymous

2162 It is our convinced view that the creation of new national demarcations in Britain through the establishment of separate Welsh and Scots Assemblies and new systems of public expenditure allocation would divide Britain and the Labour Movement.

manifesto of the Labour No Assembly campaign, 1979

2163 We have to accept that *this* concept of a Welsh Assembly is now dead and buried.

However, devolution will not die with this particular Wales Act. The rejection of the Assembly does not mean that the status quo has been fully endorsed.

editorial
in *Western Mail* (5 March 1979)

Richard Haslam

2164 Wales is generally rich in minor buildings and poor in major ones.

The Buildings of Wales:Powys (1979)

Lord Heycock

2165 The way forward for Wales is the status quo.

quoted by John Osmond in *Planet* (no. 48, May 1979)

Cledwyn Hughes MP

2166 It will be a betrayal of the work of this Government on behalf of Wales for any Socialist to do other than vote Yes.

speech in London, 20 Feb. 1979

2167 The fact is that the problems an Assembly was set up to tackle still remain and a solution must eventually be found sooner or later.

reported in *Liverpool Dail Post* (3 March 1979)

Neil Kinnock MP

2168 For the price of an Assembly we could have a new hospital or ten comprehensive schools every year.

2169 Who is prepared to give up £1 million to be bossed about by an institution in Cardiff?

2170 A Welsh Assembly would turn into yet another costly millstone around the necks of the people of Wales.

(23 Feb. 1979)

Gwen Mostyn Lewis

2171 People in South Wales are very charming, but as a crowd they are loud and coarse. We do not want to be governed by Cardiff.

in *Western Mail* (23 March 1979)

Saunders Lewis

2172 We are asked to tell the Government on St

David's Day whether we want a Welsh Assembly or not. The implied question is, Are you a nation or not? May I point out the probable consequences of a No majority? There will follow a general election. There may be a change of government. The first task of a new Westminster Parliament will be to reduce and master inflation. In Wales there are coal mines that work at a loss; there are steelworks that are judged superfluous; there are valleys convenient for submersion. And there will be no Welsh defence.

letter
in *Western Mail* (26 Feb. 1979)

John Morris MP

2173 When you see an elephant on your doorstep, you know it is there.

in response to result of Devolution referendum reported in *Western Mail* (3 March 1979)

John Osmond

2174 The metaphor of Wales as a Nonconformist, radical, one-party state, complete with a Welsh-veneered collaborating élite working at long range in London, is rapidly becoming intolerable.

'Mr Morris and the Elephant'
in *Planet* (no. 48, May 1979)

John Rowlands

2175 Something more than literature is required to save a language but a language without a literature written in it is not worth saving.

'Literature in Welsh'
in *The Arts in Wales 1950–75* (ed. Meic Stephens, 1979)

Gwyn Thomas

2176 If there is a lot of insomnia among the top layer of the aristocracy, it is because they keep waking up through the night and complimenting themselves in amazement on having stumbled across a society in which they were allowed to get away with it.

'The Subsidence Factor'
The Gwyn Jones Lecture (1979)

2177 My father and mother were Welsh-speaking, yet I did not exchange a word in that language with them. The death of Welsh ran through our family of twelve like a geological fault.

2178 Places like the Rhondda were parts of America that never managed to get on the boat.

Gwyn A. Williams

2179 In recent centuries we have progressively lost our grip on our own past. Our history has been a history to induce schizophrenia and to enforce loss of memory . . . Half-memories, folklore, myths, fantasy are rampant.

radio talk, 1979
in *Wales on the Wireless* (ed. Patrick Hannan, 1986)

Raymond Williams

2180 We are, we say, a small people, but in immediate human terms what is small, what is knowable, about twenty-five thousand people, more than we can ever talk to or know?

introduction
The Arts in Wales 1950–75 (ed. Meic Stephens, 1979)

2181 What history we were taught in the elementary school was a poisonous brand of romantic and medieval Welsh chauvinism . . . The reading was dreadful, nothing but how such and such a medieval prince defeated the Saxons and took from them great quantities of cattle and gold. I threw up on that.

Politics and Letters (1979)

2182 Suddenly England, bourgeois England, wasn't my point of reference any more. I was a Welsh European [and] I want the Welsh people – still a radical and cultured people – to defeat, over-ride or by-pass bourgeois England.

2183 The typical Welsh intellectual is – as we say – only one generation away from shirt sleeves.

— **1980** —

Max Boyce

2184 I was there!

catch-phrase

Nicholas Edwards MP

2185 Why do we in this country spend so much time talking things to destruction?

speech to Gwynedd County Council, Llanrwst, 15 April 1980

Ieuan Gwynedd Jones

2186 The Welsh language was a precious and singular possession of the masses of workers at a time when the inhuman and brutalising forces of industrialism were alienating them from nature and from society.

'Language and Community in Nineteenth Century Wales'
in *A People and a Proletariat* (ed. Dai Smith, 1980)

Jan Morris

2187 Wales suffers greatly from its stereotypes, often self-inflicted.

preface
My Favourite Stories of Wales (1980)

Wynford Vaughan-Thomas

2188 Old Swansea was never planned. It was doodled over the landscape.

Trust to Talk (1980)

Baroness White

2189 I firmly believe that we cannot hope for a healthy society in Wales unless we struggle to attain genuine bilingualism, so that at least the majority, rather than the minority, have a free choice of which language they wish to use on any particular occasion.

in *Western Mail* (10 April 1980)

— 1981 —

Anonymous

2190 Wales's greatest tragedy is that she is so far from God and so near to England.

motion before the Council of Free Churches of North Wales, 1981

Nigel Jenkins

2191 Oggy! Oggy! Oggy!
Shame dressed as pride.
The thing's all mouth,
needs a generous boot

up its oggy oggy arse
before we're all of us sung
into oggy oggy silence.

'Land of Song'

Kenneth O. Morgan

2192 The Welsh until the eighties [1880s] betrayed all the symptoms of what Marx called unhistoric nationalism.

Rebirth of a Nation: Wales 1880–1980 (1981)

2193 In 1945, and for several years afterwards, Welsh nationalism seemed to be as dead as the druids.

2194 The Welsh are, and have long been, an intensely political nation.

2195 The Welsh experience, like the Southern [States of the USA], induces a sense of humility, of the transitory, deceptive quality of political and economic achievements, of the fragility of a national culture treasured over the centuries by the common people.

2196 For all that, Wales, like Scotland indeed, also serves as a story of desperate survival against all the odds, of frequent failures and half-fulfilled aspirations, kept alive without self-destructive bitterness and ultimately with much success.

Brian Morris

2197 How, for example, does one translate 'pygmy blow-pipe' or 'exhaust manifold gasket' or even 'anglepoise lamp' into Welsh?

report on museums in Wales, 1981

Gwyn Thomas

2198 The remnant are here –
What are they but piranha
In a bowl, destroying
one another.*

'Y Cymry Cymraeg'

— 1982 —

John Fuller

2199 Marauding pop stars stress their anguish
Over the loss of the Welsh language.

I can't say it's the sort of pang which
Moves me to anger.
I bet there's no Celtic for 'ham sandwich'
Even in Bangor.

'Epistle to David Caute'

Dafydd Iwan

2200 I've been on the Education Committee
since 1933;
I know every headmaster in the county,
or rather, they know me!*

'Y Dyn Pwysig' (trans. Ned Thomas)

D. Gwenallt Jones

2201 Welsh literature will surely discover the
flesh one day; and the muse will find out
that man has got a cock.*

Ffwrneisi (1982)

Jan Morris

2202 Wales, the first place.

title of book (1982)

2203 Welsh is a life-giving language.

Wales: the First Place (1982)

2204 The language itself, whether you speak it
or not, whether you love it or hate it, is like
some bewitchment or seduction from the
past, drifting across the country down the
centuries, subtly affecting the nation's
sensibilities even when its meaning is
forgotten.

2205 Nothing is ever settled in Wales. It is a
country in flow, always on an ebbing or a
rising tide, never actually at the turn.

2206 It is showy, it is a little sentimental, some
people find it, with its invented antiquities
of ritual and costume, rather silly; but it is
unmistakably alive.

of the Chairing of the Bard ceremony at the
National Eisteddfod

2207 Water is a very Welsh element.

Gwyn A. Williams

2208 The frontiers of a Welsh nation have rarely
coincided with the frontiers of a Welsh
people.

The Welsh in their History (1982)

2209 A great deal of Welsh history has been
Welsh history with the Welsh left out.

2210 Our recent history has been sheer
melodrama.

2211 Welsh identity has constantly renewed
itself by anchoring itself in variant forms of
Britishness.

2212 We are a people with plenty of traditions
but no historical memory. We have no
historical autonomy. We live in the
interstices of other people's history.

2213 The form of Welsh personality which
historically and genuinely has existed
within a British identity seems to carry all
the stigmata of the historically transient: it
becomes a question of style, of accent, of
historically acquired manners, of half-
understood hymns sung on ritual
occasions, a question of trivialities.

2214 We Welsh of the present generation. . .
may be among the last fully to experience
an elusive but all too tangible Welshness as
a lived reality.

2215 If capitalism in the British Isles lives,
Wales will die. If Wales is to live,
capitalism in the British Isles must die.

2216 Wales is an artefact which the Welsh
produce; the Welsh make and remake
Wales day by day and year after year . . .
If we want Wales, we will have to make
Wales.

2217 Britain has begun its long march out of
history . . . We Welsh look like being the
Last of the British. There is some logic in
this. We were, after all, the First.

2218 Linguistic nationalism will dissolve us all
into warring tribes.

'Land of our Fathers'
in *Marxism Today* (Aug. 1982)

Iwan Llwyd Williams and Wiliam Owen Roberts

2219 It is painful and very difficult to create
poetry which is relevant in Welsh by now.
Poets feel very often that it is an act of
necrophilia.*

'Myth y Traddodiad Dethol'
in *Llais Llyfrau* (Autumn 1982)

161

— 1983 —

Emyr Humphreys

2220 The history of Wales, such as it is, is a
history of unending resistance and
unexpected survival.

The Taliesin Tradition (1983)

2221 The continuing existence of a Welsh
identity is in itself a remarkable historical
fact. Whether it be described as the end-
product of an inherently conservative
temperament, or as a combination of
incorrigible ignorance and stupidity, or as
a triumph of the human spirit, its existence
cannot be denied.

2222 The Methodists were to Protestantism in
several important respects what the
preaching friars had been to medieval
Catholicism.

2223 To understand a nineteenth-century
Welshman, and indeed, for a twentieth-
century Welshman to understand himself,
it is essential to know to which
denomination or religious sect his
immediate ancestors belonged.

2224 It is always the past rather than the
present that offers the best hope for the
future.

Harri Webb

2225 Let's do our best for the ancient tongue,
Its music's so delightful,
We dearly love to hear it sung,
But speak it? Oh, how frightful!

'The Art of the Possible'

2226 Where will you spend eternity?
The posters question us.
The answer comes quite readily:
Waiting for a Cardiff bus!

'Answer from Limbo'

2227 Twice I have seen my native town
By wrath and greed to ruin brought down,
Once from the sky by those called Huns
And once again by her own sons.

of Swansea
'Redevelopment'

2228 What Wales needs, and has always lacked
most

Is, instead of an eastern boundary, an East
Coast.

'Our Scientists are Working on it'

Rhodri Williams

2229 Remember the Welsh-speaking niggers.*

'Niggers Cymraeg'

— 1984 —

Dannie Abse

2230 I think of Wales as my wife and London as
my mistress.

in 'Wales! Wales?', broadcast on BBC2, 1 April
1984

Tariq Ali

2231 The Welsh Windbag.

of Neil Kinnock, but also applied to David
Lloyd George.

Anonymous

2232 Wales is closed.

graffiti on Severn Bridge during miners' strike,
1984

Jon Dressel

2233 London flickers in the parlors
of Llansteffan seven nights a week.

'Praise in the Country'

Michael Foot MP

2234 He stated his views with great persistence
and skill. He was the most powerful
opponent we had in Wales.

of Neil Kinnock's objection to devolution, 1979
quoted in Robert Harris, *The Making of Neil
Kinnock* (1984)

Raymond Garlick and Roland
Mathias

2235 What opera is to Italy, ballet to Russia,
theatre to England, symphonic music to
Germany, painting to the Netherlands,
poetry is to Wales.

introduction
Anglo-Welsh Poetry 1480–1980 (1984)

Ifor Huws

2236 My gran is a punk, she wears safety pins

And she took me to the City Hall to gob at
the Prince.*

'Punk Mamgu'

Aled Islwyn

2237 Wales hasn't got any history. She hasn't
had a history for generations. Bumbling
on, surviving from one century to the next
. . . Keeping the legends alive, that's all
recent Welsh history has been about.*

Gethin
Cadw'r Hen Chwedlau'n Fyw (1984)

Dafydd Iwan

2238 We are still here! We are still here!
Despite everyone and everything,
We are still here!*

'Yma o Hyd'

Alun Richards

2239 He [Carwyn James] was a Welshman who
made you feel glad you were a member of
the human race.

Carwyn James (1984)

Dai Smith

2240 Wales! Wales?

title of book (1984)

2241 Wales is a singular noun but a plural
experience.

Wales! Wales? (1984)

2242 The recent history of most of the Welsh
people is being allowed to drift with them
into a lobotomized anonymity.

2243 The Wales that is projected to the outside
world is not a Wales most of the Welsh
know or recognize as anything of their
own.

2244 Cardiff . . . was compounded of suburban
swank and an ineradicable accent which
cut into aural sensibilities like wire
through cheese.

— 1985 —

Duncan Bush

2245 Sometimes, to live in Wales is to know that
the dead still outnumber the living.

'The Graveyard in Dinorwic'

Lord Cledwyn

2246 Wales is infinitely worse off now than it
was in 1979, and my view is that this is an
argument for devolution, for if we had an
elected authority we might have been able
to stand up to some of the things that have
been happening in Wales, so that to that
extent the opponents of devolution were
radically wrong in what they did and said.

private interview
quoted in Hefin Williams, 'Talking about the
Referendum'
in *Planet* (no. 72, Dec./Jan. 1988–89)

Kim Howells

2247 One thing it [the miners's strike of 1984]
did was drive out once and for all the
ghosts of syndicalism which have never
haunted anywhere more than they have
haunted South Wales; and I think we
learnt that the days of a union picketing its
way to victory are long gone and were
probably long gone a decade ago.

'After the Strike'
in *Planet* (no. 51, June/July 1985)

2248 I've become very, very pessimistic about
the future of Wales, I must admit. I just
hope we're not going to become a kind of
ossified backwater like Appalachia or a
Ruritanian appendage to England, a
tourist place with industrial museums the
biggest growth industry. But there's
something, a kind of magic, that keeps us
here, I suppose, though I don't know what
it is, mind.

2249 I remember sitting in the Palladium in
Aberdare in the late sixties watching a re-
run of 'How Green was my Valley' and I
remember thinking for the first time, this is
a film extolling the virtues of scabs, full of
Welshmen with Irish accents, and it's
absolute nonsense; yet I looked around
and the entire audience had their eyes
filled with tears. In one of the most left-
wing constituencies in Britain. It's a very
curious culture, isn't it?

George Thomas MP

2250 By setting up the Welsh Office, the Labour
Government had opened up the floodgates
of nationalism.

Mr Speaker (1985)

2251 My views on devolution were an embarrassment to people like Cledwyn Hughes, Elystan Morgan, John Morris and Tom Ellis, who lived in a world of their own cocooned by nationalist aspirations.

Gwyn Thomas
2252 The Welsh have always been partial to cheese and forecasts of doom.

High on Hope (1985)

2253 I think the Welsh would have benefited from a spell of totally mindless hedonism.

2254 Hearing it [Welsh hymn-singing], I walk again among all those loved and loving people who gave warmth and beauty to the first years of my pilgrimage.

R. S. Thomas
2255 Britishness is a mask. Beneath it there is only one nation, England.*

'Undod'
J. R. Jones Memorial Lecture, 9 Dec. 1985

John Tripp
2256 I live in a country
like the crummy kitchen
behind a posh restaurant,
the cockroaches the customers
never see.

'Life under Thatcher'

Gwyn A. Williams
2257 There are roads out towards survival as a people, but they are long and hard and demand sacrifice and are at present unthinkable to most of the Welsh.

When was Wales? (1985)

2258 One thing I am sure of. Some kind of human society, though God knows what kind, will no doubt go on occupying these two western peninsulas of Britain, but that people, who are my people and no mean people, who have for a millenium and a half lived in them as a Welsh people, are now nothing but a naked people under an acid rain.

— **1986** —

Kingsley Amis
2259 He's the up-market media Welshman.

The Old Devils (1986)

2260 At last they've found a way of destroying our country, not by poverty but by prosperity.

2261 The London bastards who changed all the Welsh counties about. Even my kind of Welshman resents that. And then gave them all those crappy ancient names.

2262 They went outside and stood where a sign used to say Taxi and now said Taxi/Tacsi for the benefit of Welsh people who had never seen a letter X before.

2263 Anyway, it was Wales all right . . . There was no obvious giveaway, like road-signs in two languages or closed-down factories, but something was there, an extra greenness in the grass, a softness in the light, something that was very like England and yet not England at all, more a matter of feeling than seeing but not just feeling, something run-down and sad but simpler and freer than England all the same.

2264 When Labour councillors in South Wales start blathering about taking modern art to the people, everyone's in deep trouble.

Deirdre Beddoe
2265 Welsh women are culturally invisible.

'Images of Welsh Women'
in *Wales, the Imagined Nation* (ed. Tony Curtis, 1986)

Anthony Conran
2266 The death of Welsh would be a major betrayal of civilization.

introduction
Welsh Verse (1987)

Clive James
2267 Oh Cardiff! Dai, your homeland's
    sovereign seat,
This city of arcades and . . . more arcades
I've hardly seen yet. Is there a main street?

'To Russell Davies; a Letter from Cardiff'

Alun Richards
2268 Like the Greeks, the Welsh enjoy their woes and they nourish them in abundance, often preferring remembering to living.

Days of Absence (1986)

Ian Skidmore

2269 Beauty in Wales is received more readily through the ear than through the eye.

Gwynedd (1986)

2270 I know that practically the only growth industry in Wales has been the invention of its own history; forged – in every sense of the word – in the fires of its own powerful fancy.

radio talk, 1986
in *Wales on the Wireless* (ed. Patrick Hannan, 1986)

— **1987** —

Kingsley Amis

2271 I think it is worse to try and revive it [the Welsh language] artificially than to leave things as they are. The only recourse is to study a dead literature, or a very nearly dead literature, as a very valid and interesting academic subject: to study it, not to try to revive it or base anything in present life upon it.

radio talk, 1987
in *Wales on the Wireless* (ed. Patrick Hannan, 1988)

Anonymous

2272 Latterly, with greater knowledge has come better sense. We laugh at the Eisteddfod no longer.

editorial
in the *Daily Telegraph* (10 Aug. 1987)

Michael Bywater

2273 The Welsh are brilliant. Who else could have revived a long-dead and very silly language which was only useful for telling complex and profitable lies?

in *Punch* (30 Sept. 1987)

Tony Curtis

2274 We do no more than blow upon the embers.

'Thoughts from the Holiday Inn'

Alice Thomas Ellis

2275 Wales is crammed with aunties, and so are Cairo, Alexandria and Port Said.

'Universal Aunties'
More Home Life (1987)

Anita Gale

2276 Because it was so divisive, devolution has been a taboo subject since 1979. Now it's creeping back on to the agenda.

quoted in *Planet* (no. 65, Oct. /Nov. 1987)

Raymond Garlick

2277 What we in Wales call education
Marx defined as alienation.
Chapel too has played its part
In neutering Fluellen's heart.

'Notes for an Autobiography'

2278 Except for the genes' cryptogram,
Everything I have and am
Has come from Wales, as life's windfall.
What can it mean to own it all,
Belong to it and be at home
In Wales by right of chromosome?

2279 And certain Welsh electors
Who (the empire dead) chose to become
Colonials by referendum.

2280 In public and in private roles
A man's life turns on these two poles:
Survival and identity
Garrison the heart's warm city.
On these the life of Wales depends
Or, with the century, it ends.

2281 Apart from those in court and gaol,
What, then, happened to most of you?

'The Enigma'

Susan Mayse

2282 Back in the seventies Wales had stirred restlessly like a battered old dragon, then it had nodded off to sleep. Now it stirred again. Or was this the death-rattle?

Merlin's Web (1987)

— **1988** —

Anonymous

2283 Leave that Welsh tart alone.

Mrs Cohen
The Life of Brian (1988)

Emyr Humphreys

2284 I think the dissident is the key figure of our time.

'The Dissident Condition'
in *Planet* (no. 71, Oct./Nov. 1988)

2285 I think we all have to struggle, to a greater and lesser degree. It is part of the human condition but it is especially true in the Welsh context. We have to battle against what the Marxists describe as historical necessity.

Huw Lawrence
2286 'English?' he asked.

It had been a frequent reaction on my first visit to the island. But I found it hard to say I was English, so I nodded, and said, 'Cymraeg'.

'Deutsch?'

I shook my head emphatically.

With a pencil I drew England, Scotland and Wales on a scrap of paper and put a cross at Aberystwyth . He smiled, took hold of my shoulders and kissed me on both cheeks, and shook my hand several times.

'English', he said.

'Tourism and Crete'
in *Planet* (no. 69, June/July 1988)

Robert Minhinnick
2287 For once caravans are in place they never go away, and in fact have a mysterious sex-life of their own, multiplying like neat white caterpillars all over the hospitable *morfa* of Wales.

'Breath of the Dragon'
in Planet (no. 67, Feb. /March 1988)

A. J. P. Taylor
2288 [It is] a sordid plot to exploit Prince Charles, made for political reasons, and what is worse, for reasons of party . . . Mr Wilson is imposing on Prince Charles a sacrifice he would not dream of imposing on his own son.

on hearing that Prince Charles was to spend a term at the University College of Wales, Aberystwyth, in 1969
quoted in Anthony Holden, *Charles, a Biography* (1988)

Dafydd Elis Thomas MP
2289 Welsh culture has to be self-confident enough to take on all-comers. The idea that we can be swamped has to be rejected.

quoted by Ned Thomas
'Can Plaid Cymru Survive?'
in *Planet* (no. 70, Aug. /Sept. 1988)

Ned Thomas
2290 It is possible to allow the uniqueness of Valleys culture and yet wonder whether in modern conditions and in the English language it is possible for it to transform itself while yet, in some sense, maintaining a 'Welsh' character, a continuity of some kind.

'Can Plaid Cymru Survive?'
in *Planet* (no. 70, Aug. /Sept. 1988)

R. S. Thomas
2291 I see no other way to unity in Wales except through the Welsh language. We must start and finish with that, or all our other efforts will be of no use.*

Pe Medrwn yr Iaith (1988)

2292 Every mountain and stream, every farm and little lane announces to the world that landscape is something different in Wales.*

2293 As there is in Wales a mother tongue which is still thriving, a thorough-going Welshman can only consider English as a means of rekindling interest in Welsh-language culture and to lead people back to the mother tongue.*

2294 When I am asked: What is a Welshman? I always answer: A man who speaks Welsh. I know that many people, particularly in Glamorgan, believe that to be too restrictive a definition. Yet, I am of the opinion that to give any other answer is to set foot on the slippery slope of Britishness.*

2295 If the Welsh language were as forceful and as supple in my hands as it was in the hands of Ellis Wynne, for example, I would use it to reveal the hypocrisy, the laziness and the servility of the nation today, and to chastise them until my readers blushed from head to toe.*

2296 Is an obsession with language
an acknowledgement we are too late
to save it?

'R. I. P. 1588–1988'

Peter Walker MP
2297 I have substantial enthusiasm for the language. If I were an English-speaking

Welshman, my children and I would learn Welsh because if you are privileged to have been born the citizen of a country which has inherited not only a language but a beautiful language with a great store of literature and poetry, it is a very important inheritance, one of which you should be proud, and that is why I am so determined to create unity in Wales.

reported in *Y Cymro* (16 Nov. 1988)

Gwyn A. Williams

2298 Wales has largely been defined by forces external to itself.

'Are Welsh Historians putting on the Style?' in *Planet*(no. 68, April/May 1988)

2299 The Welsh people have lived in a permanent state of emergency since about 383 A.D.*

lecture at the National Eisteddfod, 2 Aug. 1988

2300 We as a people have been around for two thousand years. Isn't it about time we got the key to our own front door?

speech to the Campaign for a Welsh Assembly, Merthyr Tydfil, 26 Nov. 1988

— 1989 —

Anonymous

2301 The politicians have failed to defend the rights of the Welsh people. We therefore announce that all white settlers are targets for Meibion Glyndŵr. The colonists must understand that this is the land of the Welsh and not their last colony. We shall bury English imperialism.*

statement by Meibion Glyndŵr, signed Rhys Gethin, 1 March 1989

2302 It takes a very special English politician to survive and flourish in Wales among the wheelers and dealers, fantasists and place-seekers who comprise the Principality's political establishment.

in *The Spectator* (15 April 1989)

2303 There are those who would question the sanity of one who voluntarily spends a long weekend in Swansea.

in *The Sunday Times* (19 Feb. 1989)

Richard Binn

2304 In times past the Principality has always been a culinary graveyard where cooking standards in hotels, restaurants, pubs and farmhouses were as grim as gravestones in Welsh cemeteries.

A Taste of Wales (1989)

Anthony Burgess

2305 My wife died of cirrhosis of the liver. She was Welsh, and drink never did the Welsh any good – think of Dylan Thomas and Richard Burton.

in *The Sunday Times* (19 Feb. 1989)

2306 In principle I am in favour of an independent Wales . . . but the whole damn thing is so hopeless.

in *Western Mail* (3 March 1989)

2307 The world's bigger than a Welsh pub.

Dr Lewis to Reg Jones
Any Old Iron (1989)

Simon Jenkins

2308 One day devolved power will return to Scotland, Wales and Ulster. The United Kingdom will be re-pluralised. But goodness knows how much crockery will be smashed in the the mean time.

'Nationalists chafe under an Alien Yoke' in *The Sunday Times* (2 April 1989)

David A. Pretty

2309 Caradoc Evans's infamous stories of life in West Wales seem guilty not so much of malice as of understating the case.

The Rural Revolt that Failed (1989)

Fred Secombe

2310 For a split second there was an awful silence, like that at Cardiff Arms Park just before a Welsh penalty kick.

How Green was my Curate (1989)

Dai Smith

2311 Wales, unlike Ireland, has never quite caught the English Left's ear. It is as if the propinquity and sustained ambiguity of Wales is too much, too close, to grasp for those who can only hear distant trumpets.

'Relating to Wales' in *Raymond Williams: Critical Perspectives* (ed. Terry Eagleton, 1989)

David Steel MP

2312 On 1 March 1979 Scotland and Wales went to the polls on Devolution. The cause of home rule had been totally damaged by a close identification with a deeply unpopular Labour Government. A poll on Devolution became a referendum on Labour.

'A Single Vote Landslide'
in the *Independent* (28 March 1989)

Dafydd Elis Thomas MP

2313 After 1992 we will be citizens of Europe, not citizens of the UK. We will have burgundy-coloured European passports and pink European driving-licences. We will have to see ourselves more and more as Welsh Europeans.

reported in *Western Mail* (2 March 1989)

2314 I have always refused to be labelled as a Welsh Nationalist. It is not a coherent philosophy.

in *Tribune* (14 April 1989)

Ned Thomas

2315 Only a novelist could do justice to the extraordinary country we live in . . . Below the surface stereotypes of rugby and shepherds and choirs lies a most intricate pattern of power and patronage, most of them depending in the end on London for their influence.

'Man who set the Ball Rolling at S4C'
in *Wales on Sunday* (4 June 1989)

Gwyn A. Williams

2316 Clearly the struggle to defend Welsh democracy at home and to advance it in Europe are one struggle. The enemy is the same: the separatist and authoritarian British state. It is not enough to capture that Bastille: we have to dismantle it brick by brick.

editorial
Radical Wales (no. 21, Spring 1989)

— **1990** —

Ioan Bowen Rees

2317 Pessimism must be the state of mind of every honest Welsh person today.

'Wales Today: Nation or Market?'
in *Planet* (no. 79, Feb. – March 1990)

2318 We bring up our children to speak Welsh, not for the sake of the language, but for the sake of our children.

2319 To many of us, the Welsh language has become a symbol of things more important than the language even and that may be our salvation.

2320 We can take little comfort from the fact that, in principle, almost everyone is in favour of Welshness and of the language: all the enemies of Welsh have to do to extinguish it is – nothing.

2321 There is always the danger of a small nation under the thumb of a large state becoming a nation of boot-lickers. The rise of the quango in Wales today is a continuous threat to self-respect.

2322 The Welsh have had the privilege of a foretaste of a process of cultural and industrial corruption which will eventually threaten all mankind.

Dai Smith

2323 A sense of History beyond reiterated mythology is an urgent requirement for bewildered people. It could, of course, bring pain as much as balm.

'In the Presence of the Past'
in *Wales in Vision* (ed. Patrick Hannan, 1990)

Dafydd Elis Thomas MP

2324 Soon what is right for Sofia and for Riga may begin to make sense in Cardiff. And the top-heavy bureaucracy of the Welsh Office will collapse under its own weight into a form of new democracy even in Wales. Then and only then, will we as a people become part of the modern world of the twenty-first century.

'Democracy should rule here as well'
in *Western Mail* (3 Jan. 1990)

ACKNOWLEDGEMENTS

The publishers would like to thank the following for allowing the inclusion of substantial extracts:

Harri Webb, Rhydwen Williams and R. S. Thomas for permission to use a number of their poems; Raymond Garlick for extracts from his *Collected Poems 1946–1986* (Gomer); Mary Llewellyn Davies for work by T. H. Parry-Williams; Don Dale-Jones for work by A. G. Prys-Jones; the estate of Dylan Thomas for extracts from *The Poems* (Dent) and *Quite Early One Morning* (Dent); and Eben Morris for permission to use a number of poems by Idris Davies.

AUTHOR INDEX

(references are to quotation numbers)

Prys-jones, A.G. *cont.*
  1606, 1925
Prys-Thomas, Dewi 2132
Pughe, William Owen 410
Puleston, J.H. 867

Raglan, Lord 1708–10
Raleigh, Sir Walter 803
Rammell, T.W. 553
Randall, David 719
Rees, Goronwy 1585, 1816–23, 2025–8, 2030–33
Rees, Ioan Bowen 1657, 1875, 1900, 2112, 2133,
  2317–22
Rees, J. Machreth 868
Rees, John Frederick 1416, 1477, 1522–3
Rees, Thomas 626–7
Rees, William (Gwilym Hiraethog) 524
Reith, John 1478
Rhys, Ernest 1317
Rhys, Sir John 766
Rhys, Keidrych 1239, 1297–9, 1347–8, 1378–9
Rhys, Sion Dafydd 204
Richard ap Hywel 167
Richard, Henry 623, 640
Richards, Alun 1986–7, 2060–62, 2239, 2268–9
Richards, E.P. 479
Richards, Griffith 605
Richards, Robert 1400
Richards, Thomas 337
Richards, Tom 1989
Richards, William 291–2
Robert, Gruffydd 185–8
Roberts, Evan 869
Roberts, Herbert 783
Roberts, John John 792
Roberts, Kate 1118–19, 1211, 1493, 1776, 2113
Roberts, Wiliam Owen, *see under* Llwyd, Iwan
Roberts, Wilbert Lloyd 2085
Roberts, Wyn 1731
Roscoe, Thomas 487
Rosebery, Lord 767
Rosser, R.M. 1607
Rowland, David 481
Rowlands, John 2175
Rowley, Edward 1966

St David 16
Salesbury, William 178–81
Salisbury, Enoch G. 574
Samwell, David 403
Sankey-Barker, J.P. 1545
Santayana, George 1401
Sarnicol, *see* Thomas, Thomas Jacob
Saunders, Erasmus 303
Saunders, John M. 870
Saunders, S.M. 871
Savage, Richard 314
Scott, Clement 701
Scott, Sir Walter 425–6, 449
Secombe, Fred 2310
Shakespeare, William 211–17, 220–24
Shaw, George Bernard 961–3

Shebbeare, John 343
Shelley, Percy Bysshe 431–3
Shenstone, William 326
Shon ap Owen 259
Sidney, Sir Henry 193
Sidney, Sir Phillip 210
Simon, Glyn 1901, 1926
Siôn Cent 156–7
Skidmore, Ian 2269–70
Smart, Christopher 345–6
Smith, Dai 2240–44, 2311, 2323
Smith, F.E. 950, 1071
Smyth, W.H. 496
Snowden, Mrs Philip 808
Somerville, Sir Donald 1479
Southey, Robert 488
Spring, H.L. 628–9
Stanley, H.M. 671
Steel, David 2312
Stephens, Meic 1777, 1790–1800, 1876–81,
  1927, 2063
Stephens, Thomas 872
Swan, Donald, *see under* Flanders, Michael
Sypyn Cyfeiliog 147

Tacitus 3–5
Taliesin 17–19
Taylor, A.J.P. 2288
Tennyson, Lord 492–3, 523
Thomas, Ben Bowen 1379–80
Thomas, Brinley 1778
Thomas, Dafydd Elis 2034, 2289, 2313–14, 2324
Thomas, David 746
Thomas, D. Lleufer 974
Thomas, Dylan 1174, 1181, 1212–13, 1381,
  1431–7, 1457, 1480, 1546–7, 1608–33, 1658–
  60, 1882
Thomas, Edward 348
Thomas, Edward (poet) 975, 988
Thomas, George (Viscount Tonypandy) 1990,
  2035, 2250–51
Thomas, Gwyn (prose-writer) 1458, 1548,
  1586–7, 1634, 1671–2, 1711, 1779–80, 1801–
  1803, 1824–5, 1840–42, 1850–59, 1902–5,
  1928, 1969, 1991–4, 2176–8, 2252–4
Thomas, Gwyn (poet) 2101, 2198
Thomas, Howard 1417–19
Thomas, Iori 1712
Thomas, John (Ieuan Ddu) 630
Thomas, Ned 1929, 1967–8, 1995–8, 2064,
  2290, 2315
Thomas, Peter 2036
Thomas, R.D. 672–3
Thomas, R.S. 1420, 1438–44, 1465, 1549–54,
  1588–9, 1713, 1758–62, 1804, 1860–61, 1883,
  1906–10, 1930, 2037–8, 2065, 2086, 2102,
  2147–51, 2255, 2291–6
Thomas, T.H. 873
Thomas, Thomas Jacob (Sarnicol) 1190–92,
  1318
Thomas, William (Islwyn) 565–6, 689

176

Thomas, W. Jenkyn 768
Thomson, James 313
Thorpe, Jeremy 1826
Tolkien, J.R.R. 1661, 1805–6
Torbuck, John 327–8
Trevelyan, Marie 750
Tripp, John 1862–3, 1931, 2152–3, 2256
Trollope, Anthony 601
Turner, J.M.W. 386
Turner, Llewelyn 713

Vanbrugh, John 295
Vaughan, Aled 2066–70
Vaughan, Henry 261–4
Vaughan, Hilda 1086–7
Vaughan, Richard 1524, 2071
Vaughan, Rowland 250
Vaughan-Thomas, Wynford 1843, 2154–6, 2188
Verey, David 1745
Victoria, Queen 548, 638, 728, 751
Vincent, Henry 494
Vivian, Hussey 593

Wade-Evans, A.W. 1300–1, 1445, 1494
Wain, John 1970
Walker, Peter 2297
Walters, John 357–8
Watkins, Vernon 1446, 1459, 1732, 1763, 1911
Watkyns, Rowland 276–8
Watson, Sir William 889
Watts-Dunton, Theodore 784, 824
Waugh, Evelyn 1120–21
Webb, Harri 1733, 1781–2, 1807–10, 1932–44,
    1971–2, 2087–8, 2114–15, 2134–5, 2157,
    2225–8
Webb, Mary 1135
Wesley, John 318, 349, 369
Wheeler, Mortimer 1662–3
White, Baroness 2189
White, Gilbert 382
White, Walter 576
Whitman, Walt 729
Widgery, Justice 1864
Williams, David 392

Williams, David (historian) 1664
Williams, D.J. 1136–8, 1182, 1403–5, 1525,
    1590–92, 1734, 1811, 1912–14
Williams, Edward (Iolo Morganwg) 363, 368,
    387–8, 404, 573
Williams, Eliseus (Eifion Wyn) 825–6, 1114
Williams, Emlyn 1256–7, 1302, 1764
Williams, G.O. 1593–5, 1999, 2072, 2090
Williams, Griffith John 1053–6
Williams, Gwyn 2000–1
Williams, Gwyn A. 2158–9, 2208–18, 2257–8,
    2298–2300, 2316
Williams, Herbert 1844, 1865–6
Williams, Hugh 495
Williams, Iona 874
Williams, John 258
Williams, John (Ab Ithel) 562
Williams, John Ellis 1303
Williams, John Lloyd 1336
Williams, John Stuart 1884
Williams, Kyffin 2073–4
Williams, Mallt 875
Williams, Raymond 1715, 1746, 2002, 2103,
    2180–83
Williams, Rhodri 2229
Williams, Rhydwen 1827, 2039
Williams, T. Charles 876–8
Williams, T. Marchant 730
Williams, Waldo 1596–7, 1673–80
Williams, William (Pantycelyn) 331–3
Williams, William (MP) 525–6
Williams, W. Llewelyn 758, 769, 879–80
Williams Doo, Mrs 1635, 1714
Williams-Ellis, Clough 1382–4
Wood, Edward 1018
Wood, J.G. 435
Woodcock, George 1406
Wordsworth, William 401
Wykes, Thomas 123
Wyndham, Henry Penruddocke 393–9
Wynn, Sir John 237–9
Wynne, Ellis 301–2

Zimmern, Alfred E. 1598

SUBJECT INDEX

(references are to quotation numbers)

Abercwmboi 1360
Aberdare 168, 1567, 2249
Aberdaron 1723
Aberedw 659
Aberfan 1859
Abergavenny 540, 1141
Aberystwyth 575, 702, 1223, 1314, 1504, 1777, 2286
Abraham, William (Mabon) 1069
Abse, Leo 2139
Academi Gymreig (Welsh Academy) 1749
accent 803, 1336, 1448, 1480, 1587, 1636, 1904, 2244
Act of Union (1536) 171–5, 366, 1527
Adfer 2143
agriculture 119, 231, 455, 594, 854, 951, 1171, 1524, 1553–4, 1563,
Alun Mabon 578
Aneirin (see also Gododdin) 244
Anglesey 85, 716, 1726, 2111
Anglesey, Marquess of 513
Anglicanism, see Church of England
Anglicization 229, 498, 604, 994, 1372, 1500, 1538
Anglo-Welsh literature 564, 616, 1105, 1237, 1239, 1261, 1287, 1292, 1374, 1378, 1431, 1521, 1560–62, 1572–3, 1575, 1596, 1638–9, 1648, 1689–94, 1733, 1735, 1779, 1834, 1846, 1875–80, 1893–4, 1918, 2048, 2050, 2095, 2135, 2138, 2147, 2152
Aran, Yr 815
architecture 376, 912, 1094, 1121, 1383–4, 1529, 1766, 1832, 1973, 2164
Argoed 1111
Argoed Llwyfain 17–18
art (painting, sculpture), 873, 1048, 1094, 1121, 1157, 1159, 1297–8, 1362, 1399, 1441, 1487–8, 1490, 1501, 1683, 1720–21, 1731, 1850, 2008, 2046, 2074, 2104, 2155, 2264, 2269
Arthur 8, 42, 104, 196, 201, 288, 773
Arts Council 1738, 1853
Attila Rees 1622

Badon 8
Bailey, Crawshay 1139
Bala 389
Bangor 126, 563, 2199
Baptists 506
bards, see poets and Gorsedd
Barry Island 1357
BBC (see also broadcasting and television) 1102, 1345, 1412, 1493, 1738
Beaumaris 238
Bedwellty 2079
Bendigeidfran 59–61
Bendigo 1062
Bethesda 1334
Bevan, Aneurin 1426
Bible 177–8, 180, 183, 197–8, 207, 289, 352, 450, 910, 1415, 1727
bilingualism 1184, 1268, 1559, 1891, 1990, 2000, 2061, 2070, 2090, 2189
bingo 1856
Black Mountains 646
Blodeuwedd 62
Boadicea (Buddug) 562, 722
Bodnant 1544
books (see also literature) 253, 339, 1119, 1162, 1221, 1499, 1640
Borrow, George 2047
Bowen, Anne 689
Bowen, Ben 793
Boyce, Max 2191
Branwen 58
Brecon 65, 154, 894
Breconshire 886
Britain, Britons (Ancient) 1, 3, 6–9, 12–13, 15, 32, 35–41, 43–4, 67–70, 87, 138, 176, 180, 192, 196–7, 210, 240, 245, 247, 250, 268, 292–4, 326, 337, 424, 439, 568, 573, 1231, 1416, 1494
Britain (modern state & Empire) 316, 325, 629, 733, 783, 872, 1003, 1006, 1017, 1461, 1661, 1688, 1700, 1805, 1811, 2072, 2162, 2211,

Britain (modern state & Empire) *cont.* 2213,
2215, 2217, 2255, 2294, 2316
Britannia Bridge 643
Brittany 41, 311, 620, 1328
broadcasting (*see also* BBC *and* television) 1326,
1417–19, 1478, 1496, 1636, 1963, 2259
Brutus 67, 69, 143
Brut y Tywysogion 80
Brynmawr 537, 1916
Builth 680, 913
bundling, *see* courting in bed
Burton, Richard 2305
Bute, Marquess of 543

Cadair Idris 429, 661
Cadfan 29
Cadwaladr ap Cadfan 32
Cadwaladr ap Cadwallon 67
Cadwgan ap Bleddyn 66
Caerleon 201, 1052
Caernarfon 238, 376, 450, 716, 823, 1504, 1915,
2119
Caernarfonshire 398
Caerphilly 426
Caerwys 475
Calvinistic Methodists 406, 507, 591, 2129
Carmarthen 297, 1919
Carmarthenshire 519, 788, 1027, 1964, 2137
Cambria 86, 143, 196, 225, 314, 324, 348, 359–
60, 363, 403, 430, 432, 470, 543, 564, 634,
999, 1025
Cambrian strike 920, 921
Captain Cat 1610, 1614
Caratacus 1231
Caradog (conductor) 840
Cardiff 380, 397, 559, 674, 778, 804, 865, 1074,
1082, 1144–45, 1202, 1259, 1401, 1504, 1656,
1662, 1705, 1851–2, 1885, 1888, 1941, 1995,
2109, 2139, 2226, 2244, 2267, 2324
Cardiff Arms Park 2310
Cardigan 79, 105
Cardiganshire 420, 459, 519, 788, 1429, 2137
Castles 94, 375–6, 1195
Catholicism, Catholic Church 36–7, 181, 1179,
1679, 2222
Catraeth 22–3
Celts 478
Ceredigion 96, 192
Cerrig-y-drudion 712
chapels 395, 497, 687, 789, 905, 941, 966, 1039,
1058–9, 1124, 1126, 1134, 1354, 1389, 1392,
1410, 1529, 1565, 1774, 1821–2, 2079
Charles, Thomas 437
cheese 216, 916, 2252
Chepstow 682
Cherry Owen 1620
chips 1396
Church in Wales 644, 751, 1093, 1104, 1607,
1901
Church of England 276, 480, 644, 669, 706, 767,

Church of England *cont.* 799, 879–80, 1002
Cingen 33
climate 135, 151, 785, 1030, 1253, 1347
Clyro 649, 665
coal and coal-mining (*see also* miners, mining)
379, 456, 476, 496, 517, 541, 629, 676, 694,
714, 754, 823, 864, 962, 967–8, 970, 977,
1012, 1042, 1045, 1067, 1115, 1152, 1161,
1178, 1191, 1215, 1241, 1386, 1452, 1530,
1668, 1920, 2093, 2172
commerce 101, 119, 191, 527, 574, 602, 608,
621, 637, 806, 1485
committees 1670, 1819, 2056, 2200
common people, the 343, 422–3, 472, 519, 522,
530, 534, 617, 711, 920, 1048–9, 1089, 1242,
1417, 1483, 1532, 1570, 2195
Communism 845, 1872, 1921, 2110
Conservatives *see* Tories
Conwy 162, 238
corgi 1927
corruption 367, 1943, 2322
Corwen 409, 1276
counties 2261
courting in bed 477
Crawshay, Robert Thompson 690
Crawshay, William 441, 1568
Criccieth 1128
crime 536, 791, 1309
culture 615, 1461, 1487, 1503, 1511, 1516, 1585,
1603–4, 1645, 1715, 1737, 1805, 1816, 1823,
1883, 1908, 2011, 2195, 2289
Cunedda 43
Cwmbach 1845
Cwm-hir Abbey 227
Cwm Pennant 1114
Cwmscwt 2134
Cymdeithas yr Iaith Gymraeg (1885) 703,
(1962) 1922, 2021, 2077, 2122, 2281
Cymmrodorion (Hon. Soc. of) 374
Cymreigyddion Society 484, 540
Cymry, Cymro 247, 917–18, 979, 981, 1666,
2142
Cynddylan 50
cynghanedd 1977, 2138
Cymru Fydd 772

Dafydd ap Cadwaladr 147
Dai 1233, 1245, 1354, 1359, 1411, 1459
David ap Rhees (Siôn Dafydd Rhys) 365
Davies, Gwendoline & Margaret 1515
Davies, J.H. 1096
death 157, 261, 306, 369, 903, 1213, 1343, 1435,
1547, 1556, 1687, 1711, 1744, 1884, 1906–07,
1435, 1909, 2245
Demetae 14
Denbighshire 512
depopulation 434, 1108, 1420, 2103
Devolution (*see also* Welsh Assembly) 1018,
1024, 1968, 2080, 2084, 2099, 2108, 2139,
2162, 2166, 2171, 2173, 2234, 2246, 2251,

literature *cont* 622, 627, 696, 723, 739, 752, 755,
  759, 814, 823, 863, 996–7, 1034, 1037, 1049,
  1053, 1056, 1094, 1097, 1112–13, 1118, 1157–
  9, 1180, 1186, 1196, 1200, 1207, 1219, 1227,
  1249, 1268, 1279–80, 1303, 1322, 1376, 1394,
  1432, 1462, 1540, 1649, 1751, 1841, 1923,
  2066, 2175, 2201, 2271, 2297
Livingstone, Dr 671
Llan Fair 1236
Llanbrynmair 1333
Llandaf 203, 894
Llanddeiniolen 1202, 1333
Llandore 731
Llandovery College 1129, 1730
Llandrindod 324
Llandudno 894
Llanelli 922–3, 930
Llanfabon 168
Llanfairfechan 894
Llangadock 664
Llangollen 390
Llanllechid 1334
Llanrwst 450, 641, 894
Llansteffan 2233
Llanwrtyd 1745
Llanwynno 168
Lloyd George, David 797, 802, 884, 946, 964,
  1016, 1019, 1023, 1031, 1051, 1084, 1167,
  1380, 1408, 1955, 2231
Lludd ap Beli Mawr 2073
Llywelyn ap Gruffudd 113, 117, 124, 126–30,
  225, 909, 934, 1037
Llŷn 1451
Llywelyn ab Iorwerth 114
Llyfr Ancr Llanddewibrefi 142
Llywarch Hen 45–9, 425
Llywelyn Bren 136
Llywelyn Fawr 1365
London Welsh 1073, 1224, 1480, 1798
Lucius 40

Mabinogion 988, 2125
Mabon *see* Abraham, William
Machynlleth 152
Madoc (Madawg) 673, 1600, 1724
Mae Rose Cottage 1613
Maelgwn ap Rhys 105
Maesllwch castle 650
Magloconus (Maelgwn Gwynedd) 15, 43
Manorbier 84, 2106
Manx 545
Marches 110, 125, 150
Marged Uch Ifan 378
marital and sexual customs 99, 477, 502, 511,
  533–5, 697, 789, 1143, 1148, 1150, 1413,
  1614, 1696, 1780, 1970, 2201
martial prowess 1–2, 4, 8, 17–21, 24–7, 31, 41,
  51–4, 56, 78, 81–2, 89–92, 106, 114, 138, 158,
  164, 256, 259, 462, 554, 917, 954–5, 1125,
  1497, 1706

Maximus (Macsen Wledig) 11, 41, 1466
mead 21–3
Members of Parliament 524, 623, 640, 698, 839,
  909, 911, 1282, 1426, 1469, 1505, 1942, 2161
Meibion Glyndŵr 2301
Merioneth 340, 398, 430, 482, 511, 998, 1126
Merlin (Myrddin) 32, 138, 297, 1779
Merthyr Tydfil 168, 417–18, 465, 476, 481, 504,
  549, 553, 1068, 1091, 1183, 1247, 1281, 1605
Methodism 334, 395, 404, 421, 482, 592, 732,
  1838, 2222
Milford Haven 321
Milk Wood 1633
miners, mining (*see also* coal) 329–30, 955–6,
  958, 1248
minority status 620, 960, 1673, 1898, 1900,
  1953–4, 1964, 2321
Mog Edwards 1617, 1627–8
monolingualism 1173, 1651, 2145
Monmouth 221–2
Monmouthshire 407, 538, 749, 1238, 1429,
  1558, 2111
Morgan, Elystan 2251
Morgan, John 2251
Morgan, William 197, 207, 1727
Morris, John 2251
Morris-Jones, Sir John 1130
mountains and hills 76, 205, 219, 291, 298, 302–
  3, 313, 326, 340, 347, 355, 377, 383, 385–6,
  429, 430, 440, 486–7, 565, 577, 582, 652, 656,
  658, 662–3, 683, 738, 753, 795–6, 809, 815,
  837, 988, 1004, 1076, 1088, 1223, 1265, 1335,
  1344, 1667, 1674, 1686, 1732, 1775, 1786,
  2136
Mumbles 701, 786
music 97–8, 408–9, 458, 579, 699, 715, 723, 840,
  860, 878, 885, 908, 975, 981, 1065, 1094,
  1121, 1127, 1166, 1360, 1449, 1472, 1629,
  1631, 1707, 1717, 1808, 1965, 2053, 2105,
  2225

nationalism 596, 692–3, 736, 743, 745, 760, 898,
  930, 971, 1001, 1013, 1016, 1040, 1061, 1099,
  1149, 1164, 1255, 1278, 1403–5, 1414, 1424,
  1591, 1641, 1789, 1857, 1897, 1899, 1913,
  1928, 1968, 2034, 2128, 2144, 2192–3, 2218,
  2250, 2314
nationality 71, 77, 133, 247, 463, 547, 593, 599,
  613, 620, 633, 667, 697, 709, 717, 719–20,
  737, 742, 769, 782, 819–21, 835, 899, 934,
  974, 983, 1014, 1036, 1066, 1075, 1157, 1184,
  1260, 1293–4, 1296, 1400, 1477, 1491, 1523,
  1594–5, 1602, 1663, 1680, 1702, 1789, 1896,
  1972, 1986, 2221
nationalization (of mines) 1012
Neath 162, 1360
New Radnor 322
Newport 772, 2160
Newtown 991
Nogood Boyo 1632

water 2207
Welsh Assembly (*see also* Devolution) 2080,
    2163, 2167–70, 2172, 2300
Welsh Not 402, 811, 1081
Welsh Office 1370, 2250, 2324
Welshpool 576
Wesleyan Methodists 508
Western Mail 779, 800, 1013, 1941, 2044
wildness (of people, land) 83, 107, 115–16, 120,
    122–3, 140, 240, 470, 486–7
Williams, William (Pantycelyn) 349
Williams Parry, Robert 1565
Williams, D. Mathew 1234

Williams, Edward (Iolo Morganwg) 1522
Winifred Wynne 784
woad 1
women 137, 278, 295, 345, 493, 500, 552, 576,
    664, 666, 701, 784, 789, 871, 904, 1217, 1342,
    1458, 1584, 1658, 1665, 1801, 1825, 2230,
    2265, 2275, 2283
Wrexham 390
writers 484, 1750, 1924, 2039, 2041, 2049, 2082,
    2134
Wye 215, 315, 381, 401, 682
Wynne, Ellis 2295